Wounded Hearts

Jennifer Travis

Wounded

Hearts

Masculinity, Law, and Literature in American Culture

The University of North Carolina Press Chapel Hill

Manufactured in the United States of America

Designed and typeset by Julie Allred, BW&A Books, Inc., Durham, N.C.

Parts of this book have been reprinted with permission in revised form from the following works: "Pain and Recompense: The Trouble with *Ethan Frome*," *Arizona Quarterly* 53, no. 3 (1997); "The Cost of Feeling: Emotional Injury in Henry James's *The Golden Bowl*," *Modern Fiction Studies* 44, no. 4 (1998), published by The Johns Hopkins University Press; "Sexual Evidence and the Scope of Injury: Willa Cather's *A Lost Lady*," *Women's Studies: An Interdisciplinary Journal* 29, no. 2 (2000), © 2000, reproduced by permission of Taylor & Francis, Inc., <http://www.taylorandfrancis.com>; and "Willa Cather's Law of the Heart: Emotional Injury and Its Fictions," in *Boys Don't Cry? Rethinking Narratives of Masculinity and Emotion in the U.S.*, edited by Milette Shamir and Jennifer Travis (New York: Columbia University Press, 2002), © 2002 Columbia University Press, reprinted with permission of the publisher.

The paper in this book meets the guidelines for permanence and durability of the Committee on Production Guidelines for Book Longevity of the Council on Library Resources.

Library of Congress Cataloging-in-Publication Data
Travis, Jennifer.
Wounded hearts : masculinity, law, and literature in American culture / Jennifer Travis.
p. cm.
Includes bibliographical references (p.) and index.
ISBN 0-8078-2974-9 (alk. paper)—ISBN 0-8078-5635-5 (pbk. : alk. paper)
1. American fiction—History and criticism. 2. Masculinity in literature. 3. Emotions in literature. 4. Men in literature. 5. Law in literature. I. Title.
PS374.M37T73 2005
813.009'353—dc22 2005010250

cloth 09 08 07 06 05 5 4 3 2 1
paper 09 08 07 06 05 5 4 3 2 1

In memory of my father, Stuart Travis (1937–1996),
and for Mike, Miles, and Stu, with love

Contents

Acknowledgments, ix

Introduction, 1

one Soldier's Heart: The Vocabulary of Injury and the American Civil War, 23

two Emotional Equity?: William Dean Howells and the Divorce Novel, 51

three Things Not Named: Willa Cather's Lost Men, Criminal Conversations, and Emotional Auras, 79

four On Personal Quantity: Psychic Injury in Henry James's *The Golden Bowl*, 105

five The Science of Affect: Professionals Reading and the Case of *Ethan Frome*, 137

Epilogue, 163

Notes, 169

Bibliography, 189

Index, 213

Acknowledgments

From its earliest days, my work has benefited from the insight and inspiration of its readers. I am indebted to the members of my dissertation committee for their generosity and guidance: Wai Chee Dimock, Michael T. Gilmore, and Robert Ferguson. Professors Dimock and Gilmore tirelessly read chapters and enthusiastically helped me to shape my ideas. My work also has profited from so many thoughtful conversations with colleagues and friends, among them Wayne Bodle, Florence Dore, Jenna Ivers, Cathy Jurca, and Milette Shamir. I would like to thank my former colleagues at Illinois State University for their friendship and encouragement: Allison Bailey, Maura Doherty, Ron Fortune, Victoria and Charlie Harris, Rebecca Saunders, and Tori Thompson. Colleagues at the Newberry Library and participants in the Fellows' seminar helped me to think expansively and creatively about my work. My introduction and chapter 4 owe their shape to conversations with colleagues in the New York Americanist Group, including Rachel Adams, Maria Farland, Hildegard Hoeller, Gus Stadler, and Liza Yukins. Friends and colleagues at St. John's University are indispensable interlocutors, especially Bob Fanuzzi, Granville Ganter, Margaret Kim, John Lowney, Greg Maertz, Steve Mentz, Derek Owens, and Steve Sicari. Over the past few years, my writing group has been an invaluable source of intellectual energy, and for that I thank Diane Cady, Ashley Cross, Jean Lutes, and Susannah Mintz. The book's final shape owes a great deal to the readers at the University of North Carolina Press and to my editor, Sian Hunter.

I want to thank the institutions who provided time and financial support for research and writing. Brandeis University not only awarded me a dissertation year fellowship but also provided a constructive community in which I could develop as a scholar. The Newberry Library Monticello Fellowship came at a crucial time shortly thereafter and allowed me to begin the long process of transforming a dissertation into a book. The archives at the Huntington Library and its stunningly beautiful grounds encouraged me to think about pain and pleasure in new ways. The American Association of University Women's Postdoctoral American Fellowship gave me an invaluable year in which to write. The Gilder Lehrman Institute of American History supported my Civil War research at the Pierpont Morgan Library. Thanks especially to Illinois State University and to St. John's University for summer grant support and much needed release time from teaching in which to write.

I am thankful every day for the loving support of my family: my husband, Michael, and my sons, Miles and Stuart. My mother, Gail Travis, and my in-laws, Barbara and Frank Malone, were constant sources of encouragement and enthusiasm. It is a great pleasure to celebrate my many thanks and much love here.

Introduction

The Interior of a Heart

Halfway through Nathaniel Hawthorne's *The Scarlet Letter* (1850), the Reverend Arthur Dimmesdale returns to the scaffold upon which Hester Prynne stood seven years earlier, infant at her breast, awaiting punishment for the crime of adultery. Dimmesdale, "overcome" by the "great horror" of the secret he shares with Hester, emerges from his "closet" and in the dark of night proceeds to the "foot-worn" scaffold where he hopes to unburden himself of his "hideous guilt."[1] In "heaven-defying" agony, he imagines a scarlet letter identical to Hester's own burning itself into his breast "over his heart" (140). This "A" produces a "bodily" ache so "poisonous" that he is unable to restrain a cry of pain that, he believes, with some relief, will awaken the townspeople, who will then "hurry forth" and find him there (140). Dimmesdale imagines that his public exposure, bearing "the anguish in his inmost soul" in the marketplace, will relieve him of the "throb" of mental pain (136, 135). In the chapter prior to his return to the scaffold, which is appropriately titled "The Interior of a Heart," Dimmesdale makes a futile attempt at such a public admission; he uses the stage of his pulpit and the text of his sermon to relay to parishioners what he calls "the black secret of his soul" (136). He knows, the narrative tells us, "subtle, but remorseful hypocrite that he was," how his "vague confession" will be viewed (136). Each admission of sin on his part is interpreted by his flock as a lesson in contrast with his exquisite reverence. He reaches for but is unable to attain what he calls a "revolution in the sphere of thought and feeling," one that he believes will reshape his "interior kingdom" (147, 207). Dimmesdale harbors a secret that he longs to confess, but his internalized prohibitions against displaying his "interior heart" to public view prevent him from such revelation. Neither his nighttime vigil nor his daytime homily produces its desired effect. He remains in a "highly disordered mental state," suffering from "morbid self-contemplat[ion]," and a "long, intense, and secret pain" (207). Even when young Pearl recognizes the minister's suffering and implores him to appear with her mother and herself on the scaffold at noontime, he can only shudder. "All the dread of public exposure, that had so long been the anguish of his life, returned upon him. . . . [H]e will not stand with Pearl and Hester for another day" (145). Ultimately, his hideous secret remains closely guarded; despite all efforts at self-exposure, the true meaning of Dimmesdale's "heaven-defying guilt" remains a matter of private judgment between himself and God.

Contrast this with William Dean Howells's rendition of the masculine "interior of a heart" some 30 years later through his character Squire Gaylord in *A Modern Instance* (1882). In Howells's novel, the squire, like the minister, turns to a public stage to speak his heart; in the squire's case it is to rectify his daughter's defamation of character in a spurious divorce proceeding brought against her. Hawthorne's scaffold in the marketplace becomes a court of law in Howells's hand; the hideous secret, an actionable claim. Both Dimmesdale and Gaylord seek, in Gaylord's words, an "opportunity to redress an atrocious wrong" to "vindicate an . . . injured woman"; yet, only the squire is able to "unburden" his interior heart.[2] With none of Dimmesdale's reluctance and foreboding, Gaylord mounts the steps of the courthouse with "unnatural vigor"; he "stretch[es] himself to his full height" and seizes the noontime hour to publicize and "redress" an "atrocious wrong" (440). In the figure of Squire Gaylord, male pain is driven out of the closet and given public voice: "The old man's nasals cut across the judge's round tones, almost before they had ceased. His lips compressed themselves to a waving line, and his high hawk-beak came down over them; the fierce light burned in his cavernous eyes, and his grizzled hair erected itself like a crest" (440). Unlike Dimmesdale, who merely imagines his nighttime shriek calling the town toward his final reckoning, Gaylord, "fierce" and eaglelike in his focus, commands in his listeners an "appreciation of his power" (443). His courtroom sermon "summon[s] even the loiterers in the street, whose ascending tramp on the stair continually made itself heard; the lawyers, officers of the court, the judge, forgot their dinner, and posed themselves anew in their chairs to listen" (443). The squire, who speaks his heart by combining his personal feelings as a father with his professional duties as a lawyer, elicits the "electrical sphere of sympathy and admiration" that the minister only fantasizes about (443). Whereas Dimmesdale's words are duplicitous and deceiving, Gaylord's words have "iron weight," and they fall "like blows" (446).

Both men seek out public stages on which to unburden their hearts—both occasioned by a woman wronged—yet only Squire Gaylord succeeds in his desire for recompense: with rapt attention to his emotional and professional pleas, the court reverses the terms of the Hubbards' divorce proceedings. Squire Gaylord's suffering, which, as he claims, he displays on behalf of his daughter, Marcia, outstrips his adversary's, Bartley's, fictive emotional allegations. In the Reverend Dimmesdale and Squire Gaylord, male emotionalism is at a heightened pitch; in fact, both men ultimately suffer themselves to death. Yet Squire Gaylord first is able to render the public judgment of the court in his favor. He discloses and successfully prosecutes the "monstrous crime" that lay heavy on his breast (443).

Representations of masculine pain and suffering lie at the heart of some of American literature's most canonical texts; Dimmesdale and Gaylord signify substantive variations in the way masculine emotionalism was imagined and received. Dimmesdale, unable to find relief for his deeply felt wounds, agonizes himself to death in relative obscurity; the revelation of his pain and the path toward its healing are articulated and truly recognized only, Hawthorne's readers presume, in the face of God. Squire Gaylord, conversely, immediately seeks out public redress; he is confident that emotional pain and wrongful injury have public voice and accountability, and he brings this narrative into public view. For men like him and his falsely injured nemesis, Bartley Hubbard, emotional woundedness is not hidden in a closet, nor is it, to invoke Herman Melville's term, solely a matter of personal "monomaniacal" intent; instead, masculine emotional wounding becomes a question of cultural recognition and, quite often, monetary recompense.

Wounded Hearts: Masculinity, Law, and Literature in American Culture investigates the ways in which discourses on masculine emotionalism take public shape and gain cultural currency in the Civil War years through the early twentieth century, and it asks how writers such as Stephen Crane, William Dean Howells, Willa Cather, Henry James, and Edith Wharton articulate an arena of male emotional injury distinct from their antebellum predecessors. It makes a particular case for the centrality of fiction from the Civil War through the turn of the century in instituting substantive changes in the very meaning of injury, as well as in the shape, the design, and the methods of its redress. For example, the novels in this study were indebted, consciously or not, to the psychological realism of slave narratives as well as to the affective persuasions of the sentimental novel, although they perform substantially different "cultural work," to employ Jane Tompkins's phrase. When Frederick Douglass "sheds tears," for instance, when he decries his "bitterest anguish" over the "dehumanizing character of slavery" in his *Narrative* (1840), he does so always with one object in mind: heavenly freedom (19). The intense physical pains and emotional wounds that he describes are not easily repaired. The novels considered here imagine particular kinds of reparations, albeit of a substantively different sort from those imagined by their forebears. Not only do they record a history of emotional injury—from the psychological trauma of the Civil War soldier to the emotional excesses of one of the first fictional divorcés, Howells's Bartley Hubbard; and from the stoic suffering of Edith Wharton's farmer Ethan Frome to the costly wounds of Henry James's Prince Amerigo. More important, they weigh these emotional wounds by the development of cultural methods of recompense. By the late nineteenth century, the phenomenon of psychic injury animated a variety of cultural narratives; this study asks how a semantics of masculine emotional pain might be fiction generating and to what extent the changing scope of male injury across a wide discursive field employs a language of pain familiar to literary narrative. What follows might be called a genealogy of the emergence, the entrenchment, and the gendering of emotional injuries in U.S. culture.[3]

In analyzing the emerging capacity of American men to communicate their emotional wounds, this book traces the discourse of male emotionalism across a range of cultural narratives, from literature and the institutionalization of literary criticism to psychology, medicine, and the law. Methodologically, this study crosses disciplinary boundaries both in the selection of primary texts it engages and in the theoretical apparatuses it employs. This study travels to multiple locations—from battlefield to courtroom, and from early institutional debates in the university to readings of literary texts—that inspired a widening cultural discussion about the shape and texture of emotional wounds. Each chapter's internal logic draws upon arenas that may at first seem discrete or disconnected but are, I argue, intimately conjoined by their attention to and articulation of male emotional injuries. For example, in chapter 1 I read medical texts about physical and psychical wounding during the Civil War in conjunction with the debates among literary realists and their later critics about the nature of "great" wartime writing. The juxtaposition of the medical and the literary allows me to register the complex ways in which the medical anxieties about soldiers' psychological wounds were rescripted by male canonical writers in the years after the war. For writers such as William Dean Howells, Henry James, and, later, Stephen Crane, psychological wounds became the groundwork for "great" wartime literature as well as the very substance of martial manhood itself. This study analyzes the meaning of changes in the nature and substance of injury in the United States, beginning with the impact of men's bodily injuries to the puzzlement over men's newly articulated psychic injuries, from compensation for physical wounds to the insistence that words do wound. Although I am interested in how discourses about injury evolve from an emphasis on the male body to the inclusion of the male psyche, this study does not aim for a teleological account of such transformations; rather, it reads emotional injury in genealogical terms. The following chapters stress, to recall Foucault, "different scenes" where male emotional injuries are "engaged in different roles."[4] Crucial to this engagement is the vocabulary of cultural studies, with its expansion of the legitimate objects of scholarly study, its interest in the logic of discursive structures, and its linking of the study of culture to issues of social power and conflict.

In the late nineteenth and early twentieth centuries, Hawthorne's stern and unfeeling marketplace became a veritable marketplace of emotion, and some of its primary beneficiaries appeared counterintuitive to the well-entrenched (if often fictive) emotional logic of the past.[5] In this marketplace, emotional men, not sentimental women, cultivated and were rewarded for affective possessions, including such psychological states as humiliation and dishonor. Men entered courts of law to tell their stories of emotional distress, as we see Bartley Hubbard and Squire Gaylord do in William Dean Howells's *A Modern Instance* (chapter 2), and they cultivated their professional expertise to interpret stories of male pain and suffering, as we see early literary critic Bliss Perry and mid-twentieth-century critic Lionel Trilling do in chapter 5. Although emotions often are described as natural and authentic and are often associated with women, men's emotional injuries substantively challenged the construction of emotions "as part of a private life that lies outside the marketplace."[6] In fact, the recognition of men's emotional injuries did not merely denaturalize their gendering; they also occasionally reinforced emotion and gender hierarchies. For example, Squire Gaylord's distress trumps his daughter's legal claim as well as her courtroom presence to become its own form of fatherly recompense. When "injured feelings" could be shown to disrupt male sovereignty of mind, as its victims claimed in the turn-of-the-century adultery cases that form part of the subject of chapter 3 on Willa Cather's *A Lost Lady* (1923), such feelings were readily recognized and men generously compensated. This recognition that emotions could be material and compensable instituted a logic that responded to a rising masculine crisis of authority in the post–Civil War years and helped to secure a reconfiguration of masculine self-definition at the turn of the century.[7] Pain was no longer solely a cry of "hideous guilt" or bodily harm; it became a problem of both cultural compensation and evidentiary representation. Its analysis and its gendering lie at the heart of this study, and its incitements as well as consequences—what might be described as a "call to harms"—demand attention.

The investment in and masculinization of emotional woundedness pervaded America's post–Civil War social landscape, which was shaken by uncertain privilege and unstable political identity. With socioeconomic transformations brought about by emancipation, increasing pressure for women's rights, industrialization, urbanization, and incorporation, the centuries-long advantages that had been extended to white middle-class men no longer appeared self-evident. The emergence of the post–Civil War nation as a new "site of integrated social membership" (as Lauren Berlant has described the United States today) threatened robust notions of masculine personhood in the late nineteenth century, especially those that privileged the white male body as the emblem of political power.[8] Male bodies were increasingly vulnerable not only to cultural competition from previously marginalized and invisible others, but also to the onslaught of new technologies that promised progress but often epitomized bodily injury and pain. From the bloody battles of the Civil War, which first employed the rapid-fire assault rifle to deadly effect, to the plethora of injuries associated with industries such as the railroad, the white male body, once perceived as impervious, proved increasingly susceptible to assault. Although critics like Gail Bederman and Bryce Traister have contested the idea of masculine "crisis," arguing, as Bederman does, that late-nineteenth- and early-twentieth-century white men could rest assured that "people with male bodies naturally possessed both a man's identity and a man's right to wield power," it is important to recognize that "a man's right to wield power" often came to be expressed and exercised in novel ways.[9] The literal and figurative male body in pain, whether emblematic of a crisis or not, hastened men's demands for and recognition of their innermost emotional wounds.[10] *Wounded Hearts* argues that the emphasis on and public recognition of interiority and inner life, which in many instances became the particular prerogative of white middle-class men, palliated growing social and cultural threats, rescripting masculine crises as occasions to rethink and to renegotiate the grounds of masculine power and privilege.

Reading among fictional and factual narratives in the later nineteenth and early twentieth centuries, from realist literary narratives to medical and legal cases, *Wounded Hearts* examines how the exemplary early "victims" of emotional injury, white middle-class men, emerge, in many respects, against the grain of literary and cultural history, against the tendency to view women and underrepresented groups as the sole bankers of emotional wounds, and against the culturally effective naturalization of victimization. One of the most trenchant narratives in U.S. literature is the white male flight from emotion. Narratives of what Nina Baym called "beset manhood," ingrained by such critics as Henry Nash, F. O. Matthiessen, and Leslie Fiedler, have read U.S. masculinity—the tough, hyperindividualistic protagonist as well as the misunderstood and alienated American writer—against the putative coercive socializing powers and emotional excesses of women. The man of injured emotion has remained, in many respects, culturally invisible in sight of these more well-known templates of masculinity, ranging from the self-made man to the roughrider—hegemonic images of manhood and narratives of emotional restraint that have become exceedingly resilient in their narrative power. Against the fortitude of the above narratives, the study of emotion across disciplines and, in literary studies, the critique of sentiment have become paramount. Indeed, it is less the case that masculine emotions have been the subject of widespread cultural disregard than that men's use of and access to emotional territory have remained, until quite recently, largely undertheorized or ignored. Literary critics such as Julia Stern, Elizabeth Barnes, Dana Nelson, Lora Romero, Glenn Hendler, Julie Ellison, and June Howard, to name a few, have begun to reveal the complexities as well as to refute the above characterizations of closeted male emotions. With the special issue of *American Literature* titled *No More Separate Spheres* (1998), and the collections *Sentimental Men* (1999) and *Boys Don't Cry?* (2002), for instance, scholars have reframed the "repressive hypothesis" of masculine emotion to propose that affect is not banished from male experience but constitutive of some of its most characteristic manifestations: flight, competition, and bonding among them.[11] This work gives us new ways to read masculinity and new questions to ask about emotion in literary studies and beyond. This book adds to the recent critical work that writes against the separation of gendered emotional spheres and against the customary view that regards emotional sensibility as the exclusive domain of the "feminine"; it argues against the most naturalized assumptions about emotion in the nineteenth and early twentieth centuries—that women domesticated it, and men publicly disowned it—while examining how an evolving discourse on male emotional injury at that time unraveled once tidy if inaccurate associations between gender and feelings.

Inspired by debates in cultural studies, feminist and gender theory, as well as law and literary studies, *Wounded Hearts* studies the role of male emotional injuries in a growing field of emotional politics; these are wounds, I argue, that work to consolidate masculine hegemony at some times and challenge it at others. Helpful for my analysis here is Lora Romero's critique of antebellum cultural politics in her book *Home Fronts* (1997), in which she rejects univocal readings of domesticity as either always subversive or always reactionary. Like Romero's critical intervention, *Wounded Hearts* aims to record the complex and multivalent meanings of male emotional injuries. It both analyzes emergent forms of male emotionalism and interrogates the promise of recuperating male emotional expressivity by introducing some of its dangers; it asks, specifically, whether the appearance of certain forms of masculine affect necessarily challenge conventional narratives, as the literary recuperation of "sentimental men" often seems to imply. Rather than a recovery project of the emotionless, "soulless" male in literary culture, this book is an extended critique of the emotional male's practices. One of the principle ideas that connect the chapters to follow is the insistence that emotional recognition, protection, and redress must be analyzed for those moments that both strategically reconsolidate and occasionally remonstrate the hegemony of masculine victims.[12]

Scholars must expand the discussion of affect beyond the narrow confines of gender stereotypes that have defined it and must do more than simply critique the multiple ways in which affect and emotionalism have been used and to what effect. We must also think beyond conventionally fashioned expressions of emotion. While the investigation of emotion in literary studies, what Julie Ellison has labeled "Sensibility Studies," has become part of an important revisionary wave among scholars eager to recast emotional politics for the twenty-first century, scholars also must assess the degree to which the terms circulating in these debates remain static embodiments of an earlier date, with sentiment, sensibility, and sympathy gaining a degree of self-evidence despite continual changes in the emotional and cultural terrain. June Howard has expressed this danger with regard to the discourse of sentiment, cautioning, for example, against treating the "sentimental" as a reservoir for "unnatural" emotion and allowing other emotions, from anger and fear to disgust, to be "taken for granted as . . . fundamental attribute[s] of human beings" (66). Eve Sedgwick and Adam Frank take Howard's critique one step further by exposing the reluctance of theorists of emotion to move beyond the continued assertion of the discursive construction of emotion or affect while ignoring differentiations that surely exist within these categories "There is no theoretical room," write Sedgwick and Frank, "for any difference between, say, being amused, being disgusted, being ashamed, and being enraged."[13]

Mindful of these critiques, *Wounded Hearts* reads male emotionalism using a vocabulary very different from that of the more conventional categories of literary history such as sympathy, sensibility, and sentiment. It uses the vocabulary of *injury*—its notions of duty of care, its evaluations of victimhood, and its assessments of harm—as a critical discursive structure that has deeply influenced the cultural history of emotions. This especially is true, I argue, among white middle-class men for whom injury became an operable term and a more comfortable critical vocabulary through which to articulate and claim a range of emotional wounds. In fact, feminist legal theorists more recently have argued that women must seek recognition for the harms they suffer by invoking the vocabulary of injury, since this vocabulary—unlike that of emotion—has a long and legitimated history within legal discourse.[14] This study argues that men's claims of emotional woundedness appeared not only in nineteenth- and early-twentieth-century literature, but also in adjacent arenas such as the law, where debates about injury flourished and where emotional men often found a startlingly sympathetic ear for a variety of feelings, including dishonor and disgrace.

Several chapters in this study examine how literature and law entered into a dialogue about what G. Edward White has called the nineteenth century's "changing ethos of injury."[15] Largely a development of the nineteenth century, injury law (or tort law) expanded during this time to meet the huge numbers of bodily wounds caused by industrial accidents, particularly those occurring in new industries such as the railroad, that were suffered disproportionately by working-class men. Yet as legal scholars such as Morton Horwitz and Lawrence Friedman have argued, the new legal principles that accompanied this expansion, from the assumption of risk (finding that within the terms of employment, employees consent to risk, which absolves employers of responsibility for employee injuries on the job) to the fellow-servant rule (prohibiting workers from suing employers for injuries caused by their colleagues), often made the recognition and compensation of physical pains largely unavailable to those most afflicted. The narrative that is most often told about injury law—relayed in more detail in chapter 3—is one that describes the consolidation of corporate power against the very men who physically suffered in its making; male pain, in other words, was thought to languish unheard.

Literature tells a slightly different story about the recognition and recompense of male injury. I argue that the corporate economic structure that developed in the United States in the nineteenth century, one of physical injuries and material reparations, coincided with the emergence of a psychic structure (also manifest in and through the law and uniquely imagined and critiqued in literature), in which men, regardless of their economic status, could potentially capitalize on their feelings and pains. Calling upon the domain of injury law, for example, I read the cultural narratives of masculine suffering in this study, many of which focus on variations of the marriage plot, as cases of "sexual torts"; these are literary, legal, medical, and historical examples of emotional distress—ranging from narratives about male victims of female adultery and "criminal conversation" to men's legal accusations of mental cruelty and their literary fictions about divorce. I argue that these cases constitute unique (and underexamined) opportunities for the expression not only of psychic harm in the face of other forms of male pain, but also for the cultural recognition of newly visible victims of emotional and compensable suffering: men. This suffering and these early victims are particularly worth our attention in light of oft-expressed presumptions about men's emotional lives that are based on the misguided perspective that white middle-class masculinity is either emotionless or emotionally repressed.

"Sexual torts" are crucial instances of the articulation and imagination of male emotional pain; they also are instances in which the law belies what legal theorist Martha Chamallas calls its own "deep structure," since a suspicion of emotional narratives, and indeed, the insistent disavowal of emotions, subtends the law's account of itself as disinterested, unbiased, and gender neutral. For instance, Chamallas argues that when a harm is experienced by a man, injury law "highlights its tangible and objective aspects"—that is, its economic consequences—and "downplays its intangible and relational features."[16] Yet when an injury is experienced by a woman, it is "discredited as intangible and relational" (520). I argue that an examination of the shared literary and legal discourse about structures of injury encourages scholars to revise this evaluation. The literary imagination of states of injury asks readers to revisit the seemingly tangible and objective for its contextual and relational vocabularies—vocabularies that, I argue, are not mutually exclusive. Moreover, by introducing emotional injury into discussions on the relations of law and literature (a discussion that has traditionally looked to literature to provide legal reasoning with the voice of feeling), scholars may see how empathic narrative has been part of the law's own fundamental vocabulary from the start. As discourses on injury flourished not only in law and literature, but also across a variety of historical and cultural narratives, from the post–Civil War rhetoric of manhood and nation, in which interior wounds were refashioned by postwar canonical writers as evidence of a virile citizenship (chapter 1), to the more pristine professionalization of literary studies, wherein a discourse on emotional pain became a unique object of manly "scientific" study (chapter 5), the privileged and the powerful did not dissemble but rather brashly demanded recompense for the inmost interior of their hearts.

The Etymology of Injury

As the "changing ethos of injury" influenced how male emotionalism was manifest in the nineteenth and early twentieth centuries in the United States, so too have questions about its constitutive structure become vital to several current theoretical discussions, from those in feminist, gender, and critical race theory to the debates about "political correctness," the First Amendment, and the litigiousness of U.S. culture. Scholars across several disciplines now ask: Who is to be heard? Whose injuries redressed? From early political thinkers such as Thomas Hobbes, John Locke, and John Stuart Mill to more recent critical theorists as diverse as Judith Butler and Catharine MacKinnon, the prevention of injury has been considered crucial to modern notions of the state, the family, and the citizen body. Historically, the definitions of injury have taken their substance, particularly in the Lockean tradition, from their extensions in property. For Locke, the male citizen's physical body and its accompanying material extensions, the domain of property, required protection against injury; indeed, male property was injurable, although the method and design of such protection has been the subject of a long historical debate. For instance, Carol Pateman has argued in her book *The Sexual Contract* (1988) that because this political history presupposes a masculine foundation, protections against injury did not extend to women or wives in these early theories of the social contract, nor did these theories often extend their scope to consider the "originary" contract upon which such a civic structure is based: the sexual contract and/or the marriage contract. If bodily injury and one's freedom from it were a measure of masculine autonomy, a measure of male civic status, those who were never entitled to such protection (women), or, indeed, those who were denied it (again women) were also unrecognized within the civic realm of sufferers.

To trace the etymology of injury is to perceive, therefore, that its historical trajectory has taken many shapes, most designed to protect men against assaults to property and person. Hobbes in the *Leviathan* (1651), to recall an early example, maintained that only a sovereign could "defend [the people] from the invasion of Forraigners, and the injuries of one another, and thereby to secure them in such sort, as that by their owne industrie and by the fruites of the Earth" (142–43). For Hobbes, only a sovereign power could protect his subjects from outside harm. In contrast, Locke in *Of Civil Government, Two Treatise* (1690) describes a civic state developing in order to prohibit injury to its male citizens and to guarantee "such as he might appropriate to himself without injury to anybody" (134). According to Locke, it is the need for security against injury to property that justifies the limited role of the civic government, as he wrote one year earlier in his *Letter Concerning Toleration* (1689): "The pravity of mankind being such, that they had rather injuriously prey upon the fruits of other men's labours than take pains to provide for themselves . . . obliges men to enter into societies with one another; that by mutual assistance and joint force, they may secure unto each other their properties" (43). The protection of civic peace is secured through power invested in government to wield punishment, put into circulation, and offer compensation through property, the "preservation of property being the end of government" (*Of Civil Government*, 187). Property is the method, the design, as well as the object of government's protection.

Despite the attention paid to the protection of patriarchal property in the growing discourse about injury in seventeenth-century political philosophy, thoughts and emotions also were represented in this civic picture. For example, Locke's *Letter* takes as its subject the very subsumability of property with the male body and mind. Freedom of thought is defined, according to Locke, as a fundamental property right. In fact, following Locke's reasoning, the United States later included in its Constitution language protecting the mind's freedoms, most specifically in the First Amendment's liberty of conscience and thought, and the Fifth Amendment's self-incrimination clause.[17] Building upon the theories of limited government offered by early political philosophers such as Locke and, later, John Stuart Mill, liberal democracies found that civic safety was predicated upon notions of a life divided between those laws necessary to ensure public safety and the noninterference required of the autonomous male's private freedoms. Mill's *On Liberty* (1859) is perhaps the best-known evocation of this sentiment: "That the only purpose for which power can be rightfully exercised over any member of a civilised community, against his will, is to prevent harm to others. . . . The only part of the conduct of any one, for which he is amenable to society, is that which concerns others. In the part which merely concerns himself, his independence is, of right, absolute. *Over himself, over his own body and mind, the individual is sovereign*" (my emphasis).[18] The deep and necessary protection and enforcement of power to "prevent harm to others" should not interfere with the male citizen's sovereign right over himself.

While these theoretical forebears may seem a far pace from the injuries of the Civil War battlefield or the fictional divorce court, where men's troubled feelings demanded cultural and monetary recompense, they help to illuminate the groundwork of liberal political philosophies in the United States that ultimately shaped the disputes concerning the extent of the state's mandate to protect its citizens from harm. Liberal philosophy maintains, for example, that private morality (sovereignty of mind) should be guarded against intrusion and that competing notions of the good should remain outside adjudication.[19] I raise these issues not to signal this book's entrance into debates about the nature of liberalism (that ground has been amply covered and is continually contested elsewhere) but rather to register an important conceptual problem when considering the scope of civic protection against injury.[20] In the United

States, the liberal formulation of civic relationships draws a distinction between what Isaiah Berlin has called negative and positive freedom, freedom from interference and the state's obligations to actively protect its citizens from harm; this is the ground for a discussion that continues to command the attention of political, legal, and cultural theorists and continues to inspire the questions with which this section began: Whose claims of injury will be heard? What kinds of injuries redressed? To those queries we might add others, especially those that address how a cultural debate concerning the nature of injury, injury historically defined by men and the nature of their property (including women and children), came to recognize the expanding and ever vulnerable domain of the mind and the emotions.[21]

By the nineteenth century in the United States, the Lockean model of male citizenship, which linked property and personhood and in which labor and land secured personal inalienability (we might recall Mill: "Over himself, over his own body and mind, the individual is sovereign"), no longer seemed adequate. With the rise of the capitalist marketplace and with the "age of contract" coming to supplant the "age of property," as Brook Thomas describes in *American Realism and the Failed Promise of Contract* (1997), material property lost its exclusive value. Male personhood became perilously alienable, argued critics, and "potentially appropriable by market relations."[22] Herein emerged a crisis: the once powerful and protected male citizen could no longer rest assured that property conferred power; on the contrary, social status, as Daniel Bell argues of a postindustrial society, might be determined by other assets, including theoretical knowledge and technical skill.[23]

Against these economic changes, historians and sociologists of psychoanalysis from John Demos to Eli Zaretsky, have described the late-nineteenth- and early-twentieth-century emergence of psychology and psychoanalysis as a soothing antidote to the trepidation engendered by the impersonal marketplace. The institutionalization of psychology and the privileging of psychological depth became part of a new therapeutic culture in the late nineteenth century, one that met the developments of capitalism with a corresponding "expansion of inner life," especially for the white middle class.[24] Like the ideology of the sentimental home in earlier decades, which became a "haven from a heartless world," the "invention" of the psychological individual in the late nineteenth century appeared to counter the alienating effects of capitalism. Building upon Marx's theory of privatization in modern capitalism in which "therapeutic meaningfulness" resides in the "sentimentalized family" and wherein public issues are duly rewritten and, it should be noted, often fictionalized as private matters of the heart, critics of the "therapeutic culture" argued that the effective production of the "bourgeois psyche" mystified changing work relationships and expanding bureaucratic powers.[25] Theorists from Raymond Williams (who famously called the psychological the "great modern ideological system") to Michel Foucault maintained that psychoanalysis perilously took the psyche out of locations like the courtroom and placed it into the private doctor's office, an intimate sphere of relations that ultimately, in Williams's analysis, helped to diffuse public discontent for social inequities, mask diminishing corporate accountability, and discourage public methods of redress.[26] The production of the psychological self, in these critiques, serves the very capitalist structures it originally appeared to contest.

Though psychoanalysis was criticized for removing injuredness from public view, discourses of emotional injury drew upon the psychological as they pulled attention beyond the private psychological subject to locations where the dangers for injuries to the "interior of a heart" flourished. With increasing anxieties about masculine alienability in the marketplace, in other words, the meaning of injury, the cultural methods of protection against it, and the legal modes of redress for it came to be defined anew. Discourses on injury epitomized the development of what Jürgen Habermas has called in another context "privateness for an audience."[27] While Habermas uses this phrase to read the "age of sentiment" in which the exchange of literary work, most specifically letters, became a crucial site of bourgeois sympathetic identification in the eighteenth century, I invoke it to draw attention to the ways discourses of emotional injury in the later nineteenth and early twentieth centuries fashioned psychological interiority, the "privateness" of therapeutic culture, as a matter of public recognition and quite often recompense. Like the discourse of psychoanalysis, narratives of emotional injury, "privateness for an audience," were not solely impenetrable barriers against the alienating effects of capitalism; rather, the cultural production of interiority in discourses of emotional injury often overtly embraced the logic of the marketplace.[28] In their very existence, these narratives acknowledged the possibility that, as James Livingston put it, "selfhood and the market, or character and capitalism, are compatible" (150). Investment in woundedness, moreover, did not diminish men's political agency and power, as so often has been argued about the operation of women's spheres of sentiment; it occasionally masked but more often than not enhanced men. Rather than hidden away in a closet, closely cultivated at home, or shared in private with a medical professional, expressions of interiority became forms of cultural capital that were dragged into court, made the explicit cornerstone of academic institutional authority, and recast as evidence of the resilient strength of manhood itself.

A critique of the operations of male emotional injury is important, then, not only as a cultural and historical corrective, but it is also crucial given the suspicion that contemporary critical theory has registered about the politics of injury and the making of injured subjects. For example, recent work in cultural studies has become increasingly concerned about the efficacy of claims to woundedness, arguing that such claims reify the very injuries and subject positions that they are meant to relieve. Contemporary critics like Wendy Brown and Lauren Berlant suggest that declarations of injury often recapitulate disempowerment; they worry that we live in a moment of debilitating ressentiment in which woundedness, powerlessness, and emotional pain have become the hallmarks of contemporary political identity and in which empathy ("I feel your pain") becomes a political end in itself rather than a step toward social transformation.[29] Brown makes a strong case that modern states of injury, in which every instance of woundedness seems accompanied by calls for redress, work to reify the disempowered rather than to relieve.[30] For Berlant, contemporary political discourse too often trades in a "currency of distress" while it valorizes what she calls "pain centered politics," a politics that holds out the false promise that the "nation can be built across fields of social difference through affective identification and empathy" ("Poor Eliza," 2). She locates the origins of such alliances in forms of nineteenth-century sentimental women's culture and novels that she labels "the first subaltern-marked mass-cultural discourse" ("Poor Eliza," 2). The danger of the sentimental subaltern, Berlant argues (by reframing the terms of the well-known Douglas-Tompkins debate), is that its scenes of pain and suffering appear to have become ends in themselves, ends that impede progress through a "universalist rhetoric not of citizenship . . . but of the capacity for suffering and trauma at the citizens' core" ("Poor Eliza," 2). In this capacity, empathy unwittingly replaces political engagement, and the sufferers, largely underrepresented groups, bind themselves to the very injured identities that they hope to overcome.

I do not want to refute these employments of ressentiment so much as I wish to reframe them. The narratives of male emotionalism examined in this book suggest that the language of injury and suffering as well as cultural claims to pain are not only "subaltern-marked" but often hegemonic in voice and effect. Thus, while I too share Brown and Berlant's concern that cultural critique may too often trade in a currency of distress—especially, I argue, if we ignore, as we so often do, the men who trade most adeptly in this currency—this book, at its most capacious, also hopes to further complicate the ideological reaches of pain-centered politics. It argues that the rhetoric of normative masculine citizenship in the nineteenth century (developing alongside and, in some cases, supplanting sentimental culture) also came to be invested in the language of injury and suffering. The extent to which "national sentiment," to employ Lauren Berlant's phrase, may be constitutively masculine or even remasculinized in the novel and culture of the nineteenth and early twentieth centuries demands that we reassess its non-unilateral reach and complex outcomes. Suffering did become a distinct measure of social value by the second half of the nineteenth century, yet who benefited and in what capacity, like the nature and substance of emotional wounds themselves, is not always as axiomatic as contemporary debates about injured subjects at times suggest. Through the images of emotionally wounded white men spread across the pages of fiction and nonfiction alike, a national discourse on states of mind became distinctly contentious.

Wounded Hearts supplements the forms of empathic identification engendered in subaltern-marked women's novels and culture—the primary site from which affective politics often has been attributed its shape—with the forms of national sentiment that emerge in the context of male emotional wounds and their literary embodiments. As "sentimental ownership," to quote Lori Merish, at once empowered and reified domestic womanhood in the nineteenth century, this self-same ownership left the affective investments of men largely underexamined; indeed, the masculine "heart of gold" remains a well-hidden currency in need of further examination, if not of more overt circulation. The early emergence of and discourse on emotional wounds and the counterintuitive status of many of its early victims should prompt us to revisit our cultural and historical definitions of injury and its privileged narratives of bodily harm. Given its connections to women and minoritized others, it should call upon us to refine what is perhaps today too easily labeled national "hystericism" and to rethink the contemporary notion that disenfranchised

Americans are overeager to claim insubstantial wounds. By beginning to refashion the gendered trajectory of the U.S. fascination with injury and pain-centered politics, this book asks why male U.S. citizens eagerly embraced seemingly intangible (at one time, unthinkable) injuries and how these injuries became central to the cultural imagination of the twenty-first century. The broad ambition of this study is to map a struggle with a new idiom in the United States, one in which an emerging vocabulary of emotional wounds and their gendering helped to transform definitions of self as well as of nation.

Chapter 1, "Soldier's Heart: The Vocabulary of Injury and the American Civil War," traces the emergence of a new vocabulary of male psychic wounds, developing from a perplexing set of symptoms that often were disparaged and discarded among Civil War soldiers and medical men and becoming, with the help of realistic writers such as Henry James and Stephen Crane, a refined territory in need of protection and compensation. On America's foremost battlefields of pain and injury, the elusive and often shameful diagnosis of "soldier's heart" among Civil War soldiers—one of the earliest instances of what would become post-traumatic stress disorder—was remade by literary realists who, anxious about their own cultural capital, imagined male psychic and emotional wounds (and their unique capacity to render them) as the truest signs of a warrior. The chapter begins with an examination of the medical quandary over the interpretation of soldier's heart and ends with an analysis of how writers such as William Dean Howells, Henry James, and Stephen Crane embraced male emotionalism in the Civil War context as a way to reimagine and to reclaim the rhetoric of national masculinity. This rhetoric at one time presupposed the impervious white male body as its ultimate symbol, yet the presence of soldier's heart inspired new narratives of male psychological wounds that spread well beyond the original fields of battle.

Emotional injuries were as celebrated and compensated in "civilized gentleman" as they were ridiculed and dismissed in the more "delicate" sex. Chapter 2, "Emotional Equity? William Dean Howells and the Divorce Novel," illustrates how Howells, the self-appointed spokesman for postwar realism, became a prominent voice and interpreter of male emotionalism in postbellum America. Although Howells delighted in criticizing the "maudlin passions" of the sentimental novel—in which many critics have located the birthplace of the emotive—in his early realistic novel *A Modern Instance*, emotional injury takes a distinctly masculine character and shape. In Howells's novel, one of the earliest extended narratives about divorce, both the fictional divorce trial and the factual cruelty claims upon which it is based demonstrate that men who suffered from "emotional injuries" could reach out for public redress and recompense. This chapter contends that the brand of realism Howells inaugurates in *A Modern Instance* seeks to repair what he perceives to be the cultural wounds inflicted by the antebellum sentimental novel—including the cultivation of an exclusive feminine sphere of emotional excess—by constructing a realist narrative that explores an expanse of emotional injuries suffered by men. In Marcia and Bartley Hubbard's marriage, Howells has the perfect instance of such wounding. The Hubbards' once companionate marriage deteriorates in a flood of angry words and hurtful sentiments. Both Marcia and Bartley are to blame for their marital woes. Bartley, however, publicly proclaims himself a victim before the law; he capitalizes on the expanding cultural and juridical recognition of marital harm in which language and feeling, the very substance of the Hubbards' undoing, became adjudicable in new ways. *A Modern Instance* narrates an Indiana divorce battle over "words that wound," one that demonstrates Howells's insistence that American culture and, particularly, American literature are remasculinized and self-intelligibility relocated when men reclaim what many think to be the singular property of women: the emotive. In Howells's novel, emotional injury is a condition most acutely afflicting men: Ben Halleck, Bartley Hubbard, and Squire Gaylord all amplify a vocabulary of male emotionalism, while Olive Halleck, Marcia Hubbard, and Mrs. Gaylord are characterized by the want of feeling supposedly "natural" to their sex. Within Howells's realistic novel, male pain—its discursive structure and its demonstrable power—is not eschewed but rather is rendered newly readable.

Willa Cather's novel, *A Lost Lady* (1923), the subject of chapter 3, "Things Not Named: Willa Cather's Lost Men, Criminal Conversations, and Emotional Auras," also explores through domestic relations the intelligibility of male emotional injury. Her forum is not the theatrics of the divorce court, but rather the undercurrents of the adultery plot. Writing against what she sees as Howellsian realism's "overfurnishing" of masculine emotions, Cather imagines her hero Daniel Forrester's very wordlessness about his wife's adultery as constitutive of his emotional appeal. Forrester's stoic silence, however, is juxtaposed against the novel's narrator, Niel Herbert, who, in his self-appointed role as a supplier of "affection and guardianship," represents Marian Forrester's infidelities as the cause of emotional injury both to the Captain and to himself. This chapter analyzes Cather's depiction of different male responses to injury, from her characterization of the Captain not as a cuckold but rather as a victim of a modern industrial economy, to Niel's narrative displacement of this victimization onto the Forresters' domestic relations. It is Niel's narrative instead of the Captain's will that basks in emotional harm. Unlike the Captain, who is unwilling to capitalize on the potential injuries caused by his wife's adultery, injuries that were recognized and compensated well beyond the confines of Sweet Water with such legal actions as "criminal conversation," Niel, through his narrative, makes the case against Marian Forrester himself. Like the protagonist in a criminal conversation suit, which allowed men to capitalize upon the pain and emotional injuries they reportedly suffered in the private sphere—perhaps even helping to compensate for their growing economic alienation in the public sphere—Neil presents his emotional attachments as inseparable from his possessive gaze. Indeed, Niel Herbert recounts what this chapter calls a "pecuniary drama of male affect"; this drama is choreographed to privilege the male citizen's emotional life by producing and compensating the "injured male victim," while often strategically disguising how growing public investments in injury and emotional politics are gendered. Through her male characters, Niel Herbert and Daniel Forrester, Cather's novel lays bare the interior of the masculine heart.

Both chapter 3 and chapter 4, "On Personal Quantity: Psychic Injury in Henry James's *The Golden Bowl*," read against the grain of literary scholarship on these novels, which has focused primarily on the female protagonists Marian Forrester and Maggie Verver. Chapter 4 turns its attention to Adam Verver and Prince Amerigo as representatives of two seemingly competing but ultimately allied economies through which masculine power is exercised: goods and feelings. Adam is devoted to capitalist economic principles, while the prince is beholden to his "sovereign self"; he measures himself against Adam using a very "different" currency, which the prince calls his "personal quantity." At the start of James's 1904 novel, it appears that the prince's inward capital and, in turn, his manhood are devalued and effeminized in comparison with those of the rich Adam Verver's, who is able to buy and sell objets d'art and husbands and wives; yet, Amerigo, like his ancestral namesake, becomes the early explorer and colonizer of what in the novel becomes a more precious measure of the familial economy: its calculus of emotional pain. At the start of *The Golden Bowl*, the characters conspire to prevent pain and injury; they work to maintain the integrity of precious objects and of surface relationships. Maggie, in fact, rejects the prince's discourse on interiority, his "private subtlety" at the novel's start. This changes, however, with the revelation of a fatal crack in the golden bowl and, with it, a flaw in the characters' designs. In the second half of the novel, wounds and feelings, part and parcel of the prince's "sovereign personal power," and once disavowed in favor of Adam's surface aesthetics, become the very currency upon which economic and familial relationships are renegotiated, a renegotiation that ends largely in the prince's favor. This chapter not only rereads the discourse of masculinity in the novel; it also places the characters' changing dialogue and evaluation of injury in the context of a larger debate about the recognition and protection of "emotional life," articulated most famously in Samuel Warren and Louis Brandeis's 1890 article "The Right to Privacy." Unlike Warren and Brandeis, who tell the story of the inalienability of the psyche and its withdrawal from the marketplace, James's characters, using the self-same language of the law, as Maggie does on the prince's behalf, expose how the psyche is made material, compensable, and ultimately alienable in the hands of those with power.

Realistic novels like those of Howells, Cather, and James often employed technical discourse and expertise from such diverse fields as law and psychology in order to imagine their own works' engagement in affective politics. At a time when psychologists and neurologists were making house calls to the emotionally injured, and law courts were hearing cases of irreconcilable emotional wounds, literary realists as well as the male literary scholars who began to interpret their work annexed the emotive and the psychological. Literary critics, for example, staked claim, as they newly defined their place within the university (indeed, within the nation itself), to a unique capacity to interpret, analyze, and teach the lay public how to comprehend a vast and novel territory of emotional wounds. Chapter 5, "The Science of Affect: Professionals Reading and the Case of *Ethan Frome*," takes the critical reception of Edith Wharton's novel as an occasion to map the process of scholarly debate about the subjects, objects, and gendering of psychic pain: What were readers to do, Wharton's early reviewers asked, with what seemed like the gratuitous presentation of emotional pain, especially male emotional pain, in the novel? For the early critics of *Ethan Frome* (1911), the rendering of pain, particularly in the figure of Ethan Frome, and the problem of discerning its "ends" became an intricate puzzle, one that caught readers in its unraveling. More was at stake in these reviews than the reputation of an individual novelist, however. If the presentation of male psychic pain was a problem for the largely male critics of Wharton's novel, for a growing public of readers at the turn of the twentieth century the discernment of pain was central to a culture that was increasingly asked to extend its capacity to understand and compensate psychological wounds.

How to read emotions and the pain that often accompanied emotional wounds, especially how to read emotional wounding wisely, became a matter of growing debate in literature, law, medicine, and psychology in the late nineteenth and early twentieth centuries. Wharton dramatizes these debates within the novel itself, asking its readers to judge the competition of suffering that ensues among the novel's characters, Ethan, Mattie, and Zeena. The narrator of *Ethan Frome*, moreover, registers the compulsion and the anxiety about reading and interpreting pain; he interviews various townspeople about Ethan Frome and his "frozen woe," and yet he is still perplexed by the indecipherable sorrow in Ethan's face. Despite the trouble that Ethan's pain evokes in its narrator and in the novel's male critics, literature, many of these same critics later argued, provided an eye onto a world of emotion at a time of increasing demand to expand cultural understandings of the emotive realm in such areas as the social sciences, medicine, and the law. As the United States moved into an increasingly disciplinary world in which literature and criticism appeared to command less of a role, professional literary scholars asserted the importance of novel reading for precisely its ability to navigate, articulate, and train readers in the analysis of feeling. This chapter expands upon the reading of pain and injury thematized in Wharton's novel to examine how, with the institutionalization of literary studies, male literary critics capitalized upon growing public anxieties accompanying the expansion of affect. Fashioning themselves far beyond the professorial training of taste, male literary critics instituted the reading of emotional pain (and their self-appointed authority to interpret affect) as a cultural mandate for all civic-minded men. While *Wounded Hearts* could be described as part of the legacy of this cultural mandate, it reads male pain not as a consolidation of power but rather with an eye toward its operations. It seeks new ways to fashion the enduring debate about emotion, injury, and the gendering of wounds.

Death from a broken heart is no sentimental idea, but a terrible reality. . . . A sudden emotion may indeed stop the pulsations of the heart as instantaneously as a sword thrust or a bullet.

—W. A. Hammond, M.D., surgeon general of the U.S. Army, "A Few Words about the Nerves," The Galaxy *(1868)*

one

Soldier's Heart

The Vocabulary of Injury and the American Civil War

The National Body

As Jacob Mendes Da Costa, a Philadelphia doctor, entered one of the many military hospitals that had sprung up to treat the war wounded, he expected the overwhelming number of casualties; indeed, the crowded hospital ward was becoming one of the regular sites of the war. What he was not prepared for was the kind of injuries he found. "Shortly after the establishment of military hospitals in our large cities, I was appointed visiting physician to one in Philadelphia, and there I noticed cases of a peculiar form of functional disorder of the heart."[1] Along with the brutally battered bodies that came off the battlefields and onto the examination tables were patients whose injuries were not easily detected by the blood upon their bodies, soldiers who were suffering not from the mutilation that had claimed so many lives in the bloodiest and most deadly war in U.S. history, but from a seemingly invisible, though no less painful, injury of heart. Da Costa encountered patients in these military hospitals who suffered from what he called "irritable heart," a set of perplexing symptoms that became known throughout the divided nation by the name of "soldier's heart."[2]

Like William Henry, a private in the 68th Pennsylvania Volunteers who was afflicted with a "soreness in the cardiac region," "a constant dull pain," and occasional strange attacks of "giddiness," Da Costa's patients offered no evidence of lesions in the area of the heart or elsewhere. Da Costa concluded that their symptoms must be a functional disorder of the nervous system: "It seems to me most likely that the heart has become irritable from its over action and frequent excitement, and that disordered innervation keeps it so" (2). Like other military surgeons who were confronted by a growing multitude of soldiers complaining of symptoms for which there were no apparent physical wounds, Da Costa couched his diagnoses in the available physiological terms. With the overwhelming number of physical injuries that plagued the divided nation, it was hard for Civil War surgeons to imagine the nature of pains that were not physical in origin.[3] Da Costa and other doctors searched in vain for physical reference points that could explain these soldiers' ailments, although Da Costa notes that he "could find but extremely few instances in which a wound had even seemed to be the starting point" (38). Soldier's heart, often characterized by cardiac pain, digestive disorders, shortness of breath, and sleep disturbances—symptoms that have since been understood within the context of psychological disorders—emerged from the "clinical soil" of the battlefield (Da Costa, 17).

The Civil War, with its visual and verbal record of devastating physical injury, may seem a deeply vexed historical landscape from which to begin a project of mapping discourses of male emotional wounds. After all, "the gallant Dead" were piled randomly, as one soldier described, from "Plains" to "river," and the shock of violent bodily injury was everywhere. Inch by inch—whether amid railway crashes or among shrapnel wounds—the very circumference of wounding within the national imaginary confirmed its corporeality. As the health of the nation was imagined as a collective of robust bodies, so too was the nation at war routinely envisioned as an injured body: "A desperate enemy is stabbing at the heart of the nation, the capital and clutching at the nation's throat, the Mississippi river," exclaimed Harry Bellows, future president of the Sanitary Commission.[4] Not only was the discourse of bodily health a vehicle for addressing national debates from slavery to secession; at times of crisis and in times of war the body often became the sole index of national prowess. As Elaine Scarry would argue much later in *The Body in Pain* (1985), reciprocal physical injury is "the obsessive content of war" itself.[5] Given the Civil War rhetoric of the injured national body, the existence of soldiers who suffered wounds that could not be readily documented by the surgeon's eye, whose wounds could not be circulated within this national rhetoric, presented a complex problem for those involved in the treatment of the wounded if not for the war effort itself. Against the multitudes of "injured flesh," these barely tangible psychic injuries emerged to become their own symptom of national crises in the war years and those following. Indeed, the appearance of soldier's heart during the Civil War prompted an unusual conflict: within the larger battle for re-union of the national body, another battle for the soldier's mind, and, by extension, the national psyche, was taking place.

This chapter traces the emergence and transformation of the vocabularies of engagement from soldier's heart's perplexing set of symptoms, which were often disparaged and discarded, to the written record of the literary martial men who heroized and reclaimed them. Amid the wartime rhetoric of nation, which depended upon a heroic masculinity—the unassailable male body with demonstrable strength and requisite manly silence—a soldier's heart sounded faint; yet the subtle articulation of such pains, their far-reaching resonance, challenged conventional notions of war, manhood, and the self. I begin with the medical doctors who were presented with the daunting task of interpreting soldier's hearts, as well as the shame and distress that attended these diagnoses, and end with the writers and critics who remade them into evidence of the very meaning of martial manhood itself. Such heartfelt wounds became central to realist writers such as William Dean Howells, Henry James, and, later, Stephen Crane, who would initiate a long lament over what they saw as the absence of "great" Civil War writings and who would adopt a discourse of *emotional injury* in the Civil War context as a way to reclaim and ultimately to remake the rhetoric of national masculinity. To them, the invisible injuries of soldiers' hearts could become the injuries of the nation. Through their work, men for whom physical injuries often were badges of honor might come to understand and perhaps even to esteem a different figure of wound. This is the story of how the scourge of the soldier became the power and promise of the literary man.

The Nervous Man and the Man of Nerve

It is hardly surprising that the Civil War would be taken as a "literary touchstone for manhood." "Exhortations to masculine nation-building," as Elizabeth Young notes in her book *Disarming the Nation: Women's Writing and the American Civil War* (1999), "tended to exclude women, both white and black, from its narrative," while such exhortations mythologized the war as "the province of male fighters and [the] war novel as the creation of male writers" (1, 2). Yet the models of masculinity emerging from the war were not as univocal as this description suggests.[6] The exhortations of soldier's heart challenged dominant critical narratives about Civil War manhood and its rhetoric of national masculinity, demythologizing the province of "male fighters" and "male writers." Of course, it remained deeply antithetical to the idea of martial manhood, especially Civil War manhood, to suggest, as Civil War commander and historian Harold Porter inadvertently did in his magazine article titled "The Philosophy of Courage" (1888), that the nervous man rather than the man of nerve was a central character on the American landscape during and immediately after the Civil War.[7] The centrality of the "nervous man" continues to surprise even today. Eric T. Dean Jr. argues in *Shook over Hell: Post-Traumatic Stress, Vietnam, and the Civil War* (1997) that Civil War historiography most often reads the conflict in one of two ways: righteously or heroically. Despite the recent return of social historians to the war's many battlegrounds and participants, variations on these two lines of argument have tended to eclipse the Civil War soldier and veteran as a "psychiatric victim."[8] Critics must address this absence, as Dean argues; I would suggest that critics must also attend to how the presence of the psychiatric victim inspired new narratives of manhood, especially among those who adopted and adapted his cause: the male canonical writers of the postwar years. A nascent language of wounds and a working vocabulary about injury were embraced by realist writers for whom the project (and subsequent legacy) of remembering (and re-membering) the Civil War soldier became paramount.

Soldier's heart was felt well beyond the fields of battle. This chapter examines three discursive fields of action for recording its development and deployment: the medical, the personal/autobiographical, and the fictional. Each of these narrative arenas simultaneously struggled to address male psychic injuries, and each spoke to the commingling and codependence of seemingly disparate discursive realms. Medicine often would adopt the language of literature, memoirs and letters would appropriate the style of popular sentimental writings, and realist novels would aspire to remake and reclaim a version of martial manhood through newly emerging psychological notions of the "real." All struggled with how to translate seemingly invisible suffering into national glory, and all demonstrated how deeply vexed and doubly bound the language of injury could be. This chapter charts several sites in a genealogy of injury: the relationship between bodily wounding and psychic wounding; the transformation of narrative techniques to describe injury, from the soldier's self-described lack and shame to literary renderings of pain's presence and power; and, attending this, the literary quarrel between the language of "sentimental wounds" and the vocabulary of "realist injury" through which fiction writers struggled to make personal and public, to invoke Raymond Williams's phrase, new "structures of feeling."[9]

The concept of injury became a battleground during the Civil War. The growing number of sufferers who did not bear its physical signs became the invisible underside of a conflict that was captured by what Alan Trachtenberg has called "the memorializing gaze of the camera"; the large-scale wounding in the Civil War was occasion for the first massive attempt at accounting for the physically wounded through the photographic lens, capturing battle wounds well beyond the fields of battle.[10] Recent studies of Civil War photographs have described the effects of the camera's medical documentation, detailing, for example, how photographs of the war wounded acted as evidence of one's veteran status, ensuring that the physical injuries captured by the camera would be compensated. The physically ravaged carried their own self-portraits of suffering to prove their status not only to posterity but also to the pension boards.[11] The new technology of the camera was witness to and evidence of a degree of suffering previously unseen by the general public. Mathew Brady's images of the war dead and wounded gave people the capacity to view not only the physical injuries and material losses of the war but also, for the first time, the increasing capacity of the nation's new technologies to inflict such damage. Never before had there been visual images of men with bullet holes draping their bodies, images that made the devastation occasioned by technological invention all the more real. Oliver Wendell Holmes Sr., writing in an 1863 *Atlantic Monthly* article about the new technology of the photograph, "Doings of the Sunbeam," called these wartime photographs, in stark opposition to the cheery title of his piece, the "terrible mementos of one of the most sanguinary conflicts of the war."[12] If part of what made Americans "civilized" was their technological prowess, Holmes suggested, this power of invention also allowed Americans to betray civilization by destroying one another, a destruction they then were given the capacity to view. For Holmes, Brady's war photos not only capture the magnitude of their subject matter but also elicit painful psychological responses in their viewers. "It was so nearly like visiting the battlefield to look over these views," Holmes writes, "that all the emotions excited by the actual sight of the stained and sordid scene, strewed with rags and wrecks, came back to us, and we buried them in the recesses of our cabinet as we would have buried the mutilated remains of the dead they too vividly represented" (12). The technology of the camera "replicates" painful feelings in those who do not see or engage in the battle firsthand. For Holmes, such feelings must be buried or hidden in a "cabinet" (his furniture for the unconscious) because they are "repulsive, brutal, sickening," and far too unnerving. Ultimately, photography captured the stunning capacity for technology not only to represent but also to inflict grave damage on soldiers' bodies—and occasionally on the minds of those who viewed the wounded—as well as on the war-torn landscape of a nation.[13]

The physical wounds recorded by the camera were as much a record of bravery and service (and thus compensation) as a record of horror. Such wounds were for the victor signs of honor ("to die for one's country"), for the vanquished the visible signs of defeat. Indeed, the "glory of being shot at," if not wounded, was touted by Private Alfred Bellard of Company C of the 5th Regiment of New Jersey in his diary as a "military ambition."[14] War wounds had currency (especially if one survived them); they were the very "language of manhood," as Susan Griffin has noted about Henry James's deeply painful (lack of) wartime experience.[15] Given what a viewer of the Civil War photograph, like Holmes, imagines must be the magnitude of physical pain suffered by the injured soldier, we might ask how Da Costa's patients, soldiers who suffered no visible "manly" wounds, could be recorded for posterity? Who bore witness to wounds that did not assault the lens of the camera with its daunting detail of physical pain? How could the wounded infantryman represent his psychic pain, offer evidence of his suffering, when the body defined the dimensions of cognizable harm for a nation at war?

As the perplexities surrounding soldier's heart suggest, war wounds were penetrating far deeper than the surface of the lithograph or photographic plate. The photograph made the physical ravages of war shockingly immediate; yet these physical injuries were accompanied by psychological wounds that were often difficult to enunciate if not impossible to replicate on film. Horace Porter's *Century Magazine* article "The Philosophy of Courage" (1888) suggested that the record of a soldier's feeling, if not a testament of fearlessness and tempered emotion, must be considered a record of shame. The article, which offered a reply to growing public questions about the feelings of men in battle, tried to ease what Porter took to be the problem of male "nervousness" (wanting as Holmes did to bury feeling in a cabinet) by waxing poetic on the attributes of courage: "Courage . . . is universally recognized as the manliest of all human attributes; it nerves its possessor for resolute attempts, and equips him for putting forth his supreme efforts. A once popular farce set forth these two opposite traits in human nature under the title of 'The nervous man and the man of nerve.'"[16] Porter's promotion of courage aside, his satire is telling; although the Civil War is often described as a point of emergence for a martial vision of manhood, one that is ultra-virile (and from which years later Teddy Roosevelt and his band of crusaders might inspire America's citizens to conquer the world), there were other sides to the images of manhood emerging from the modern battleground and beyond. Men could be puissant and imperialistic, yet so too were they struggling with fragility and nervousness, although less often are these visions of masculinity analyzed in such terms. In fact, the "unwritten war," a phrase that has become quite contested in Civil War literary scholarship, sustains some of its resonance when it comes to the "nervous man" of the Civil War battlefield.[17] A soldier's heart beat faintly.

By the time Porter was writing his assessment of soldierly feeling in 1888, male nervousness had entered full force onto the cultural scene; in fact, multiple intangible injuries were manifest by warriors and civilians alike. In the decades immediately following the war, vigorous attempts were made to repair masculine fragility as nervous men appeared on the doorsteps of doctors who believed that activity and work would "re-man" even the most tender and "civilized" of hearts.[18] Postwar men, described as newly effeminized by peacetime and business culture, were instructed to quit mental work for a time and to reinvigorate their bodies with everything from roughriding in the West to working on the railroad. According to doctors such as George M. Beard and S. Weir Mitchell, the new life of the mind, rather than the soldiers' life of the body, was making these men soft, "womanly." In 1869, two years before Da Costa published his findings on "irritable heart," George M. Beard, a New York neurologist, coined the term "neurasthenia" to describe a host of complaints that he heard from patients soon after the war, who ranged from those experiencing emotional distress and anxiety to the seemingly incurable "insane." With the rise of neurology as a medical specialty in the years after the Civil War, neurasthenia thrived, as Tom Lutz has abundantly detailed in *American Nervousness* (1991), particularly among civilians, many of whom did not engage in battle.[19]

Mitchell, best known as the villain in Charlotte Perkins Gilman's story "The Yellow Wallpaper" (1892), was one of the earliest specialists in the treatment of soldier's heart.[20] Mitchell's infamy may be attributable to his authorship of the rest cure and the women patients whom he sought to recuperate, yet he was also the author of the camp cure, a formula for men to go roughriding through the West to ease their overly fragile nerves.[21] Mitchell was given full discretion during the war over two large hospital wards in Philadelphia by Surgeon General William A. Hammond, and his experience there helped him to formulate the new emphasis on nervousness that exploded onto the cultural scene in the last decades of the century.[22] Mitchell's study and treatment in the military hospitals of injuries to the nerves and the central nervous system are detailed in his first major work, *Gunshot Wounds and Other Injuries of Nerves* (1864), in which he describes his patients as men "who have been shifted from one hospital to another, and whose cases have been the despair of their surgical attendants."[23] These men, "left among the wards," exhibited "strange instances of wounds of nerves. Most of them presented phenomena which are rarely seen, and which were naturally foreign to the observation even of those surgeons whose experience was the most extensive and complete."[24]

Like Da Costa, Mitchell struggled to find diagnoses for the curious wounds he would witness; reluctantly, he was led from physiological to nonphysical explanations. Along the way, Mitchell turned to fiction writing. In an early story, "The Case of George Dedlo," for example, Mitchell writes of a soldier who exhibits "strange instances" of nerves when he loses limb after limb to battle wounds. The story, which Mitchell's narrator claims at the outset will be published elsewhere as a "psychological statement," follows Dedlo and his hallucinations of bodily wholeness as he progressively becomes physically disabled.[25] Rather than end his account where those soldiers suffering with phantom limbs were often found, the "Stump Hospital," Mitchell ends "The Case of George

Dedlo" at a spiritualist meeting, where Dedlo's limbs reappear from the dead to carry him away.[26] The story's sudden transformation from factual to fantastical is telling. The "war neuroses"—from cases of nerves to soldier's heart—became a matter of increasing perplexity to its early physicians; it provoked bewildered responses and inspired creative steps among those obligated to treat it. George Dedlo's pain, like the pain Virginia Woolf would later describe in her essay "On Being Ill," "taper[s] into mysticism."[27]

Despite the growing medical interest in neurology and the increasing caseloads of "intangible wounds" for leading doctors such as Da Costa, Mitchell, and Hammond, the discussion about wartime trauma was scarcely audible outside the wards of their Philadelphia hospitals. The hushed whisper and muted vocabulary in which these wounds were described reflects their ethereality. In the *Medical and Surgical History of the War of the Rebellion* (1888) (the six-volume cumulative account of battle wounds and treatments ordered by Hammond), an exasperated surgeon implores his colleagues to refine their language so that there are "fewer vague descriptions of shock and of conditions of indefinable, indescribable anxiety and nervous depression."[28] If the Civil War and the trouble of emotionally damaged men made a profound impression upon Mitchell's life and the work, it occasioned not so much a "cure," as other manifestations of psychological illness would in later years, as a discreet cataloging of its sufferers' symptoms. "No elements will impress the neurological student more," claimed one physician, "than the diversity of theories presented: their wide range of interpretation, their multiplicity of symptomology, incongruities of description, lack of definite detail."[29] Doctors, sensitive to the demands of masculine dignity, were hard-pressed to come up with "inoffensive terminology," as Elaine Showalter has argued about the nervousness of middle-class men during the First World War. The coming into vogue of the term "hysteria" in the decades after the Civil War likely would have offended veterans, especially given the coincidence of their symptoms with those of "hysterical" women who were becoming ostracized and, indeed, pathologized.[30] How were these medical men to put these injuries into seemly words, and what words, moreover, should they use?

Physicians had puzzled for nearly two centuries over soldier's heart's nearest relative, "nostalgia," a disease labeled as early as 1688 by Johannes Hofer, a German medical student, that continued to present itself among soldiers during the Civil War. Cases of nostalgia, recorded everywhere from Switzerland and Scotland to Ireland and Lapland since the seventeenth century, had reportedly "reached epidemic proportions" in the French army by the turn of the eighteenth century.[31] Men suffering from the disease, otherwise known as "homesickness," were susceptible to fits of weeping, mental dejection, loss of appetite, anxiety, irritability, and more general wasting away. According to Hofer, not only did separation from the homeland initiate these symptoms, but an "afflicted imagination" often was to blame as well (156). In a letter home to his wife, Sallie, Civil War soldier Edward Ogden writes of one such case, "Have just passed through a great excitement, one of our boys, a fine intelligent fellow was taken with temporary insanity during last night, and we had a terrible excitement in camp during the time, myself and Mr. Mason have been detached to take care of him." This same "boy," described as a temporary "lunatic" by Ogden, when put "under the influence of the quietness of a farm house, where we took him, and the kind care of the old lady Mrs. Walter [became] much better." Ogden, himself under the influence of such events, writes: "There is no mistaking the fact that I am really home sick, we have finished our duty and I am anxious to return to my family and business."[32] While Ogden credits Mrs. Walter's kindness in opening her home to the young soldier's recovery, he also employs the model of homesickness to express concern for his own mental state.

Like the ailing national body that became mobilized as part of the North's wartime rhetoric, homesickness became a condition that demanded the language of "re-union." We see this in the Civil War soldier's desire for the war's end and his return to "family and business," and we see this in the Old Homestead stories that filled the nation's magazines in the postwar years, which staged national re-union as an extension of individual romance.[33] In the military, however, the diagnosis of homesickness was complicated by the conjecture that many Civil War soldiers were fighting at or near home, not merely for home or the imagined ideal nation, and thus many surgeons resisted the possibility—afflicted imagination aside—that homesickness was a viable explanation for their patients. "In nostalgic cases," claimed Assistant Surgeon J. Theodore Calhoun of the United States Army, "some derangement of [bodily] health, as a rule, preceded the mental phenomenon."[34] Though Calhoun went on to describe nostalgia as "associated with some other [unnamed] morbid condition . . . of a serious character [in which] mental depression seemed to destroy the recuperative power," the difficulties of definition and intangible etiology meant that the cases of Civil War nostalgia were reported infrequently.[35] In the *Medical and Surgical History of the War of the Rebellion*, nostalgia is briefly described in a small section titled, "On Certain Diseases Not Heretofore Discussed." Even Mitchell somewhat hastily dismisses nostalgia as a substantive diagnosis for American soldiers in favor of a frontal attack on some of his German colleagues of neurology. In his address "The Medical Department in the Civil War" (1914), he concludes: "Cases of nostalgia, homesickness, were serious additions to the peril of wounds and disease, and a disorder we rarely see nowadays. I regret that no careful study was made of what was in some instances an interesting psychic malady, making men hysteric and incurable except by discharge. Today, aided by German perplexities, we would ask the victim a hundred and twenty one questions, consult their subconscious mind and their dreams as to why they wanted to go home and do no better than let them go as hopeless."[36]

Mitchell's flip rejection of psychoanalytic methods of analysis belies the seriousness with which he treated these "addition[s] to the peril of wounds and diseases" during and in the decades following the war. His ironic lament over the loss of "nostalgia," his suspicion of psychoanalysis, his infamous prescriptions for other writers, mainly female, to cease and desist, must be attributed to the protection of what he saw as his own expanding territory of the nerves and mind. The ability of modern warfare to perpetuate psychological wounds and the doctors' difficulty in adequately accounting for them became a central condition of the Civil War, in which neuroses spread through hospital wards with few versed in a language—what would ultimately become the language of psychoanalysis—designed to interpret, to analyze, or to repair such wounds. What nerve doctors such as Mitchell and Hammond were often hard-pressed to explain in medical terms came to be translated into a literary idiom, where their brand of nostalgia seemed far more at home. Hammond, who became a professor of nervous and mental diseases at Bellevue Hospital in New York, also wrote fiction in the postwar years. His interest in madness and the psyche continued in stories such as "A Candidate for Bedlam" and "A Madness Most Discreet."[37] As for Mitchell, his experience in the Civil War was a determining influence in his life not only as a medical writer but as a novelist, and many of his novels draw upon medical themes. Literature was Mitchell's therapeutic ground for working through his questions about the nerves and the psyche; through novel writing he sought to fill with language and voice what was a notable absence in medical circles. For Mitchell, a literary idiom imagined what a medical vocabulary lacked; thus, literature became a central stage upon which his vocabulary of neurological injury might unfold.

Mitchell's novel *In War Time* (1884) tells the story of a young doctor named Wendell who aids wounded patients at a military hospital in Philadelphia and the Morton family for whom he continues to care after the war.[38] The Civil War in this novel not only occasions Mitchell's descriptions of the war's overwhelming physical wounds—it begins, as many Civil War novels do, in the hospital ward—but it also occasions Mitchell's exploration of how emotional wounds profoundly affect men: men and men only in the novel are beleaguered with pains, from troubled psyches to strange, undiagnosed illnesses. Mitchell's doctor is so overwhelmed by medicine's somatic vocabulary that he ignores his own troubled psyche. Yet, the novel makes interiority a battleground for the doctor; we learn, for example, that he is in a fierce war with depression: "He was without much steady capacity for resistance, and yielded with a not incurious attention to his humors . . . being either too weak or too indifferent to battle with their influence, and in fact having, like many persons of intelligence, without vigor of character, a pleasure in the belief that he possessed in a high degree individualities, even in the way of what he knew to be morbid" (16). "Morbidity" here is a code word both for depression and, in the language of nostalgia, "ailments of a wounded imagination." For instance, when Wendell should be consumed with professional duties, he is easily distracted and delayed from work: the sight of a mulberry tree with its "reptilian vileness of texture and color" leaves him incapacitated (5). Despite these "morbid individualities," Wendell is given a dual role as caregiver for sick men and guardian of one of the war's orphaned children. By consciously staging a meeting ground of gender roles, medical doctor for soldiers and domestic caregiver, the doctor's increasingly unmanageable psychological symptoms seem to be explained by Mitchell as attributes of his more effeminate nature.[39] Yet, they are not pathologized by other characters as such, nor is Wendell's domestic work suspect because of its hint of effeminacy. Wendell's "wounded imagination" does become crucially life threatening for those under his care, however, culminating with the mismanaged health and tragic death of Edward Morton, the major's son. Through the doctor's errors of medical and personal judgment, Mitchell writes a full-length fictional case study of the medical man's psyche. In fact, Mitchell's doctor might be considered prescient: by the end of the 1880s, Mitchell's colleague George Beard would find that at least 10 percent of his patients were medical doctors searching for relief from similar and still unmanageable ills. Amid a growing science of bodies and a nascent science of minds, literature became an experimental ground. Through his literary efforts, Mitchell accommodated wounds that his medical colleagues often were a bit hasty to dismiss; he expanded the scope of cognizable injury to include not only the wounded soldier but also his worn and weary caretaker. As notions about the psyche moved gingerly from the Civil War camp onto the novel's page, the language of the medical imagination became a transitional moment toward a fuller conception and narration of the psyche.

Physicians, surgeons, and analysts struggled with how to define and to describe a missing variable, the psyche, and with how to give substance and validity to what was misunderstood, unrecognized, and often disparaged as a fundamentally effeminate flaw. When Charles S. Myer renamed soldier's heart "shell shock" by the First World War, for example, he did so in order to protect the manhood of soldiers experiencing emotional tenderheartedness; Myer linked their emotionality to the proximity of exploding shells despite the fact that many of its victims had not seen battle. Although physicians understood that even the most virile of men could "crack" under the extraordinary pressures of war, an entire military literature sprang up in order to combat what was perceived as the growing threat of costly psychological wounds. What began with two small hospitals in Philadelphia devoted to the study of symptoms in pursuit of a name had become an international laboratory by the First World War, as the world watched its wounded men returning from other battles with a new and indecorous diagnosis. Medical officers from around the globe recognized what Civil War physicians earlier could only vaguely intimate: with modern warfare, the number of wounds to the nervous system "greatly increased."[40] That same year, at the Fifth International Psycho-Analytical Congress in Budapest, Freud's well-known student Sándor Ferenczi detailed modernity's party to pain: "The mass-experiment of the war has produced various severe neuroses, including those in which there could be no question of a mechanical influence." He argued that neurologists, however, were guilty of a most severe omission in their findings (Mitchell's earlier attack did not go unrebuffed): "Neurologists have likewise been forced to recognize that something was missing in their calculations, and this something was again—the psyche."[41]

By the First World War, psychic injuries were not read as ailments of a wounded imagination, nor solely as "perils" in need of an effective medical cure. To the public, men suffering psychic wounds were degenerates and sissies, and to many military men the distrust of the injured psyche became so great that complaints of such wounds were called "compensation hysteria." According to Sándor Ferenczi's study of psychic injuries during the First World War, those who suffered from "severe" neurosis "were for the most part those who had an *interest* in being able to prove an injury" (my emphasis).[42] In Freud's introduction to Ferenczi's work, he famously concurs: "The part played in dealing with mental conflicts by the primary benefit from being ill ('the flight into illness') were observed to be present equally in the war neuroses and were accepted almost universally."[43] Despite the efforts of Freud, Ferenczi, and other analysts grappling with the complexities of traumatic experience —and their analyses were not meant to dismiss but rather to instruct—psychological injury was disparaged within the military and among the public as evidence of malingering. In a few brief decades, from the opening of Mitchell's nerve hospitals to the explosion of psychic wounds in subsequent conflicts, the language circulating about the male psyche was remade from "strange instances" in need of study to suspicious currencies in need of strict regulation.[44]

Compensation Hysteria: The Literary Currency of Psychic Wounds

Given the requisite nature of bodily wounding as a measure of military compensation (including the evidentiary photograph), and as Horace Porter suggests, of masculine courage, it may be no wonder that writers and critics in the post–Civil War years lamented the lost record of psychological wounding; such wounding seemed silenced by the overwhelming physical destruction.[45] Indeed, the medical quandary over soldier's heart that I have briefly detailed was matched if not exceeded by a literary cost accounting that also found its slightly more refined vocabulary bankrupt despite the number of journals, letters, and diaries written during the war. For example, William Dean Howells, the much-hailed dean of American letters in the postwar years, repeatedly bemoaned what he saw as the paltry sum of valuable literature to emerge from the conflict: "Every author who deals in fiction feels it to be his duty to contribute towards the payment of the accumulated interest in the events of the war." Yet the war, Howells proclaimed, "not only left us the burden . . . of a national debt," but left a debt that the nation's literature, staggering "lamely," has scarcely repaid.[46] Despite the numerous fictional and autobiographical accounts of the war, which inspired critic Edmund Wilson to memorably query in the opening of his celebrated study of Civil War writings, *Patriotic Gore* (1962), "Has there ever been another historical crisis of the magnitude of 1861–1865 in which so many people were so articulate?" few of these many authors, Howells repeatedly lamented a century earlier, "treat the war really."[47] In 1864, one New York newspaper editor concurred when he asked, "Is this tremendous epic we are now living to bring forth naught but trash unutterable and bombast?"[48] The war, according to literary critic Henry Beers in 1900, has distinguished itself through "the grandeur of high convictions, and that emotional stress which finds its natural utterance in eloquence and song," and thus must produce "great" sentiment, if not at the time of battle, then certainly in its aftermath.[49] Yet this "sentiment" seemed to many critics to take the form of overzealous patriotism in Civil War diaries and memoirs, memoirs that are often snapshots rendered years after the events or representations of willful memory written to exculpate soldiers or tout bravery; regimental history often appeared the same. Even close to a century after Howells, critics continued to mourn the lack of "great" literature to emerge from the nation's most definitive conflict.[50] In a 1984 review essay titled "The American Literature of War," David Lundberg joined Daniel Aaron (*The Unwritten War* [1976]) and Thomas Leonard (*Above the Battle* [1978]) in finding that Civil War literature was mostly "artificial and shallow." "Apparently Civil War veterans preferred to remain stoically silent about suffering," Lundberg writes.[51] He is quick to point out, rightly, that soldiers "wrote about what they went through in a manner expected of them," a manner that was not yet characterized by expectations to narrate the wounded psyche (375). In the massive outpouring of writing intended to narrate the war, wounding did not include a fully textured conception of the psyche or a conception of psychological suffering that has become, at least since Freud, the prerequisite for communicating emotional pain. Although the record of injury is everywhere, these records appear to lack what some critics might call emotional depth.

It is not my intention to confirm or condemn the judgments of critics about the aesthetic value of the literature to emerge from the war; in fact, there have been a number of recent studies by Kathleen Diffley, Elizabeth Young, and others that aim to challenge the above evaluations.

Nor is it my intention to review this literature in detail, or to introduce readers to the vast sea of wartime accounts. I want to take the critical expectations for "depth" and "realism" in opposition to "artificiality" and "shallowness" as a different context through which to frame the quandary over psychological wounds and the vocabulary of injury in the Civil War years. The lack of intimate narrative about suffering by soldiers at war, as Lundberg claims in his review article, does not adequately describe the record of wounding that plagues almost every page of every diary and memoir; his estimation, rather, describes a retroactive expectation for a narrative of a more intricately textured sort. Literary critics from Howells and Beers at the turn of the twentieth century to Aaron and Leonard toward that century's end were not calling merely for "strong sentiment"; they were searching for stories of psychological along with physical struggle, searching for and trying to understand an amplified vocabulary of wounds (shocks of a different kind). The debt that Howells and other critics of American literature since them have presented for repayment was not in accumulated words alone. What these critics desired to read as the stuff of literature (the emotive and the psychological) emerged out of what was often taken, at least by the military with its traditional image of the martial man, to be the shame of the nation.[52]

If physical wounding always carried with it some degree of honor, soldiers were expected to remain "stoically silent" when it came to the nonphysical injuries of the heart and mind; for the Civil War soldier, these wounds by necessity were to be buried in talk of duty, courage, and manhood. The crushing presence of bodily injury in memoirs, histories, and letters therefore seemed matched, as Howells would famously lament, by a disturbingly silent psychological record. Chronicling his thoughts of battle in his diary and his letters home, for example, Oliver Wendell Holmes Jr. makes clear that his physical injury is a necessary sign that he has "done [his] duty," and he is "very anxious [his family] should know that."[53] On what he believes to be his deathbed, Holmes notes to himself and his potential reader, "I am proud . . . I couldn't be guilty of a deathbed recantation—father and I had talked of that and were agreed that it generally meant nothing but a cowardly giving away to fear" (28). What it meant to be a warrior, if not a man, in the midst of conflict was to bear wounds, even death, with little show of anxiety. "Civil War soldiers," argues Gerald F. Linderman in his study *Embattled Courage* (1987), could not "draw on that reassuring conviction of mid-twentieth century soldiers that battle fear was 'normal.' Instead, the terrors of combat seemed to grow larger because so often they were suffered wordlessly."[54] This loss of language, this silence, was understood as necessary discipline and good breeding. John F. Kasson describes that manliness in nineteenth-century America meant the suppression of one's feelings: "Command yourself," *The Illustrated Manners Book* enjoined its male readers in 1855. "The man who is liable to fits of passion; who cannot control his temper, but is subject to ungovernable excitements of any kind, is always in danger."[55] In addition to the demands of gentlemanly dignity, the demands of manliness were at stake: to be injured in wartime was considered "manly," and physical wounding was a sign of masculine strength not only of body but also of character. Even many years after the war, Holmes would tell a Harvard audience, "The book for the army is a war-song, not a hospital-sketch" (despite the overwhelming presence of the latter).[56] The Civil War for the later Justice Holmes became "a figurative crucible" for the "test of individual manhood."[57] Ironically, Holmes would record his near-fatal injury and hospital stay throughout his life, bearing not the physical wounds that had healed but wearing what was called the soldier's mustache; this signaled upon his body the make of a warrior.[58]

John Carlos Rowe has called war's fetishization of physicality its "perverse invocation of the body."[59] During the Civil War, this "perversity" was omnipresent in soldiers' diaries and letters; it often eclipsed the forms of psychic injury that accompanied it. Feelings of pain and injury were difficult, if not impossible, for their narrators to describe. For instance, Daniel Chisholm, a soldier in the 116th Pennsylvania, repeatedly declares in his letters that any description of suffering is inadequate to the experience of it: "I cannot describe the suffering of this night," and again, "My suffering I could not describe."[60] Rufus Dawes laments in his diary, collected as *The Sixth Wisconsin* (1890), of the horror endured by his brother, who had his jaw and half of his face blown off, and yet Dawes can only offer the banal observation, "The misery of that night's ride was indescribable."[61] Readers of Civil War letters, diaries, and memoirs are repeatedly presented with such phrases: "To tell you how we feel is impossible"; "Nobody at home can form the least idea of the hardships that a soldier has to go through."[62] "I don't know," Robert Shaw likewise writes to his mother, "whether you will like to hear about these things or not for they are horrible to see or to think of—but such scenes show us, more than anything else, what war really is."[63] The reader never quite learns the dimensions of the "real" war either for those wounded or for Shaw himself: "I was surprised to see that the men even who had the worst wounds didn't seem to suffer much. There's no need to go into an account of my feelings" (185). This self-proclaimed lack of vocabulary to express "feelings" becomes particularly striking considering that pain and suffering (and its indescribability) is a common idiom to many of those engaged in battle. For example, Christian Epperly wishes that his wife could see because he certainly cannot tell her about the horrors of war: "You don't know half the harrows of this war and the distruction of thing [if] you was here one moment you could see anuff to Satisfy your mind that waar is one of the most distressing things that man ever had to contend with."[64] Despite many soldiers' distrust of their ability to describe the scenes of war—yet another recurring trope to mark many of the war narratives—there is awareness not only of audience but also of a need for precisely the kind of writing that these soldiers most often felt incapable of producing. Men like Dawes's commander, Colonel Bragg, often bemoan their inability to adequately convey their experience: "Of all I have gone through, I can not now write an intelligent account. I can only tell my wife I am alive and well. I am too stupid for any use" (Dawes, 284).

The disappointment expressed by Bragg is a small example of the absence that Howells and other contemporary critics would lament. "Firsthand accounts were ultimately vitiated by the delicate priorities of a feminized cultural ethos," writes Diffley, describing the conventional view. Without the spare skill of Hemingway or the emotional "urgency of a Wiesel," she continues, many writers "closed the shutters of a national reckoning against the shock of Civil War" (xi). Critics prior to Hemingway held fast to this assessment, beginning with Howells, who claimed that the "young lady writers in the magazines" failed to treat the war "really and artistically."[65] That a feminized ethos dictated narrow emotional experiences is misleading, however. As both Diffley and Young amply demonstrate, women's accounts of the war did not close but rather cast wide open the landscape upon which the Civil War was written. From Louisa May Alcott's hospital sketches to S. Emma E. Edmonds account of Civil War cross-dressing, women's experiences and representations were diverse, despite remaining largely "unwritten" among the war's later historians and critics.

Among women writers, Harriet Beecher Stowe is most credited for having written the Civil War and shaped this "feminized ethos," although her wartime narratives often sought a path different from that of her cohorts. In a letter to James T. Fields describing the inception of her idea for a series called "House and Home Papers," she depicts "a sort of spicy sprightly writing that I feel I need to write in these days to keep from thinking of things that make me dizzy & blind & fill my eyes with tears so that I cant see the paper I mean such things as are being done where our heroes are dying as Shaw died. . . . I feel the need of a little gentle household merriment & talk of common things—to indulge which I have devised this."[66] Stowe self-consciously sought to displace the pain of battle for the reading public, and her talk of "common things" became her most successful wartime writing, appearing, as Joan Hedrick describes, during the "darkest days for the Union army" (312). In fact, more than one-third of the 300 Civil War stories published in magazines during and immediately after the war were Old Homestead stories, indicating the appeal of "restorative domestic values" (and the accompanying assumption of a feminized ethos) at a time when these values were at their most vulnerable.[67] For Stowe, replacing the dreadful with the quotidian, the dangerous with the domestic, and the potentially psychological with the overtly sentimental was a logical narrative strategy; it was a strategy that the wartime soldier/writer used.

What also appears to remain unwritten in accounts of the Civil War is the complex and emotional responses of soldiers to the work of women writers. War writings may connote battle scenes and stratagems, yet many, following the lead of civilian writers like Stowe, served as witnesses to the more "domestic" daily side of war, a side not purely about bearing weapons, mapping battle sites and tactics, or recording the war's extraordinary terrors, much to the chagrin of critics like Howells. Many such soldiers, for instance, were familiar with Stowe's infamous call to arms through her portrait of slavery, *Uncle Tom's Cabin* (1852). Elisha Hunt Rhodes in his *Chronicle of Daily Life in the Union Army* even likened images of field hands and the sprawling plantations described in his diary to Stowe's novel.[68] Likewise, the more incisive accounts of the war in Rhodes's diary rely on the pastoral rather than the purely military: "Today we found a bee tree in a grove near camp. The tree was promptly cut down and found to be well stored with honey. What a treat it was to us. The bees charged on the Regiment and accomplished what the Rebels have never done, put us to flight" (83). That diary writers were influenced by the language that was available, particularly the strategies of domestic displacement, becomes apparent through the number of tableaux found in the diaries and letters. "Having become somewhat domesticated in our new position," writes Private Wilbur Fisk, "I see no better way of employing one of the fairest mornings here that Virginia ever saw than by writing a line or so to my always welcome visitor, the Freeman."[69] Fisk goes on to describe the making of living spaces for the soldiers, detailing how "some of the boys fix themselves up stands for writing-desks, and cupboards for their cups, plates, and fragments of rations" (190–91). John Faller writes of cooking and food preparation and is quite taken with a stove, which, he tells his sister, "is drawing like a little steam engine."[70]

The life of the soldier at war certainly seeps into talk of "household merriment," as Alfred Bellard reminds readers on nearly every page of his diary. Food is often scarce and almost always stolen, as are some other staples. Bellard speaks of "freshly killed cattle," apples and pears, and tobacco ("we of course helped ourselves to a few bunches") (145). Some of the war diaries, although punctuated with the numbers of wounded, helped to displace, as Stowe suggested they might, the anxiety of wartime through the focus on commonplace "domestic" scenes, combating homesickness by re-creating home. Whereas such a style of writing could encompass tears and portraits designed to "tug at the heartstrings," these domestic displacements did not offer the soldier (especially given his code of silence) a model for the expression of subtle displays of feeling. For example, the titles of the collections exceeded their content in making use of emotive language, including "Mother, May You Never See the Sights I Have Seen," "Unspoiled Heart," and "Blue-Eyed Child of Fortune."[71]

Given that soldiers like Rhodes were aware of the descriptive categories employed by sentimental writers, why did the language of emotional injury seem to appear reticently and stiffly in the writings from the front? Why, in other words, would Howells (and literary critics for more than a century following) feel emboldened to claim so little for their literary store? Certainly suffering was literary and even nonliterary subject matter well before the Civil War soldier even thought to lift his pen. Had not Stowe's portrait of slavery been the epitome of national horror if not its most vocal anguish? That Eliza, George, or Tom was not a literary model for the military man's portrayal of his own soldier's heart speaks to the extent to which a certain ethos of emotional wounding had been circumscribed by the confines of gender and race at midcentury in the United States. Tom was presented by Stowe as a martyr of silent suffering, and Eliza, a picture of womanly pain; the drama of Little

Eva's death would be looked to by generations as the ultimate expression of suffering and sacrifice. Still, these characters were slaves, women, and children, and the expression of suffering that was reserved for a woman or a slave was not a model for the white man, who (unlike these others) was representative of the nation. Whereas Stowe deployed sentiment as a unifying and universalizing mode of national cohesion, the very antidote against homesickness, a "warrior" like Oliver Wendell Holmes Jr. was quick to dismiss (rather rudely) its efficacy: "Doesn't the squashy sentimentalism of a big minority of our people about human life make you puke?"[72] Sentiment was a term of derision by Holmes's time, one that originated, as June Howard reminds us, "in the reaction against the elevation of emotional sensitivity to the status of a moral touchstone" (71). Holmes's overblown response not only reflects the suspicion of what he sees as socially constructed sentiment; it also reveals the anxieties felt by men of letters over the strong presence if not predominance of women in the Civil War literary marketplace. Sentimentalism and the women who were credited with embodying it became representative of the dangers of excessive feeling.[73]

If sentiment was stigmatized by men of letters such as Howells and Holmes as manipulative, inauthentic, and "juvenile," its putative opposite, emotion, was embraced as natural, authentic, and fundamentally human. By labeling and rejecting the sentimental, in other words, these male writers were not disavowing emotion but rather capitalizing on a false dichotomy in which "squashy sentimentalism" appeared in opposition to authentic emotion; this dichotomy allowed men to reclaim an emotional style that seemed to them more real. Although the numerous fictional and nonfictional accounts of the war—the literature that attempted to bring home the conflict in personal terms—did not seem to offer Howells the kind of realistic account that he was venturing to strategize for his own work and for a nation of readers, those writers who joined his lament began to rewrite and to remake the meaning of "emotional sensitivity" itself. Against national sentiment and its bodily discourse (epitomized by Harriet Beecher Stowe, her eyes filled with tears) these writers—among them Henry James and, later, Stephen Crane—cultivated a form of national suffering inspired by emergent definitions of emotional injury and personified by the soldier with a wounded heart. Accompanying the charge of nationhood, for these writers, were newly conceived expectations for self-representation, expectations in which one's interior life and one's psychological status were coming to figure prominently. In seeking some definitive *emotive* voices to issue from the war's many battlegrounds, they were reflecting the growing awareness that not only was the war between the states a national turning point from which they urged a novel field of literary representations, but also one that would inspire a new psychic and, most important to them, manly territory for dispute. In other words, the kind of interior wounds that inspired so much medical debate during the Civil War came to define realism's "martial men." Despite the overwhelming language of physical scars that appeared to mark the national discourse on masculinity, these writers would remake physical injuries into scars of interiority, albeit cultivating a language of emotional woundedness that would become "visible, legible, and governable."[74]

In this quest, Howells and his cohorts not only sought a version of martial manhood different from the national sentiment cultivated by so-called juvenile sentimental writers; they also sought a model of the "realistic" and "artistic" that would exceed the literary strategies of the "authentic" warrior as well. Perhaps this sentiment is summed up best by Stephen Crane, who, upon reading many firsthand accounts of the war in preparation for his own attempt at a war narrative, *The Red Badge of Courage* (1895), exclaimed that the Civil War soldiers/writers "spout eternally of what they did, but they are as *emotionless as rocks*!" (my emphasis).[75] Neither the female pen nor the "authentic" soldier's voice could satisfy the desire for a Civil War vocabulary that included the intangible heart of the soldier. Howells, James, and Crane therefore considered their "realistic" writings a correction not only to the sentiment that they saw as excessively felt and obtrusively present but also its equivalent absence among martial men. Despite the mysteries of soldier's heart, these writers used it as an occasion to rewrite professional and martial authority; their writings crucially reworked rather than retracted the embattled terrain of the emotive.

The Lament of the Literary and the Making of Martial Men

When Howells lamented the lack of a "realistic" (read psychological and emotional) register of wartime writing, he indicated implicitly that the source of shame for the worn and weary soldier was the new mark of realism for the literate and literary man. For Howells it was a matter of language, of putting intangible injuries into words; in attempting to do so, he and his cohorts adapted the mysteries of science against the marketplace of sentiment and did so on precisely the most gendered of grounds: the emotions.[76] Through the Civil War soldier, invisible hurts of the most "obscure" kind were rendered by later realists more readily readable. Henry James used this strategy repeatedly in early stories such as "The Story of a Year" (1865), "Poor Richard" (1867), and "A Most Extraordinary Case" (1868). In the last story, James attempts to narrate wounds received not in battle but in the conspicuous absence from it.[77] In fact, James appears to make what he famously describes as his "obscure hurt" more tangible by putting it within the body of one who is expected to be hurt, the Civil War soldier. James writes about the pains he feels, perhaps the conflicted feelings he has about not going to war in light of his brothers who did, as if he too were a warrior.[78] He imagines his own injuries as a battleground and crucially constructs them within a Civil War framework.

In "A Most Extraordinary Case," Ferdinand Mason, a wounded Civil War soldier, is found near death in a dark hotel room by his aunt, Mrs. Mason. Upon finding him alone, she insists that he return with her to the country and be nursed back to health. In the country, where Mrs. Mason lives with her adopted niece, Caroline Hofmann, Ferdinand reluctantly and against stern cautions falls in love. When Miss Hofmann does not return his insinuations of interest and instead engages to marry the young doctor who has been nursing Ferdinand back to health, Ferdinand abruptly takes a turn for the worse. Although he had just been out "chatting" at a dance, he dies within hours. It is a "most extraordinary case," Dr. Knight notes, because "the man was steadily getting well" (484). Yet without the affections of Miss Hofmann, Ferdinand's soldier's heart overcomes him. James foreshadows Ferdinand's mysterious interior wound throughout the narrative, suggesting, for example, that his illness was never physical in character: "It had been his fortune never to receive a serious wound"; his health just "broke down" (466). The psychological character of his hurt is confirmed by Ferdinand's own lament about his injury: "To have broken down in his country's defense, even, will avail him nothing. . . . She needs a man who has defended his country without breaking down—a being complete, intact, well seasoned, invulnerable" (474). Though Ferdinand's manhood is questioned in these moments of self-reflection—to his own mind a soldier's heart does sound faint—his status as soldier also simultaneously erases any suggestion of effeminacy. Dr. Knight is brought in to care for Ferdinand's modern war illness; according to Mrs. Mason, Dr. Gregory, the town physician, "only knows how to treat old-fashioned, obsolete complaints. Anything brought about by the [Civil] war would be quite out of his range" (464). Dr. Knight likewise offers Ferdinand more acute psychological insights: "You take things too hard." . . . "You were devoured with the mania of appearing to take things easily and to be perfectly indifferent" (471). He cautions Ferdinand: "You have opposed no resistance; you haven't cared to get well" (465). The psychological diagnoses that Knight employs ultimately are adopted by Ferdinand who, in turn, dismisses his earlier concern over his own vulnerabilities: he "had not been a soldier for nothing. . . . He deserved his injury, and he would bear it in silence" (480–481). It is his silence not in war but in love, however, that appears to kill him. Readers may recall Surgeon General Hammond's verdict for those with seemingly indescribable wounds, published the same year James's story appeared: "Death from a broken heart is no sentimental idea but a terrible reality."

The language of psychic injury allowed James to imagine the afflicted martial man in an alternative way: rather than tears, painful silences would speak, and emotional injury or the injuries of the heart would be adopted as a nonsentimental form of realism. Like James, writers from Howells to Crane found themselves profoundly unnerved by the war and imagined fictionalized responses to such "problems" as desertion and the traumatized veteran's return home; yet few of them were participants in its many contests. "By avoiding the most profound event of the century," writes David Shi in *Facing Facts* (1995), Howells and others were "denied the badge of martial experience confirming their masculine identity."[79] Howells left the country as ambassador to Venice, trailed by thoughts of the war and guilt for not having served.[80] And though the war did have a tremendous impact on the James family, with two of the brothers seeing battle and severe injury, Henry himself did not serve.[81] James's and Howells's absence of wartime experience has led critics to interpret their work as riddled with anxiety over their lack of martial manhood. This reading has mistakenly fueled critical perceptions of realism as radically different from emotional literature, a desperate attempt to distinguish itself from an "effeminate" sphere of sentiment. To the contrary, the relatively new psychological stakes of war, with newly emerging symptoms like soldier's heart, allowed men like James, Crane, and Howells to enter new masculine territory—to participate by conceptualizing war injuries as mental battles—to be martial men.

It is precisely this transformation from physical to psychological, from the technologies of combat to the trenches of the mind with all its attendant anxieties, that Stephen Crane narrates in *The Red Badge of Courage*. The novel portrays a soldier in battle by a writer not even born at the time of the war to answer the question that Horace Porter claimed was on the public's mind for decades after the war's end: "How does the soldier feel in battle?"[82] T. W. Higginson describes the conventional reception of Crane's novel: "The wonder is that this young writer, who had no way of getting at it all except the gossip—printed or written—of these very old soldiers, should be able to go behind them all, and give an account of their life, not only more vivid than they themselves have ever given, but more accurate."[83] Stephen Crane publicly cultivated such a response when he claimed that he took up the topic of the Civil War from his dissatisfaction after reading a series of first-person accounts of the war published in *Century Magazine* (in which Porter's article appeared) titled "Battles and Leaders of the Civil War": "I wonder that some of these fellows don't tell how they felt in those scraps!" Crane self-consciously searched for the mark of the warrior that is psychological and emotional in kind. Yet a story about psychic pain of the kind that Crane longed for, one that was not "emotionless as rocks," was difficult to document. As the fictional youth Henry Fleming in Stephen Crane's story comes to recognize, physical wounding is the most powerful visible sign of a warrior.

Crane's novel reads something like a tale of "desertion" of the kind disparaged by Horace Porter in his description of courage: "I saw a company officer desert his men, and run to the rear, as pale as a corpse, trembling like an aspen, the picture of an abject craven. . . . He was past all shame; he was absolutely demented" (250). Despite what Porter calls the officer's dementia, he is quick to come to his defense, making clear to his readers that the officer (like enlisted youth Henry Fleming) could and did prove himself in the end: "The man was no coward at heart; he had for the moment, in army parlance, 'lost his grip' under that first murderous fire" (250). Stephen Crane's novel is perhaps the most well-known fictional tale of losing one's "grip," in which Henry, a common soldier, enlists only to find himself fleeing at the first sustained engagement in battle. The narrative follows Henry's feelings of relief at his first instincts to escape and, later, the emergence of his shame: "He was amid wounds. The mob of men was bleeding. Because of the tattered soldier's question he now felt that his shame could be viewed. He was continually casting sidelong glances to see if the men were contemplating the letters of guilt he felt burned into his brow."[84] When he tries to sneak back into a brigade by joining a march of soldiers who, he notices, have been severely wounded, he also recognizes that his own injury-free body is the most conspicuous. The only way for Henry to rejoin his brigade, if not to regain his self-respect, is for him to don a physical injury: "He wished that he, too, had a wound, a red badge of courage" (40). After a chance incident in which he is assaulted by another seemingly "demented" soldier, Henry is blessed with just this. In other words, the red badge is visible sign, one that is necessary to the vocabulary of engagement and to the stakes of the battle; this, at all costs, Henry must bear.

What accompanies this narrative displacement of the object of wounding (from the enemy to the self) is Henry's more painful epistemological and linguistic crisis. His emotions, he repeatedly decries, make him "feel strange" (9). And he tries to find this strangeness, this "anxiety" of "heart," in his comrades to no avail (10). He struggles to "fathom a comrade with seductive sentences," to probe the "secret" and the "unseen" (9). Yet "he of the injured fingers," the "tattered" soldier, offers no "kindred emotions"; indeed, Henry finally pronounces himself a "mental outcast" (10, 14). For Henry, the evidence of bodily injury conveys value: physical wounds and "torn bodies" are "peculiarly happy," have "passion," and he imagines "the magnificent pathos of his dead body" to relieve the "pain of his thoughts" (40, 43, 14). Crane's novel redefines the war narrative not solely through its focus on the traumatized psyche (a commonplace critical observation), but by questioning what it means to have a language about injury and to bear evidence of it. For example, the most devastating engagements for Henry are mere *talk* about physical wounds rather than their actual infliction: "The simple questions of the tattered man had been knife thrusts to him" (46). "It might be inside mostly," says the tattered soldier, "an' them plays thunder. Where is it located?" (45). "Yeh might have some queer kind 'a hurt yerself. Yeh can't never tell. Where is your'n located?" (45). Henry's wounds are "inside," "queer," and unlocalizable according to the idiom of battle. He believes that most of the nameless soldiers he encounters will read his fear as cowardice and his mental battles as a loss of will. The soldier's questions, the probing of the interior of a hurt/heart, the fixing of its location, are devastating to Henry: "They asserted a society that probes pitilessly at secrets until all is apparent" (46). Henry wants to talk about fear—his "unknown quantity" (a phrase that Henry James will later use to describe Prince Amerigo's psychic wounds in *The Golden Bowl*), yet he cannot. Like Oliver Wendell Holmes Jr., Henry must test his will, his reason, with "mathematical" proofs (6). *The Red Badge of Courage* tells the story of uncertainty and internal conflict, the "brilliant measurings of his mind" that no "red badge" can adequately represent (86). Crane calls the soldier harboring such "measurings" in his later story "The Sergeant's Private Madhouse" "the trembling victim of an idea."[85] Amid the tales of wounded limbs, shot organs, and bruised bodies, Henry finally buries "the red sickness of battle" beneath a captured Confederate flag; his wounded soldier's heart emits a double sound: shameful for the soldier yet ultimately heroic for his writer (100).

The Red Badge of Courage has often been read as an imprecise account of the Civil War because it lacks accurate narrative detail about the war's many battles; yet as a tale of psychic distress it is deeply rooted in this conflict. It recognizes an important and often unarticulated link among the multitude of red badges that marked many of the wounded soldiers in the war. Psychological wounds exploded like a canon onto the stage of the bloody struggle. In the figure of Henry Fleming, who "wonder[s] at the number of emotions and events that had been crowded into such little spaces," such spaces would become iconic (86). Crane's novel would remake Henry's intimate suffering as a model for the national ego; his "privatized state of feeling" would become the most "authentic" representation of national heroism itself.

The Civil War occasioned what might at first seem an unusual alliance of military, medical, and literary languages that fashioned a new vocabulary about injury. Although the overwhelming presence of bodily injury often obscured the psychological suffering that accompanied it, the challenge of recognizing, compensating, and treating the injured of heart was a shared problem and a joint task. Those who studied and maintained the war wounded and those who imagined a literature to describe it were partners in representation, if it was a strange partnership at that. What was clearly a battle staged over feeling on many fronts continued to be staged in its aftermath by the neurologists and surgeons who served during the war, as well as among literati like Howells and James for whom realistic literature was a vehicle to provide some respite for obscure hurts. The impact of the wounded psyche or soldier's heart, as we shall see in the following chapters, spread rapidly. Like Crane, the writers who did not engage in the battles of the Civil War often waged their own campaigns within and against both the social injuries of the nation and the personal injuries of the heart. For writers such as Howells and James, "injury" and its *emotional* stakes were a deep manly concern. Crane's rallying cry for the Civil War psyche confirmed that men of letters were invested in a new language of complex and capacious wounds. Although the injured body and mind of the Civil War soldier did not become Howells's intimate subject matter, he too sought to redraw the boundaries of personal and political injury; indeed, his call for the "real" resulted in a project in which the war between the states became a match of gender, one that intimately questions the boundaries of affection and discord. Howells's novel *A Modern Instance*, the subject of the next chapter, examines the emergence of a new category of injury, injury to feelings, and one of its early modes of reparation: divorce. This chapter examines how realistic novels are informed by a quandary of feeling, particularly male feeling, and the dynamic of legal and literary evidence that brings this feeling to light. With Howells's morphing of the martial man, we move from the battlefield to the law court and from war wounds to words that wound.

While the present battle is not being fought with rifles and artillery, nevertheless the casualties are serious. In one instance there are the shell shocks of trench life, in the other the shell shocks of family life—and in both, emotional breakdowns.

—*Smiley Blanton, M.D., and Woodbridge Riley, "Shell Shocks of Family Life,"* Forum *(November 1929)*

two

Emotional Equity?

William Dean Howells and the Divorce Novel

Marital Shell Shock

As surely as men suffered psychic wounds on the Civil War fields of battle, both men and women in the decades following the war were "casualties of combat" in the home. The modern marriage frequently was described as a contemporary battleground. Among the major causes of the "present-day nervous disorders with their attendant matrimonial difficulties and ultimate separations and divorces," argued Smiley Blanton and Woodbridge Riley in *Forum* magazine in 1929, were the "conflicts and sex taboos" that resulted from "the patriarchal family" (282).[1] Women, they proposed, had been increasingly "shell shocked" by the denial of their capacity in a more "liberated" culture, while their husbands grew "moody, sarcastic, and irritable" and suffered from battle "headaches and fatigue" when their wives demonstrated success outside the home (286). As pressure was put on patriarchal relations, all, in effect, were its victims. The diagnoses of a new breed of literature on the exploding subject of divorce celebrated the rights of women, lamented the wrongful disempowerment of men, cautioned about women's fickle loves, and found numerous victims "legally murdered" by the divorce courts among men and women alike.[2] As women's opportunities expanded in the decades following the Civil War, and men's hegemony seemingly narrowed in their wake, men trod, occasionally uneasily, on grounds that women had previously patrolled, and vice versa. Consequently, a plethora of early-twentieth-century studies maintained that the modern marriage was filled with emotional trench warfare. "In the main the nervous husband does not differ greatly from the nervous housewife," suggested Dr. Abraham Myerson in a 1921 *Ladies Home Journal* article. "There is in both the same fatigue, easily arising and hard to dispel . . . a restlessness that makes every noise the prelude to an explosion and enhances an excitement into a soul-disturbing event. There is the same uncontrol of emotion, and in both . . . that weary struggle between fear and hope which gets nowhere."[3] When it came to emotional "uncontrol," men and women were not on conflicting sides, these analysts of male-female relations contended; rather they were in the same brigade.

Deeply concerned with the effects of the "emotional" and "soul-disturbing" challenge to conventional gender roles, many doctors helped to crystallize for public consumption their convenient cause: the nation's marital breakdowns. Yet the frenzy over divorce began years if not decades before several of these disquieted pronouncements. When William Dean Howells chose the subject of divorce for one of his earliest "realistic" experiments, *A Modern Instance* (1882), he joined a wave of interest in an explosive issue that quickly was recognized as one of the foremost shell shocks of family life. Anticipating Dr. Myerson's proposal that men and women suffer from the same emotional "uncontrol," Howells insisted to the public and to his publisher, James R. Osgood, that both Marcia and Bartley Hubbard, his fictionalized and fractious couple, were "equally to blame" for their marital woes.[4] Neither blame nor equity (although Marcia hails from a town by this same name) for conjugal conflict is the real subject matter of Howells's novel, however. As if forecasting Henry Fleming's acute sensitivity to the danger of words in Stephen Crane's *The Red Badge of Courage*, *A Modern Instance* imagines a growing theater of injury, the American divorce court, where words do not solely represent pain and suffering but are in themselves recognized as uniquely capable of intimate and irreconcilable injury. In Howells's narrative of the shell shocks of marital life, the battlefield becomes a court of law, and those men with war wounds suffer emotional and increasingly verbal injuries of heart.

From Howells's small New England town that he calls Equity to the law courts of Indiana, these emotional injuries are surprisingly nonequitable; throughout Howells's novel and the several legal cases that inspired it, emotional wounds are primarily, if not exclusively, suffered by men. Through his representation of an Indiana divorce and its expanded recognition of marital harm, Howells gives texture and voice to a burgeoning domain of injury, one in which language and feeling are adjudicable in new ways, and he depicts the capacity for such injury as a condition most acutely afflicting men. *A Modern Instance* gives us men who are wounded by their passions (Ben), their foibles (Bartley), and even, as we shall see with Squire Gaylord, by patriarchy itself. In fact, male wounds are a paradigmatic problem in *A Modern Instance* and demand a vast sea change, from the cultural vocabulary necessary to understand pain and injury to the kinds of questions asked and reparations offered to those who experience it. Howells believes that American literature and culture will be remasculinized and reinvented when men reclaim a domain of injury that many readers and critics schooled in stereotypes about the sentimental novel think the singular property of women: injured emotions.

Howells explores the newly emerging image of the male sufferer in *A Modern Instance*, a novel that helped to indicate and, indeed, to occasion a shift in the laws of feeling. This shift, which G. Edward White has called "the changing ethos of injury," was especially prominent in the nineteenth century.[5] From transformations in tort and divorce law to medical mysteries such as soldier's heart and its successes like anesthesia, the management of pain and injury became paramount across American culture. "If happiness was the key word of the eighteenth century" (life, liberty, and the pursuit of happiness), writes Wai Chee Dimock, "pain might well be the key word of the nineteenth."[6] For Dimock, the most capacious forum in which this key word is spoken and received, its concepts questioned and often left unresolved, is the realist novel. With close attention to another of Howells's realist experiments, *The Rise of Silas Lapham* (1885), Dimock argues that pain in the novel is broadly represented as the culture's recognition of and responsibility for pain conspicuously narrowed in the world outside its fictional borders. The novel in its form and substance resists what Dimock calls the "dream of objective adequation" structuring other fields interested in pain management, such as the law, in which conflict ideally is resolved by balancing the scales of justice and is characterized by the desire to minimize and to control emotion (151). The novel, Dimock argues, values the "residual" rather than the "instrumental"; as such, it gives pain and injury a large and expansive voice. Nan Goodman takes up a similar analytic terrain when she argues against the inevitability of an economic model structuring the rise of legal accounts of injury, accounts that aim to minimize the scope of legally actionable harms. Like Dimock, literature, in Goodman's reading, helps to register the "contingencies rather than the exigencies of legal history."[7] The novel, both critics suggest, provides an alternative account of institutional culture, one that is less tidy and resolute than its legal counterparts and that offers an incomplete vision of how the world becomes. Howells's *A Modern Instance* appears to fit quite nicely in this rendering of the novel's extended capacity for imagining pain; it narrates a comparable kind of novelistic expansion, especially the expanded capacity not only for injured emotions but for the male emotions it so deftly imagines. Drawing upon new scientific interest in affect within arenas such as medicine and the law, arenas that at one time seemed to shun emotion, Howells reauthorizes emotion in *A Modern Instance* in unexpected ways. In fact, realist fiction, as Howells imagined its reach, did not merely stand in opposition to the instrumentalism of the social sciences; it became a domain at once expansive and instructive, one most suitable, as we shall see in *A Modern Instance*, to analytic and authoritative accounts of emotion.

For Howells, the growing cultural conversation about divorce became an occasion to explore a burgeoning class of emotional injuries and the role that language and literature played in their evolution. *A Modern Instance* opens the private sphere of marital relations to public scrutiny by representing the proliferating issue of divorce; as it does so, it reiterates, rewrites, and seemingly makes real a critical recognition: novelistic language has the power to wound well beyond the dimensions of its covers. Howells manages his intervention in a mounting cultural debate about the wounding potential of words not as literary critics before him have, by touting the novel's moral vacuousness or its unique ability to cause harm by encouraging mindless fancies, but rather by narrating the novel's capacity to characterize and evaluate the increasing seriousness with which language and feeling are recognized and assessed. Howells records the nature of injuries that for him are no less real because they occur in realist fiction than psychic wounds were unreal because they were invisible upon the bodies of Civil War soldiers some two decades earlier. This chapter examines Howells's representations of and investments in the cultural quandary over emotional injuries, which Mari Matsuda and Richard Delgado have labeled in a different context "words that wound." Such injuries form a constitutive place in Howells's construction of a new novelistic "sense of the real."[8] Injury is not only the cause of action in Howells's divorce drama; it is also the term, this chapter argues, upon whose refinement the very status of Howells's realist project rests.

Words That Wound

The idea that language has the power to injure may sound self-evident. From Shakespeare to Howells, writers have reminded us that as beings of language we are equally capable of being undone by it; after all, the tongue is sharper than the sword.[9] That language has the ability to inflict harm is far from a static truism, however. The degree to which words wound, the estimate of their damage, and the punitive costs that they warrant are still much-disputed issues, particularly today among critical race theorists, gender theorists, and First Amendment advocates. Critical race theorists argue, for instance, that hate speech should be adjudicable precisely because this speech perpetuates social injuries: alienation, exploitation, and exclusion among them. Other theorists, such as Judith Butler (*Excitable Speech*) and Wendy Brown (*States of Injury*), have doubts about the efficacy of an expanded domain of speech-based injuries and voice concern about juridical forms of redress. Though this contemporary debate is not my immediate focus, the questions it inspires about language's capacity to yield violence and its analysis of who should be protected against it resonate in Howells's work.

Juridical redress, linguistic (mis)appropriation, injured identity, and emotional vulnerability are all substantive issues in *A Modern Instance*; the injuries that Howells's characters suffer broaden cultural conceptions of injured subjects as they also unsettle them. Of course, speech-based injuries were hardly new in the United States in the 1880s; law courts had litigated language for centuries in Britain and later in the United States, where early libel cases formed the groundwork for debates about First Amendment speech itself. Injury, in such cases, often remained narrowly interpreted, however. Following Blackstone's legal commentaries, defamatory speech was injurious in American common law if it failed the test of truth, despite the "harm done to a person by publication of facts that he or she strove to keep private."[10] Not until 1843 did the British Parliament, and in turn, a revised Blackstone, discard truth as an indisputable defense in civil defamation cases. Judges in Britain and the United States increasingly privileged privacy over truth in adjudicating such cases. As Milette Shamir describes, through civil defamation suits, a "new language of privacy" emerged, one that recognized that language, regardless of its truth-value, can be "potentially harmful to private life" (759). By the time Howells took up his pen to write his tale of divorce, perceptions about language, injury, and emotion were changing dramatically in an effort to meet a more modern culture; in fact, individuals, the culture and its courts recognized, could be harmed in new ways by words. This burgeoning recognition gave new emphasis to emerging yet imprecise concepts, from privacy to emotional injury.

I briefly introduce these issues to underscore that this cognitive arena was circulating not far from Howells's own interests in realism and his chosen subject, divorce. Howells, who was concerned with representing the "facts" of American life, also was well schooled in a debate adjacent to the legal one, a debate that similarly expressed concern for the capacity of language to incite injury; literary fictions were hardly strangers to disputes about the threat of sharper tongues. In critiques of the novel since its emergence as a genre, certainly from its earliest appearance in the Republic, the language of novel writing was considered injurious and its reception dangerous, for reasons ranging from the novel's supposed encouragement of sexual licentiousness to the reader's threatened seduction by false ideas. The Reverend Samuel Miller, a Princeton educator, pronounced "with confidence" that "no one was ever an extensive and especially an habitual reader of novels, even supposing them to be all well selected, without suffering both intellectual and moral injury."[11] The "intellectual and moral" injuries decried by Miller and his cohorts were not suffered by men and women alike, however; the primary victims of the novel's seductions in these early critiques were thought to be women. As Cathy Davidson recounts in *Revolution and the Word* (1986): "To control female minds and feminine sexuality, the novel—its earliest critics would unanimously agree—had to be kept out of the wrong hands."[12] Literary fiction was considered a threat to the stability of the nation: women were the first warriors to fall in the war of words. Such inflammatory evaluations, starting from the earliest days of the novel, continued in somewhat different form in Howells's critical circles at the turn of the twentieth century, when writers such as Henry James and Edith Wharton self-consciously wrote against the dangers of "feminine" fiction while they also were influenced deeply by it.

To claim that emotional injury has a central place in Howells's ethos of realism may seem rather contentious; much of the critical discourse about Howellsian realism has portrayed him as well schooled in the history of the novel and, accordingly, quite wary about the efficacy of emotion, which was characterized most often as excessive sentiment. In fact, the readings of realism that emphasize its opposition to the sentimentalists of the prior generation are remarkably resilient. Critic Edwin Cady, who was largely responsible for reigniting interest in Howells in the mid-twentieth century, introduced a largely psychosocial critique of his work, arguing that Howells's own failures of masculine performance, his exceedingly effeminate nervousness, made him incapable of fulfilling his realist vision. "Life-long psychological difficulties left Howells with a neurotic condition which literally made it impossible for him to know and understand as realities the portions of pain and filth and terror in human living with which a major writer must be at least vicariously intimate."[13] What might be called the anxiety critique of Howellsian realism has been taken up repeatedly in different theoretical guises by literary critics such as Alfred Habegger and David Shi. Shi's description of the literary scope of realism is representative: Howells's and James's "strident attacks against feminine sentimentalism resulted in part from their continuing efforts to assert their own manliness. Gender anxieties permeate their fiction and criticism. Before the Civil War, Howells observed, the male writer had been a heroic figure, but afterward he was dismissed as a 'kind of mental and moral woman, to whom a real man, a business man, could have nothing to say.'"[14] As a critical manifesto, realism, argues Michael D. Bell, was Howells's attempt to cultivate a robust version of masculine ideals and to differentiate himself from the effeminacy of the artist.[15] No doubt Howells's perception of male writers' "mental and moral" womanhood, as Shi describes, suffused his anxiety about wartime literature, the literary store that he and his cohorts found bereft of the "mental and moral" emotions of war, as I have argued previously. As a result of these affirmations of gender anxiety, however, the role of affect in the construction of a new postwar "heroic" masculinity has remained obscure among Howells's critics, despite evidence that Howells actively opposed revalidating stereotypical transcripts of gender, especially those in which women alone are the voices of moral authority, sympathy, and feeling.

Literary interest in male emotions until quite recently has tended to remain eclipsed both by a critical tradition that has been inclined to take gender as the dividing measure of America's emotional economy —the very syntax of separate spheres—and one that elevates popular wisdom on the inexpressibility of men's emotions to the status of self-evidence. Though this chapter agrees with the central argument of Bell's book—that realism is differently defined and understood among its very different practitioners—it questions his and other critics' readings of Howellsian machismo, which Bell states this way: "To be a realist or a naturalist in this period was to provide assurance to one's society and oneself that one was a 'real' man" (6). What it means for Howells to be a "real man" was not to eschew effeminacy, as difficult and fluctuating as that term may be, but rather to repossess emotion by carefully designating men as the repositories of feeling. Howellsian realism, in other words, remakes rather than rescinds the "forbidden phases of the . . . emotional nature" (22). Although real men, according to Bell's reading of Howells, are "men who handle language as a burly carpenter hefts his tools," real men in Howells's novels, and certainly in *A Modern Instance*, as we shall see, deal "stabs" with words for emotional effect (22). Bell, Habegger, and Shi rightly contend that Howellsian realism, and for that matter the realism of James and Twain, is built upon the social foundations of gender; yet it remains important to address how Howells breaks with the popular prescriptions about affective politics by repositioning feeling as acutely localizable regardless of gender. Howells and his earliest reviewers, for example, likened *A Modern Instance* to the work of the most famous sentimentalist, Harriet Beecher Stowe. A *Century Magazine* review exclaimed that "since *Uncle Tom's Cabin* there has appeared no American work of fiction having a stronger and wider moral bearing, or of greater power to affect public sentiment. . . . [The characters] are addressed to the hearts and consciences of men and women in all grades of society and in all parts of the country."[16] Howells heartily embraced this reading, proclaiming in a letter to a friend that since slavery there has not been a theme more "intense and pathetic" for the novel. Rather than repudiating "feminine" feeling as so many of Howells's more contemporary critics have maintained he does, Howells's novel advocates a different texture of feeling, one with a scope and affect that, he hopes, will go well beyond the novelist's pages.

This said, it is important to acknowledge that Howells lent his voice and reputation to the voluminous excoriations of the sentimental novel, often deeming it "injurious." Although he finally may have considered sentimental fiction a margin less pernicious than his historical forebears did, he too supported the critical evaluation that sentimental fictions were potentially dangerous for young women and young men alike. Howells vehemently professes his preparation to discard what he calls the "maudlin affection" of the popular novel on numerous occasions in his collection *Criticism and Fiction* (1891), and he describes this kind of novel as "poisonous; it may not kill but it will certainly injure" (47, 50). Throughout his work, Howells fictionalizes this disavowal. For example, in one of his best-known novels, *The Rise of Silas Lapham* (1885), Howells depicts a scene at the Corey dinner table where several characters poke fun at Miss Kingsbury's enthusiasm for a novel called *Tears Idle Tears*.[17] In Howells's account, *Tears* is less threatening for its social disruptions (as the Reverend Miller would claim) than its lack thereof. Idleness, leisure, and dilettantism (and any accompanying tears) have no place in Howells's ethos of realism, which, as Amy Kaplan argues, "unites its practitioners . . . through the mutual recognition of a common identity rooted in the productive sphere" (17). Christopher Wilson characterizes this ethos as a "masculine ideal of authorship," an ideal that seized upon technical expertise and scientific knowledge as models for professionalization (Wilson, 10). In employing a scientific rather than a sentimental vocabulary (exalting expertise and dismissing fancy), Howells found himself not only redefining authorship but also remaking rather than reneging emotion, for it was precisely the sphere of emotions that these fields, from medicine and psychology to the law, were coming to address.

Contrary to Howells's self-fashioned antipathy toward sentiment and "idle" affect, an antipathy much fetishized among his critics, Howells's literary brand of realism initiated in *A Modern Instance* navigates and amplifies the effects of the emotive, engaging and revising newly professionalized and technical renderings of affect. Howells may be decidedly against emotive excess (as *Tears Idle Tears* suggests), yet he writes about the local incarnations as well as the specialized practices of "emotion work" across gender and genre lines.[18] What is significant about Howells's criticism of his predecessors' sentimental vocabulary and his insistence on its injuriousness is that unlike earlier critics of the novel, who were quick to criticize its noxious effects on the "fairer sex," Howells's criticisms also emphasize the injuries affecting young men. "I believe fiction in the past to have been largely injurious," he writes. "The positive injury that most novels work is by no means so easily to be measured in the case of young men whose character they help so much to form or deform."[19] Howells cultivates new voices of emotional authority in *A Modern Instance*, a novel in which he seeks to compensate for and repair what he perceives to be the injuries done by the sentimental novel (primarily to women) by creating a fiction that reveals the range of emotional and linguistic injuries suffered by men.

Ben Idle Ben

Howells reintegrates emotion into the novel by relocating what he understands as the abuse of affect (the excess of emotion that he takes as the scourge of sentimental fiction) in a realist idiom, one in which feeling is intimately connected to other social discourses and is quite often spoken through the mouths of men. He does this in *A Modern Instance* through the social issue of divorce, in which emotional injury is rendered intelligible if not on a grander scale than sentimental fiction, then perhaps on what Howells takes to be a more "realistic" one. He does this by joining the forces of literary and extraliterary culture—in this case, the culture of law and literature—suggesting that each commits something to the other, and, subsequently, thematizing this correspondence in his novel: "The hour of the night had come when a lawyer permits himself a novel."[20] At the end of a long business day, novel reading is not only a needed respite for a lawyer, in this instance Ben's friend and legal counsel, Atherton; it also becomes a narrative upon which to extend emotive and reasoning skills. It is to the teachings of the novel that Atherton turns when Ben Halleck interrupts his friend's nightly reading to theorize his own injury of heart: "Isn't there a theory that women forgive injuries, but never ignominies?" Ben asks. "That's what the novelists teach," Atherton replies, "and we bachelors get most of our doctrine about women from them. We don't go to nature for our impressions; but neither do the novelists, for that matter. Now and then . . . in the way of business, I get a glimpse of realities that make me doubt my prophets" (283). Lawyers like Atherton read novels; from them they learn about women's responses to injury. Bachelors like Ben also read novels, and from them they adapt their "doctrine" about women. Yet as their conversation suggests, Atherton's "business" and Ben's experience indicate that the novelist "prophets" may be wrong. Although novel reading frames their perceptions and the questions that they ask of each other, Atherton also glibly concedes that novels may have led them astray. Noting that readers may be misguided by novelists' representations of the female gender, Howells offers the conversation between Ben and Atherton as an extension of his own literary critique. Howells's novel, after all, is most certainly not solely a "doctrine about women." The exchange between Ben and Atherton is not meant to spurn readers into considering a dismissal of the novel's teachings, a theme to which Howells will return, but rather to make readers conscious of the distinctions between "novels in the past" and the novel they now read, especially in its contributions to and theories about injury.

Were a reader to amplify Ben Halleck's philosophy of injury ("Few of us have the courage to face the consequence of the injuries we do, and that's what makes people seem hard and indifferent when they are really not so") as a means by which to enter a discussion of male wounds in Howells's novel, it might be most fruitful to begin with the trial scene at the end of the novel, in which facing the consequences of injury would seem to be the novel's climax, one that involves men rapt in legal argument seeking the recognition of injury and its just recompense (250). In this scene, Squire Gaylord argues with vehemence, if not sheer vengeance, to reverse the terms of the Hubbards' divorce suit, claiming that it is not Bartley who has been unjustly harmed but rather Marcia who suffers the graver injury. To and for whom, a reader might ask, does Ben's somewhat enigmatic philosophy apply, as he waits, a bystander at a trial in which he too is intricately emotionally invested? Are we meant to hark back to this pronouncement while Ben stands watching Bartley Hubbard slip cautiously out of the back of the courtroom? Is Howells suggesting that Bartley is a less brutish and a more bathetic character to whom the reader is supposed to extend sympathy? Or is this philosophy meant more for Squire Gaylord, whose seeming "courage" at facing injury makes him seem "hard and indifferent" to Bartley and "cruel" in the eyes of Olive Halleck (422)? These questions and several others certainly emanate from Ben's declaration; yet I wish to query the resonances rather than the consequences of Ben Halleck's privileged term, "injury," in Howells's novel.

The complexity of *A Modern Instance*'s trial scene and the status of its injured subjects is a topic to which this chapter will return; however, I want to begin analyzing some of the complexities of this key term, "injury," by recalling a much smaller exchange, in which Ben's philosophy about injury is relayed by his mother to Marcia Gaylord. Although less theatrical than the novel's climactic trial, it is one in which the problems that the trial ultimately renders begin to take shape. This scene comes precisely at midpoint in the novel, when Mrs. Halleck reveals the event of Ben's own disabling physical injury, his "piteous" "lame" leg, to Marcia Gaylord. Mrs. Halleck professes that she cannot stand to let Marcia believe that Ben has always been "a cripple," and she explains that Ben's injuries were a result of a physical assault (249). "'What seemed the worst of all,' Mrs. Halleck continued, 'was that the boy who did it, never expressed any regret for it, or acknowledged it by word or deed, though he must have known that Ben knew who hurt him'" (250). Since early boyhood, Ben has borne the outward sign of physical injury and bodily difference. Marcia's father and lawyer, Squire Gaylord, lets Marcia know that "he couldn't have got any damages for such a thing anyway"; there is as yet no structure in place to compensate or demand "responsibility" for such an injury (294). The novel, however, rejects the focus on Ben's physical disability in order to depict the difficulty and significance of wounds for Ben that are not physical or compensable but exceedingly emotional in kind.[21]

If the problem accompanying injury is the novel's primary motivating condition (we might recall that Bartley inflicts a harm similar to Ben's on Henry Bird, and this originally breaks off Bartley and Marcia's engagement), the reader learns that Ben's primary concern is not his physical disability but rather his wrenching injury of heart: he pities the appalling marriage that he feels Marcia has submitted to, while he secretly desires her for himself. Indeed, Marcia and Bartley's marriage first and foremost makes Ben "sick at heart" (286), and, using language that he adopts from personal perceptions about his own physical injury, he judges it to be a "hideous deformity" (246). By projecting his vocabulary about his physical and disabled body onto his emotional perception of the Hubbards' alliance, he underscores a conceptual affinity: both body and psyche are subject to the infliction of disabling pain and injury. Yet Ben's pronouncements about the Hubbards' marriage, unlike his more philosophical speculations about injury, are considered melodramatic by Atherton. As exaggerated as they at first may seem, Ben's sentiments are indicative of the novel's preoccupation with emotional well-being, especially in marital relations. To Ben, Marcia and Bartley's union is monstrous not because Bartley is a philanderer, a poor wage earner, or a substance abuser, all possibilities within the realm of the novel; rather, Ben perceives a lack of affective partnership between the couple. He is convinced of their incompatibility based on a want of *emotional equity*, a lack that, he holds, will hasten their demise.

Ben's assessment of the Hubbards initially may seem uncharitable; yet his critique, based upon a belief in companionate marriage, is hardly unusual. While in pre-romantic unions, Elaine Tyler May writes, "husbands and wives neither expected nor hoped that their spouse would provide them with ultimate fulfillment in life, or that the home would be a self-contained private domain geared toward the personal happiness of individual family members," such expectations had dramatically changed by the middle of the nineteenth century. The Hubbards indicate and Howells's novel substantiates that "personal happiness," if not necessarily achieved in marriage, ultimately is expected by its contracting parties.[22] From the novel's start, both marriage and the rituals of courtship that lead to it have changed significantly; the narrator tells us that it is a time when "youth commands its fate," when children make their own amorous decisions, and parents are relegated to the background (7). When the novel opens, Bartley and Marcia are "alone together and all of the other inmates of the house [are] asleep" (7); the narrator informs the reader that "the situation, scarcely conceivable to another civilization, is so common in ours" (7). For the Hubbards, the road to marriage is no longer a matter of "convenience and necessity," what anthropologists have characterized as the first business arrangement; it is a contractual bond of affection, what Walter Benn Michaels, invoking Edith Wharton, has called the "contracted heart."[23] In modern marriage, writes Michaels, "the contract as the expression of 'desire' doesn't only unite form and feeling, it undoes the possibility of an opposition between them" (522). Desire and the desire for the marriage contract, in other words, become one and the same.

The equivalence of love and law, what Michaels describes as the "implication of love in property," not only sustains its relevance with the possibility of contracting *in* but also of contracting *out* through divorce. With divorce, property and love once again appear alienable, and, as we see in Howells's novel, the negotiated currency of love and affection seems rescued from neglect. More than the element of amorous independence delegated to the youth in Howells's novel, a designation that began much earlier with the rise of companionate marriage, the novel depicts desire as a condition for romantic union as well as the crucial substance upon which it may unravel. As social historians observe, the increase in divorce is a symptom as well as a constitutive requirement of affective relations.[24] Different expectations in marriage inevitably led to greater disappointments, explains Norma Basch in *Framing American Divorce* (1999). Unlike companionate marriage, which, as Howells confirms, was "commonplace," wounding the "feelings" of a spouse and "destroy[ing] his peace and happiness" were only emerging in the late nineteenth century as sufficient grounds for the termination of affective legal bonds.[25] Who benefited from such an expansion and in what capacity continues to command the attention of scholars across a variety of fields. Although scholars often focus on women's roles when they query how divorce reframes power in marital relations, they must also ask how men stake claim to emotional property as a way to assert power. More to Howells's purpose in his novel, however, readers might ask how the "robust" language of literary realism and its interest in emotional authority touches the heart of these new legal transformations.

In Howells's divorce novel, the arguments between the Hubbards that the reader is privy to, arguments that become punctuating points in the narrative, substantially injure the emotions.[26] The Hubbards' quarrels, rather than being instigated by family finances or drunkenness, as might be the occasion for one bout, are about feelings, jealousies, and misdirected words. Bartley, in the Hubbards' first major argument of their marriage, flies spitefully at Marcia: "I thought it might remind you of a disagreeable little episode in your own life, when you flung me away, and had to go down on your knees to pick me up again" (258). (This is an accusation he continually returns to.) The narrator is sure to tell the reader that "these thrusts which they dealt each other in their quarrels, however blind and misdirected, always reached their hearts: it was the wicked will that hurt"; these thrusts leave them both "bleeding inwardly" (258). In the Hubbard household, ill will and harsh words define the essence of marital trouble. In the confrontation that leads to the final separation, wounds are once again foremost meant to injure the feelings of the other. Bartley rails at his wife: "You were tolerably shameless in getting me; when your jealous temper made you throw me away, you couldn't live till you got me back again; you ran after me. Well, I suppose you've learnt wisdom, now" (258). Bartley, it seems, has an uncanny ability for unselfconscious self-criticism. His statement suggests that Marcia's biggest mistake is her desire to have him back. Howells calls these verbal spars "stabs" and tells us that although "each had most need of the other's mercy . . . neither would have mercy" (346).

Despite the Hubbards' emotional sparring, readers of *A Modern Instance* immediately will recognize Ben Halleck as the novel's most vocal spokesperson of acute suffering; he agonizes over the horrors of the Hubbards' marriage and repeatedly seeks out Atherton to help work through his troubled psyche. In one of Howells's more didactic exchanges between the two men, the lawyer suggests that in the Hubbards' failing marriage there may be a "plea of blame on both sides" (286). Ben, chastised by Atherton for overly pitying Marcia, challenges:

> "Imagine the case reversed!"
>
> "It isn't imaginable."
>
> "You think there is a special code of morals for women; sins and shames for them that are no sins and shames for us!"
>
> "No, I don't think that. I merely suggest that you don't idealize the victim in this instance. I dare say she hasn't suffered half as much as you have." (286)

Although Atherton is emphatic in his disavowal of unilateral blame for what will be the Hubbards' ensuing divorce, Howells's novel presents a "case in reverse" not only as imaginable but as substantially actionable. In other words, it introduces "sins and shames" and a degree of suffering that is more degendered than a novel-reading public may at that time have seen. Against the sentimental novel, which according to Howells played to the passions and seemed to its detractors to excessively imagine women, children, and slaves as its objects of sympathy, Howells draws upon divorce law and the discourse about emotions developing in the social sciences in order to extend the scope of potential sufferers to include fathers and husbands. Through the issue of divorce, Howells imagines legal and professional interest in their emotional well-being. "The case reversed" is a case for the novel as well; if Atherton is right that Ben's suffering outweighs anything Marcia Hubbard is permitted to feel, not only is marital blame more diffuse than at first glance, but so too is the domain of suffering and the path of its recognition. The sphere of emotions requires the attention not only of the sentimentalist but also of the realist professional.

Unlike the woman that he has come to his lawyer to talk about, Ben is most fully—and often pathetically and excessively—a slave to his emotions as well as his prejudices. Readers discover this when Ben first sees Flavia, the Hubbards' daughter. He instantaneously reads the child as "an element of [Marcia's] misery in the future" (246). Howells is sure to note that a few moments later Ben is "flushed, ashamed of the wrong his thoughts, or rather his emotions, had done" (247). The point here is that Ben's thoughts and emotions are never two separate entities. Emotional suffering is a semipermanent condition for Ben. On one occasion, after assisting an inebriated Bartley home, Ben cannot shake his mortification: "I hadn't been at pains to look them up since the thing happened, and I had been carrying their squalid secret around for a fortnight, and suffering from it as if it were all my own" (283). Ben's statement is telling, for it is "all his own"; Ben later relates how Marcia "made me ashamed of the melodramatic compassion I had been feeling for her," for she felt none of it.

If only to emphasize Marcia's seeming distance from the "natural" feeling of her sex, Ben, on their trip to the Indiana divorce court, dramatically observes that Marcia's sorrow finally "had unsexed her" (431). That sorrow has the potential to "unsex" its subject, radical as it may seem in a novel about marital relations and in a novelistic tradition in which women are routinely portrayed as the voices of sorrow, is commonplace in the world that Howells creates. The characters that readers might expect to be the harbingers of feeling are more remarkable for their want of it. Olive Halleck, for example, is given the voice of reason to counterbalance her more emotional brother, and her friend Clara is counseled more than once in the novel to be "sympathetic" (222).

Readers often have noted that the novel builds the Hubbards' separation and divorce on what seems to be the character deterioration of Bartley; yet Howells does not neglect to describe and amplify the excessive jealousies and passions of Marcia. Both are to some degree responsible, although it is not until their meeting in the somewhat shaky structure of the divorce court that such responsibility is given shape. Howells confirms the judgment against Bartley and Marcia in a letter written to James Osgood in 1881: "I propose to take a couple who are up to a certain point almost equally to blame for their misery; their love marriage falls into ruin through the undisciplined character of both."[27] (That Howells calls their union a "love marriage" emphasizes that "love" as a prerequisite for companionate marriage has not been wholly naturalized.) Such sentiments of "equal blame" and equal responsibility permeate the characters' evaluations of the Hubbards in the novel as well. Atherton, who describes Marcia as "honest, sensible, and good" (213) midway through the novel, pronounces her "passionate, narrow-minded, jealous" by the novel's end (453). And when Olive is ready to dismiss Bartley, surmising, "Nothing is easier than to be a good husband," Mrs. Halleck comes to his defense, exclaiming, "Ah my dear, wait till you have tried" (232). (A chance, of course, she will never get.) Howells's description of the Hubbards' relationship also shifts. Fairly early on in the novel Howells describes the Hubbards' marriage by its days "wanting of suffering," calling these "the happiest of their lives"; yet this happiness soon falters. Bartley at the beginning of the relationship bestows upon Marcia the traditional role of womanly "influence": "You have always influenced me for good; your influence upon me has been ennobling and elevating" (13). Although Marcia at one time responded, "I will try to be kind and patient with you. I will indeed" (137), both Bartley's patience and Marcia's influence wear away as time passes. If Bartley once "did his best to be patient with [Marcia's] caprices and fretfulness . . . instant in atonement for every failure" (232–33), he grows utterly self-absorbed and narcissistic. Marcia's "nerves" soon undo her (182), and Bartley's soft reproaches begin to harden. As Bartley's "instant atonement" becomes plaguing curses, Howells tells the reader that "Marcia's temper fired at his treacherous recurrence to a grievance which he had once so sacredly and sweetly ignored" (258).

Although the ultimate ground for the Hubbards' divorce legally appears to be abandonment—only after Squire Gaylord's legal intervention does the ground become Marcia's abandonment by Bartley and not the other way around—the novel indicates to its reader that there are other bases building in favor of the separation: the Hubbards' growing emotional separation, disinterest, and just plain dislike. It is significant that Bartley brings forward a divorce case based on the ground of abandonment. In the years 1867–1906 in Indiana, women brought forward nearly 5,000 abandonment cases compared with fewer than 40 brought by men.[28] Thus a reader well schooled in the divorce debates then proliferating in magazines and papers would find Bartley's legal action for abandonment unusual; it immediately draws attention to itself as a ruse or spurious claim. The emotional injuries that spark the marital problems in the Hubbard household increasingly were recognized by law courts under the versatile category of "cruelty" as a ground for divorce. Actions for "cruelty" centered on a spouse's "pain," "torment," and "misery," feelings that courts came to recognize but also were continually puzzled by.[29]

Imagine the Case Reversed

What for the lawyer, Atherton, is an unimaginable philosophical query about the possibility of male woe ("imagine"!), was a growing voice in courtrooms across the country, particularly in Indiana, where both women and men sought divorce not solely on the grounds of adultery or abandonment, but also for the less demonstrable but equally serious ground of cruelty, which alleged physical or emotional abuse. In the latter nineteenth century there was a noticeable increase in men seeking divorce on grounds that could only seem "unmanly" to a modern student of such cases who is well conditioned in normative gender roles. Historian Robert Griswold infers that these men surely found the admission that they had endured cruel treatment "difficult": "A 'real' man should be able to control his wife, and if he could not, far be it from him to seek redress from agents of the state."[30] The expanding grounds for divorce for those seeking just such redress was one of the primary sources of controversy about marital breakups in the nineteenth century, however. It became the impetus for Howells's novel.

A Modern Instance, which spends most of its several hundred pages mapping the inevitable deterioration of the Hubbards' marriage—matched only by Bartley's own demise—quickly ends as a divorce novel, and at its time of publication, if not inception, it was one of the earliest. While critics have debated whether Howells wrote his novel as a rigid condemnation of modern morality or as a more complex description of its aspersions, it is his engagement in the debate that is paramount.[31] Howells, who called his novel an "Indiana divorce case," simultaneously celebrates and censures divorce suits in a state where legal separations were more easily accessible and readily granted. According to Lawrence Friedman, lax divorce laws in Indiana and, later, Nevada attracted a "tourist trade," people with money who would spend it living briefly in states willing to grant easy divorces; this explains Bartley's short residence in the state of Indiana.[32] By the 1880s many people in the United States were talking about the subject of divorce, with Indiana foremost on their minds, an interest that Howells capitalized upon.[33] Indiana was a notorious destination for obtaining a divorce, where from an early date the grounds for divorce were more expansively defined than in other states. In a heated exchange in the *New York Tribune*, Horace Greeley charged that Indiana was a "free love" colony because of its liberal divorce laws.[34] Likewise, the district recorder of Indiana, answering an inquiry from a man wondering if divorce proceedings had been filed against him, responded, "I think we have divorced half of the citizens of your State, so that if we continue in the same train, I imagine, in a few years we shall exhaust the marriages of New York and Massachusetts."[35]

In Indiana the divorce rate more than doubled from the year 1870 to 1900. Whereas in most states the grounds for divorce continued to be actions claiming adultery or abandonment, in Indiana there were also grounds citing drunkenness, failure of the husband to provide, impotence, cruel and inhuman treatment of either party by the other, and the conviction of either party in an infamous crime.[36] Though divorces were increasingly granted in several states on the grounds of adultery or abandonment, they less often were granted on grounds such as "cruel and inhuman treatment" in these states, especially when the cruel and inhuman treatment was of word rather than of deed alone (*cruel* usually meant life threatening). Therefore, it is significant that Howells chooses Indiana as the site where the Hubbards' marriage would theatrically end; it is one important site where the push toward "no-fault divorce" begins to take hold. Although "fault" was still assigned and categorized in order to terminate marriages in Indiana, it was found in a variety of actions and, more important, in words—"causes" for divorce that in the main still were considered mute. In fact, an "omnibus clause" actionable in Indiana until 1873 granted law courts full discretion to grant divorce for "any cause" in "any case."[37] Though such cases came under intense scrutiny and prolonged debate, and ultimately the omnibus clause was repealed, these cases shaped Howell's fascination with the subject. The highest number of divorces in Indiana were brought upon the ground of *cruelty*, defined in *Graft v. Graft* (1881), one year before Howells published his novel, as giving "pain, willing or pleased to give torment, vex or afflict or cause grief or misery."[38] What might cause such pain and inflict such injury was often the occasion for dispute, although a skillful lawyer might convince a sympathetic jury that language itself had the capacity for such grievous torment.

Because "no-fault divorce" was not actionable until the twentieth century, the legal grounds for divorce often were understood as fictitious precisely because emotion and affective relations were not encompassed by the law.[39] Howells fictionalizes in the 1880s the problem that Roscoe

Pound would pose in his 1910 essay "Law in Books and Law in Action": "We know that in many parts of the country, at least extreme cruelty has become a convenient fiction to cover up that incompatibility of temper that may not unreasonably exist between a respected [man and his wife]" (21). So the question is, How are communities to behave in light of such fictions? Howells responds to this query by making the hero of his divorce story bring forward a suit on a fictitious ground most often sought by women. Thus Howells draws attention to divorce not only as a "realist" social phenomenon but also as an occasion for nonmimetic discrepancies. The cause of action for the Hubbards' divorce and its just cause are decidedly distinct, a fictional distinction that we are privy to in Bartley's claim of "abandonment" by his wife. Abandonment, as we have seen, is Bartley's cover for the growing "incompatibility of temper" that results in his departure and, eventually, the Hubbards' divorce. "Essentially, strict divorce remained on the books," Lawrence Friedman explains. "In some states, it was very strict indeed; New York, for example, confined the allowable grounds for divorce essentially to adultery. But the practice altered drastically. After the 1870s the most important changes in the divorce system were hardly reflected in the statutes. These changes took place through the culmination of thousands of small, obscure, individual actions."[40] Cruelty cases brought by men, as Howells's novel indicates, were not solely convenient "fictions" intended to extend the cause of action for divorce to more emotional grounds; such cases also signaled a cultural change that permitted and even favored men's testimony of emotional harm.

Many of the "small individual" actions to which Friedman refers were coming to be defined under the umbrella of cruelty, which was expanding in scope and recognizing new victims.[41] According to Griswold, from 1867 to 1906 a total of 39,300 men received divorces on the ground of cruelty. Next to nonsupport, cruelty cases increased more sharply than cases based on any other cause in these years. "Comparing the years 1902–1906 with 1867–1871, divorces granted to wives on the ground of cruelty jumped 960 percent, and to husbands 1,610 percent."[42] Whereas the cruelty cases decided in favor of women consisted mostly of cruelty and habitual drunkenness or cruelty and neglect to provide, for men the ground of cruelty was more subtle and expansive, including "cruelty and incompatibility of temper," "cruelty and lewd conduct," and "cruelty and refusal to cohabitate"; women were not granted divorces on these charges.[43] Michael S. Hindus and Lynne E. Withey argue that "liberalized [divorce] laws . . . were put to uses that had not been envisioned by the lawmakers responsible for them."[44] This is especially true given that the original motive for the cruelty clause in many states was the protection of women, and yet divorces granted to men on the ground of cruelty were increasing more quickly than for women. Griswold cites more than a tenfold increase in the number of cruelty suits brought by men in the years 1880–1906. Between "1867 and 1871, men nationwide received 800 divorces on the ground of cruelty; between 1902 and 1906, by contrast, they received 13,678 such divorces."[45] Men were no longer solely at fault in cruelty cases. They too could be victims of fault, a status that the law valorized and that men increasingly sought out.

Fathers and Sons(-in-Law)

It is first Bartley, the modern professional man, and then Squire Gaylord, the antiquarian country lawyer, who demonstrates just how the legal arena may be a place in which male feeling is given voice and recognition. The reader witnesses, for example, how the law is quick to endorse Bartley's vulnerability (and does little to check the substance of his claims). Although Bartley originally seeks the divorce against Marcia, in the trial scene at the end of the novel it is Squire Gaylord and Ben who demand the divorce for Marcia. When Squire Gaylord successfully reverses the terms of the divorce proceedings on Marcia's behalf, she is stupefied, even after she learns of the action and accusations of her estranged husband. Marcia rises from her chair crying, "Never. Let him go. I will not have it. I don't understand. I never meant to hurt him. Let him go. It's my cause" (445). Marcia leaps toward her father, who in a state of shock suffers an attack that will eventually kill him. The lawyer's illness, rather than Marcia's agency, becomes the focal point of the scene, and like Little Eva's deathbed scene in Harriet Beecher Stowe's *Uncle Tom's Cabin*, his attack is among the most dramatic and excessive displays of feeling. Marcia's divorce, sought to protect her character, is not, finally, her cause.[46] What the reader is left with from the trial scene at the end of Howells's novel is not that justice is finally achieved for Marcia, but rather that male feeling, at one time largely absent or ineffably mute as a descriptive cultural category, is given substance and voice.

That men are a repository for feeling in Howells's novel transcends the generational division that has defined father and son-in-law, the lawyer and the newspaperman. Squire Gaylord and Bartley Hubbard often are read as two opposing poles of manhood, with two very different professions and aspirations; yet what most strikingly joins them is their positions as emotive centers in their marriages. Bartley Hubbard, who is characterized as the more "modern" man, the man who works in journalism as opposed to pursuing a respectable legal career, is most certainly a man of exacting feeling, even if this feeling often leads him astray. Bartley is characterized throughout the novel as "longing for sympathy" when, Howells tells us, "he experienced any mental or physical discomfort" (23). Each episode in Bartley's life and career is accompanied by its requisite demand of sympathy. Even after he rises to the pinnacle of professional success in journalism, readers are not surprised to find that he "shed[s] tears" when Marcia locks him out of their bedroom after an argument (271). Bartley repeatedly invokes emotional language, including drawing attention to "what hurt [him]" (167) and valuing "affectionate intimacy" (100). He does this to such a degree that emotional language functions as a form of Homeric epithet for Bartley in the novel, following him whenever his name is mentioned. Bartley's ambition is not just in journalism but also in sympathy; this is affirmed by the novel's narrator, who validates Bartley's sensibilities: "In this civilization of ours, grotesque and unequal and imperfect as it is in many things, we are bound together in a brotherly sympathy unknown to any other" (174). Howells seems to be more sympathetic to Bartley (he admits that Bartley was to some extent a self-portrait) than critics have previously thought. Even Mark Twain found Bartley an engaging character, one in which he saw himself, "He is me . . . and I enjoy him to the utmost uttermost, and without a pang."[47] In putting forward such an interpretation of Bartley, I do not mean to suggest that he is a character deserving sympathy in the novel; Howells is clear to indicate that Bartley's use of emotion ultimately is excessive, and his perversion of sympathy finally serves to discredit him in readers' eyes. For example, Bartley is unable to extend the sympathy that he so demands throughout the novel to Kinney before and after stealing his story for publication. It is important that male emotionalism is a strategy for Bartley throughout the narrative, however; it indicates its centrality both for the "hardhearted" journalist as well as the much-maligned literary domestic.

Though Bartley may be considered guilty of abusing affect in the novel, the affective role of father and husband is strikingly affirmed, perhaps even celebrated, in the Gaylords' relationship. According to Howells's description of the Gaylords' marriage, there is no "equity" of emotion but rather a stunningly unequal distribution of feeling, with Mrs. Gaylord throwing "more and more the burden of acute feeling upon the husband" as the two grow older (89). More surprising is not that the squire would feel "enough" for both he and his wife as they age, but that the lawyer has always been the repository of feeling in the marriage: "It was not apathy that she had felt when their children died one after another, but an obscure and formless expectation that Mr. Gaylord would suffer enough for both" (89). Howells suggests that when Mrs. Gaylord finds "herself upon the point of experiencing a painful emotion of sympathy" she "save[s] herself" by transmitting the impetus of such feeling to her husband (292). Unlike his wife, Squire Gaylord is acutely aware of the demands of his heart. He describes his relationship with Marcia as one of "intimate sympathy," and he believes that the "sole pleasure" in his life is the happiness of his daughter (97). When he contemplates Marcia's romantic desires, he desperately tries to ease what he sees as dual "pangs of heart": Marcia's for Bartley and his for his daughter's romance, of which he strongly disapproves (97). It is because Squire Gaylord refuses to extend this same heartfelt sympathy to Bartley Hubbard that Bartley describes Marcia's father as a man who "has his emotions under control—not to say under lock and key—not to add, in irons" (243). This, we must realize, is Bartley's most potent insult.

Through Howells's characters Bartley Hubbard and Squire Gaylord, readers see the literary and legal embrace of male feeling. Howells also is quick to convey the dangers of feeling's immoderation. For example, with his secondary characters we see that Atherton is too severe and Ben suffers too much. Whereas novels may once have been unreliable sources for the recognition of injury (forcing Atherton and Ben to "doubt" their "prophets"), now readers see that law courts also may be dubitable spaces for emotional expression. Though the novel initially presents a reversal of authority between novelists and lawyers with regard to feeling (with "nature" and "business" in a more fruitful alliance than nature and novels), readers also witness in Marcia's divorce case at the end of the novel the unfortunate and unscrupulous excesses of the law. By the narrative's close, readers may believe that neither the courtroom nor the lawyer's office can occasion reasoned debate; perhaps Howells's novel should supplant these sites as the voice of realistic emotion.

Verbal Cruelty

Injury is a key term for Howells in the evolving status of the novel from sentimentalism to realism. As Howells reinvents the nature of affliction and the cost of injury, he also foregrounds the very capacity of language and of words to transmit such a change. The novel is neither a dangerous entity to be read with caution, as earlier critics of fiction maintained, nor a fictional linguistic space in which social issues like divorce come to fruition without "real" consequences. Along with Ben, Atherton, and the law court, readers are encouraged to analyze the substance of emotional injury claims as well as the objects of its recognition. Howells's novel imagines a case, a modern instance, in which strong feeling and verbal sparring structures his characters' marital demise. Literary language, this modern instance suggests, helps readers to analyze the increasingly material power and cultural substance accorded to words.

In 1882, the year in which Howells published his presentation of the unruly Hubbards, a Michigan appeals court in the case of *Whitmore v. Whitmore* delivered the opinion that a woman can irreparably injure the feelings of a man. In this divorce case, the court found it "extreme cruelty warranting a divorce for a wife to causelessly humiliate and disgrace her husband" by "applying vile and vulgar epithets to him and dogging him."[48] According to the court, the husband dramatically suffers under the weight of words. Consequently, law journals began to publish articles expressing wonderment at these new findings. Irving Browne wrote in a *Central Law Journal* article titled "Oral Cruelty as a Ground of Divorce" (1898) that he was frankly perplexed at the "acme of tenderness [that] has been reached in this country" in the numerous and proliferating cases of cruelty as a ground for divorce. Browne is not concerned about women's claims, but rather about those cases brought by men who suffer at the mere words of their wives; he is astonished that "the husband is regarded with more tenderness than the wife."[49] Through these male "victims," law courts came to recognize a relatively new category of injury, injury to emotions and "mental feelings." They began to acknowledge the importance of verbal language to impart such feeling. Words do wound.

Consider another instance. In an 1883 case that Howells might have invented himself, A. Carpenter—husband, lawyer, and U.S. Army colonel—brought divorce proceedings against his wife for what he argued was an elaborate literary plot to undermine his character, a plot that he claimed was carried out through her diaries and anonymous letters sent to newspapers. The court agreed:

> It was formerly thought that to constitute extreme cruelty, such as would authorize the granting of a divorce, physical violence is necessary; but the modern and better-considered cases have repudiated this doctrine as taking too low and sensual a view of the marriage relation, and it is now very generally held that any unjustifiable conduct on the part of either the husband or the wife, which so grievously wounds the mental feelings of the other, or so utterly destroys the peace of mind of the other . . . utterly destroys the legitimate ends and objects of matrimony, [and] constitutes "extreme cruelty" under the statutes, although no physical or personal violence may be inflicted, or even threatened.[50]

The legal change in the scope of afflictions, from the subjects extending feeling to those demanding sympathy (and winning lawsuits), accompanied the recognition that emotion now required legal protection. The proliferation of cruelty cases, especially in states like Indiana where Howells stages his novel's final divorce trial, were decided less on the direct physical evidence of harm between spouses than on their hurtful feelings. Published a year before Howells's novel, Joel Prentiss Bishop's 1881 *Commentaries on the Law of Marriage and Divorce* suggests that "mental suffering is the keenest and most enduring of all pains" and that courts must acknowledge that "words produce more permanent estrangement than violence."[51] He wonders, however, how "mental feelings" are to be grasped in light of their apparent intangibility: "The test whereby to determine whether it is cruelty or not—is not a tangible substance; it is a mental condition, created in persons other than the one accused" (648). For Bishop, the question is how to convey the evidence of injury when, unlike most behavior warranting legal action, the conduct is not defined by one particular act. "With no one act pre-eminently reprehensible, [the conduct] may consist of the entire course of life. The case oftenest occurring is where the entire life is connected with and gives color to a few significant acts and words. But the entire life cannot be written down in specific averment. How, then, shall the allegation be?" (645).

This problem of definition, representation, and evidence is the subject Howells takes up in his first foray into realism, his self-consciously "realistic" instance of modern life.[52] The problem Howells poses for himself in representing the Hubbards' case is revealed in the trouble he had deciding upon a title for his novel, one that he changed from *The New Medea*, to *A Married Life*, *Marcia Hubbard's Marriage*, *An American Situation*, *Commonplace History*, and *The Light of Common Day*. He considered his story commonplace history, mythic drama, and newly visible social plight. Howells recognized that wounded feelings and the ability for "mere" words to impart harm commanded the attention of extraliterary social narratives. Wounding words were not only recognized but also validated by the seeming voice of reason: the law. Howells draws upon a cultural history in which the courtroom is a privileged space for working through social issues, while he also criticizes its centrality in "truth governing."[53] He shows readers that the law cannot always be trusted as one of culture's most reasonable voices; even in the more scientific professions, emotions may lead one astray.

That Howells was looking for a legal situation in which the causes for marital discontent were expansively defined and unpredictably decided (where narrative and the power of the word might prevail) is evident in his correspondences with Maurice Thompson, an Indiana railroad engineer turned lawyer and budding novelist. According to Thompson's letters, Howells was interested in visiting an Indiana courtroom to witness a divorce trial firsthand. Howells was not looking for any divorce case, however; he was looking for cases decided under the Indiana "omnibus clause," which, as mentioned earlier, gave the courts full discretion to grant divorce for "any cause" in "any case." Although this particular clause was repealed in 1873, well before Howells even began his novel, he was unaware of this when he began considering his subject. As late as 1881 Thompson wrote to Howells suggesting that he might help him with the trial scene: "If it chance that I discover no divorce cause pending under the old regime, you may draw on me for a minute description of the kind of court scene that you want."[54] Of course, there would be no cases pending under a clause that was repealed in 1873, and Howells never did take Thompson up on his offer to act as a court reporter (although Howells did spend a week with Thompson in Indiana); nonetheless, the increasing presence of cruelty actions suited Howells's purpose well. These cases indicated to Howells just how the texture of male sentiment and the claims of suffering and cruelty might take shape, and they highlighted the near indiscernibility between the fictional and the real in the seemingly most realistic and reasonable of environs: the law court.

Divorce in *A Modern Instance* is not merely a convenient fictional tool for Howells, one through which he breaks with the novel tradition by forgoing the marriage plot to focus on marital exits. (Indeed, he also abandons the adultery novel, one of the more common narrative devices in the nineteenth century and subject of the next chapter.)[55] More important, divorce, and particularly the cause of action for cruelty, which legal scholars conceded "cannot in the nature of things be defined," permits Howells to offer into evidence the critical recognition that real-life situations often invoke, if not require, a fictional vocabulary. Literary invention in this case is closely aligned with legal narratives and may help to structure its very methods of recognition and recompense.[56] Howells's mix of legal and literary "fictions" permits him to recuperate a domain of feeling that in his mind had been lost to the literary "bestsellers" and women authors, retrieving for realistic literature that which had been corrupted by the "novel [that] flatters the passions" (*Criticism and Fiction*, 46). Howells does this by presenting emotionality as multidimensional and quite often masculine in character. Like legal actions for divorce that focused on the emotions as valid criteria for social change, change would not take place solely through what Howells and several other critics dismissed as the "private" patience and influence exerted by the female population, but rather through the affective extension of sympathy and responsibility that was masculine in shape and kind. Howells's novel ushered in a new fictional disposition in which words were recognized not solely for their ability to heal, to instruct, or to extend sympathy, but for their "realistic" and manly potential to wound.

Nebraska is particularly blessed with laws calculated to regulate the personal life of her citizens. They are not laws that trample you underfoot and crush you but laws that just sort of cramp one. Laws that put the state on a plane between despotism and personal liberty.

—*Willa Cather,* Lincoln Evening State Journal *(1921), in* Willa Cather in Person *(1986)*

three

Things Not Named

Willa Cather's Lost Men, Criminal Conversations, and Emotional Auras

If William Dean Howells's characters Squire Gaylord and Bartley Hubbard render the divorce court a dramatic stage for disputing the law of the masculine heart, Willa Cather's characters Captain Daniel Forrester and Niel Herbert in her 1923 novel *A Lost Lady* perform a more muted and minimalist drama of male emotions. More than forty years after Howells published his realist experiment in which he reenvisioned the gendering of emotional wounds, Willa Cather writes a spare and sympathetic portrait of men who appear to suffer, at least within the pages of the novel, largely in silence. Cather's novel looks back with nostalgia to the post–Civil War landscape of Sweet Water, Nebraska, and to the pioneers who built the transcontinental railroad in order to unite the landscape and its people. This is a far different vocation than Howells's pioneers in Indiana who, at the same time, were battling to undo marital unions. Yet Cather's novel, like Howells's, seeks to reinvest emotion, especially masculine emotion, with literary and cultural value; it too imagines and revises some of the very conditions upon which pain and injury were coming to be newly defined. *A Lost Lady* casts the injured male psyche not only as a subject for recognition, but also for potential safeguard and reward; in so doing, it invites readers to revisit and even to resituate men's newly compensable emotional wounds.[1]

A Lost Lady is a novel about adultery. Through the omniscient narration of Niel Herbert, one of the novel's most acutely wounded men, Cather tells the story of the enigmatic and unfaithful Marian Forrester and her loyal husband, Daniel, an aging railroad pioneer. Captain Forrester is a victim of the modern industrial economy; he is physically injured, no longer capable of managing the rigorous work of railroad expansion, and he is displaced by younger, more financially astute businessmen. Through Niel Herbert's narration and his self-appointed responsibility for the Forresters' "affection and guardianship," the kinds of injuries that the Captain suffers, injuries that were growing in number yet often unrecognized in the public sphere of corporate economy, seamlessly are displaced onto domestic relations.[2] Niel presents Marian Forrester's infidelities as the cause of personal and emotional injury both to the Captain and to himself; indeed, Niel, unlike the Captain, will capitalize on these injuries: they provide the need for his narrative itself. Niel's narration not only indulges his sense of personal injury and betrayal; it indicates a larger cultural drive toward the reconceptualization of injury, from cultural concern over its physical manifestations to acknowledgment of its psychical counterparts. As the rising number of corporate and industrial injuries were unacknowledged and uncompensated in the public sphere—Captain Forrester is representative of mounting alienation in this regard—domestic injuries, among them the nation's adulteries and divorces, superseded them in urgency and scope.

For example, at home, male emotional distress (but not female) was given legal substance and thus loudly was heard. Niel, the apprentice lawyer, speaks in muted tones that would seem to befit the narration of what the culture beyond the novel would call "criminal conversation." Contrary to what the words might seem to imply—stolen whispers and inaudible secrets—criminal conversation designated the noisy and outspoken cataloging of emotional property in legal actions that became the vocal equivalent of "unspoken" adulteries. Criminal conversation allowed a husband, who could not legally sue his wife for damages in an adultery case, to press a third party, the "seducer," for damages over the husband's loss of consortium, or the "right" to sexual relations with a wife. These tort or injury cases allowed men like Captain Forrester to capitalize on the pain and emotional injuries they reportedly suffered in the private sphere, perhaps even compensating for their growing economic alienation and financial failures in the public sphere. Criminal conversation cases narrated pecuniary dramas of male affect in which the "property-man" became a hero. Much like Howells's theater of divorce, criminal conversation cases were choreographed to privilege the male citizen's emotional life by producing and compensating the injured male victim.

This chapter examines this melodrama of male affect, first through the figure of the Captain, who appears heroic in his very resistance to it, and then through the figure of Neil, who initially embraces this pecuniary drama but ultimately casts it aside. For Cather, the unspoken threat of "criminal conversation," with its cataloging of emotional property, underscores the conditions from which the novel must articulate its antithesis: the revival of a lost, seemingly immaterial, emotional terrain. The lost emotional terrain that Cather privileges as the novel's cultural work is not one of words or of material recompense. Cather wants to write a novel that embraces the "presence of the thing not named, of the overtone divined by the ear but not heard by it . . . the emotional aura."[3]

For Cather, "emotional aura" is best defined by what it is not. It is not, for instance, a product of her predecessor William Dean Howells's realist legacy; indeed, Cather launches a critique of this legacy, which she reads as too fraught with words. For Cather, the writer's purpose is to "leave the scene bare for the play of emotions, great and little"; thus, despite Howells's early attempts at reauthorizing and regendering emotion in realist fiction, in Cather's estimation, the realist novel has failed miserably ("Novel Démeublé," 43). In her essay "The Novel Démeublé," published shortly before *A Lost Lady*, Cather argues that the drive of realists to catalog "the fact, the thing, the deed" has left the novel "over-furnished": "The novel, for a long while, has been over-furnished. The property-man has been so busy on its pages, the importance of material objects and their vivid presentation have been so stressed, that we take it for granted whoever can observe, and can write the English language, can write a novel" ("Novel Démeublé," 1). "The property-man" in all his exquisite detail has evacuated the "emotional penumbra of character" ("Novel Démeublé," 40). Cather writes to recapture an "emotional penumbra" by divesting the "property-man" of much of his property, by imagining his growing physical and financial frailties, and by implicitly critiquing what the novel does not name but everywhere recalls: the cultural drive to catalog his emotional life as one more piece of furniture.

If the above description rings at all familiar for readers of *A Lost Lady*, it is because the character Daniel Forrester is Cather's anti-property-man. As we shall see, he resolutely refuses to name "the fact, or the thing, or the deed" of Marian's adultery, and he remains heroic in his financial divestment and physical decline, all of which increase his "emotional aura." In the shadows of Cather's title character in *A Lost Lady*, Marian Forrester, and often in the background of much critical debate that has focused on the enigmatic, dutiful, and yet unfaithful wife of the great railroad man, Daniel Forrester embodies the novel's language of loss and emotional gain. In fact, Niel and the narrative assure readers more than once that it is Marian Forrester's "comprehension of a man like the railroad-builder, her loyalty to him," that "stamped her more than anything else" (65). For Cather, Captain Forrester is representative of the novelist's "backward" glance, her nostalgia for a "lost" historical moment. His character represents the author's sense of her own writing in the year prior to the novel's publication; she claims it is for the "the backward, and by one of their number" that the sketches and her essay "The Novel Démeublé" appear.[4] The Captain may be a vestige of the lost pioneer days, but he also exemplifies the kind of emotional shadowing and understatement that Cather privileges as the novel's more contemporary work. He is heroic in this understatement; not only is it his "habit" to "talk very little," but also, unlike Howells's Squire Gaylord, he refuses to speak what he "know[s]" (82, 39, 99). The Captain, the novel everywhere reminds us, is a master of things not named.

Cather's phrase "the thing not named" commands attention well beyond Captain Forrester's silence about Marian's adultery. For example, it is repeatedly invoked by contemporary Cather critics in order to illuminate the currents of same-sex sexual desire in her oeuvre.[5] Adultery in *A Lost Lady* taps into the same undercurrent of Cather's sexual things unsaid. Unlike the cultural silencing of same-sex sexual desire that commands its love "dare not speak its name," however, the compulsion in heterosexual adultery cases at the turn of the century was to speak, to name, and to toll. Thus, the Captain's acknowledged wordlessness, which adds to his emotional appeal within the pages of the novel, does so precisely because it invokes and implicitly critiques another thing not named in those same pages: criminal conversation and its pecuniary narratives of male emotional pain. Cather's novel does not prescribe but rather illuminates the workings of this unnamed adultery plot as she writes against its insistence on overfurnishing emotion. In the antipathy between the novel's things not named, the criminal conversation that is actionable yet not pursued, and Daniel Forrester's things not named, his stoic silence about his wife's affairs, emerges his and Cather's cultivated "emotional aura."

It is crucial that Captain Forrester rejects any action, legal or otherwise, for which his financial profit might mean ruin for another, even someone as threatening or, to use Niel's word, as "evil," as Frank Ellinger (37). The novel's most stunning instance of this is the Captain's refusal, after a Denver bank in which he is heavily invested fails, to sacrifice the railroad laborers' life savings in order to keep his pension, a pivotal decision about which more will be said in the pages to come. What must be noted immediately, however, is the presence of Judge Pommeroy, the Captain's lawyer and friend, who accompanies the Captain to Denver and whose professional services are always on call. Cather's novel declares the importance of the legal arena by populating its supporting cast of male characters with lawyers, judges, and those studying for careers in the law. Judge Pommeroy, Captain Forrester's closest friend in Sweet Water, is also Niel Herbert's uncle under whom Niel is studying law. Indeed, the novel's lamentation over the heroic decline of the early railroad pioneer is paralleled by its depiction of the characters Judge Pommeroy and Ivy Peters, whose differences represent the decay of the legal profession.

What the novel illustrates as "lost" are the high-minded scruples of the lawyer called Judge and the triumph of unscrupulous materialism embodied in the cruel young boy turned lawyer, Ivy Peters. In fact, when the Judge and Captain return from their trip to Denver in which the Captain "strip[s]" himself of his fortune while the other railroad executives and their lawyers cash out, the Judge turns to his nephew, Niel, and counsels him against a career in the law: "I can't see any honourable career for a lawyer, in this new business world that's coming up. Leave the law to boys like Ivy Peters, and get into some clean profession" (76, 77). Like the railroad executives, Ivy Peters capitalizes on the Forresters' financial straits; Peters plants grain in the Captain's prized marsh. "By draining the marsh Ivy had obliterated a few acres of something he hated, though he could not name it, and had asserted his power over the people who had loved those unproductive meadows for their idleness and silvery beauty" (89). Ivy Peters also assumes Marian Forrester's power of attorney after her husband's death, displacing the honorable Judge Pommeroy (89). Ivy is "smooth" and "unprincipled," and he has business savvy (76, 128). He is precisely the lawyer who might "name" Frank, Marian's lover, and make him pay for his criminal conversation. Yet the Captain, like Judge Pommeroy, rejects the dealings of such unscrupulous professionals; he stands against the new brand of American materialism, which, in light of actions like criminal conversation, threatens to make masculine emotions into one more piece of furniture or bale of wheat.

Although the Captain rejects legal action that seeks to quantify emotions and make them as "productive" as his once idle meadows, Cather's novel capitalizes upon the vocabulary of injury that criminal conversation actions partake in and are inspired by. Readers see through the Captain and Neil that male wounds hardly remain idle, for instance. Before I turn to criminal conversation, its commodification of masculine emotions, and its importance as the unspoken adultery plot that underpins *A Lost Lady*, it is crucial to note how the language of injury and accident marks pivotal moments of plot and character development in Cather's novel. Injury and the response to it become a means of social and interpersonal cohesion for the novel's characters, from Niel's fall in the Foresters' grove, which initiates his voyeurism and "guardianship" of the Forresters, to the Captain's fall from his horse, which effectively ends his railroad career and brings him and Marian to Sweet Water year-round (69). Indeed, readers will remember that it is Marian's injury, her fall from Eagle Cliff, that leads to her meeting the Captain: "She noticed she suffered less when Captain Forrester carried her. . . . 'It was Captain Forrester I wanted to hold my hand when the surgeon had to do things to me. You remember, Niel, he always boasted that I never screamed when they were carrying me up the trail. He stayed at the camp until I could begin to walk, holding to his arm. When he asked me to marry him, he didn't have to ask twice. Do you wonder?'" (143). The Captain's ability to mitigate Marian's physical pain makes their union appear inevitable to her. She describes how prior to her accident she "noticed him [Forrester] very little" and was "off every day with the young men" (141). Afterward, it was only the Captain whom she "wanted" (141). Marian heals from her injuries and the couple marry; however, within a few years a similar accident "cut[s] short the Captain's career as a roadbuilder" (23). After the Captain's disabling fall—for Marian is it is "as if one of the mountains had fallen down"—he "never suggest[s] taking a contract for the railroad again," and the couple, who spend their winters in Denver and their summers in Sweet Water, make Nebraska their permanent home (31, 23).

It is significant, given the repeated role of accidents in the novel, that Cather builds the town of Sweet Water and the Forresters' lives together around the industry most notorious for injury: the railroad. Cather follows in the footsteps of several U.S. writers who by the turn of the twentieth century would imagine the railroad as the cultural barometer not solely of industrial promise, but also of an evolving politics of pain and recompense. In the first paragraph of Cather's colleague Stephen Crane's story "The Monster" (1898), for example, a child who fancies himself a railroad conductor behind schedule causes the destruction of a peony, an accident that anticipates the thematic disfigurement of Henry Johnson that is to follow.[6] From Frank Norris's *The Octopus* (1901) to Theodore Dreiser's *The Titan* (1914), the railroad became a national symbol of seemingly infinite capacity inseparable from egregious harm.[7]

Forrester, a lifelong railroad man, embodies this dualism. For example, the young Forrester finds the land in Sweet Water where he wishes to build his dream home while he is working tirelessly as a "driver for a freighting company that carried supplies across the plains" (42). "Once, when he was driven out of the trial by a wash-out, he rode south on his horse to explore, and found an Indian encampment near the Sweet Water, on this very hill where his house now stood. He was, he said, 'greatly taken with the location,' and made up his mind that he would one day have a house there. He cut down a young willow tree and drove the stake into the ground to mark the spot where he wished to build. He went away and did not come back for many years; he was helping to lay the first railroad across the plains" (42). Despite years of intermittent sickness, responsibilities, and discouragement, Forrester eventually "[buys] the place from the railroad company" and twelve years later returns with his new wife, Marian, to build his house (43). The Captain tells the story of Sweet Water to dinner guests who have stopped over from their railway trip west (27). At Marian's urging, and despite the Captain's protests, he ends his narration with what she calls his "philosophy of life," a philosophy in which Sweet Water and the railroad are parallel dreams: "We dreamed the railroad across the mountains, just as I dreamed my place on the Sweet Water" (44, 45). In the Captain's dream, the railroad is an industry of promise; it helps to build his home and the town of Sweet Water, just as it helps to keep the Forresters connected with friends and acquaintances who often find it "agreeable to drop off the express and spend a night" as they pass through town (3, 4). "In those days" the narrator tells us, "it was enough to say of a man that he was 'connected with the Burlington'"; he was part of the "railroad aristocracy" (3). On the very first pages of Cather's novel, however, the narrator describes two classes of male citizens who emerge from the railroad's westward expansion: "There were two then distinct social strata in the prairie States; the homesteaders and hand-workers who were there to make a living and the bankers and gentlemen ranchers who came from the Atlantic seaboard to invest money and to 'develop our great West'" (3). Captain Forrester, the railroad man and gentleman rancher, makes his fortune on this railroad and becomes associated with the latter group of men (4). Unlike most gentlemen ranchers, he does not forget the former; for all of the railroad's promise, the Captain acknowledges that it also leaves behind broken dreams and broken men.

The Captain's philosophy, which Marian urges must be "heard again," recognizes that some people "get nothing in this world" (44): "'My philosophy is that what you think of and plan for day by day, in spite of yourself, so to speak—you will get. You will get it more or less. That is, unless you are one of the people who get nothing in this world. There are such people. I have lived too much in mining works and construction camps not to know that.' He paused as if, though this was too dark a chapter to be gone into, it must have its place, its moment of silent recognition" (44). As much as the railroad initially brings the Captain riches and comfort, for others it is only dangerous work with little reward. In fact, the Captain is not immune to the changing fortunes associated with the railroad. Within the first few pages of the novel, readers learn that the Captain's dream is primarily nostalgic: the railroad that has built up the Captain's town has also begun to leave it behind. The Forresters have far fewer visitors than in the early railroad days; the Burlington was "drawing in its horns, as people said, and the railroad officials were not stopping off at Sweet Water so often" (24). This leads to the Captain's increasing isolation and to Marian's overt discontent. Against the dream of the railroad and its making of the Sweet Water homestead is the Captain's "silent recognition" of its failures.

Not long after the dinner party, a bank panic threatens to destroy Forrester's railroad hands financially. His "pleasant labors" in his garden at Sweet Water are interrupted by the news that the Denver bank in which he invested his savings has failed; the Captain, along with the "day labourers, many of whom had at some time worked for [the] Captain," stood to lose their savings (68, 74). In this sole instance, Captain Forrester refuses to remain silent. Forrester, the Judge tells Niel and Marian upon his and the Captain's return, "was the only well-known name among the bank officers, it was the name which promised security and fair treatment to his old workmen and their friends" (74). When the other directors unfairly want to refund only a portion of the depositor's money, the Captain does "what a man of honour was bound to do" and honors their notes by cashing in his own government bonds, mining stocks, and other securities (75). "With five of the directors backing down, he had either to lose his name or save it. The depositors had put their savings into that bank because Captain Forrester was president. To those men with no capital but their back and their two hands, his name meant safety. As he tried to explain to the directors, those deposits were above price; money saved to buy a home, or to take care of a man in sickness, or to send a boy to school. And those young men, bright fellows, well thought of in the community, sat there and looked down their noses and let your husband strip himself down to pledging his life insurance!" (75). In this new world of "business," laments Judge Pommeroy, the "smooth members of the bar like Ivy Peters" protect themselves first and see no responsibility for the welfare of others. In fact, Cather names Captain Forrester's lawyer "Judge" as an ironic comment not only on the depravity of new business dealings (which lack "proper judgment") but also on the status of judges in the mid-nineteenth century, whose judicial power helped to encourage these same business interests (Horwitz, 205). Against this complicity, Cather's Judge helps the Captain make socially responsible but poor fiscal judgments, bringing Captain Forrester close to bankruptcy. Indeed the Judge, who regrets his role "out there as the Captain's counsel" because he is unable to persuade the Captain to save himself, admires the Captain's sense of responsibility and "duty of care" to his former workers and the bank's current depositors (76).

This episode emphasizes that the Captain, a contractor who built "hundreds of miles of roads" for the railroad, cannot forget the "dark chapter" of the railroad's expansion; he wants to see that his men are not those who "get nothing in this world." The Captain is sensitive to the myriad of injuries, industrial and financial, suffered by those laborers whom he has employed over the years (4). His sense of duty, which extends well beyond its legal call, is also a residual response to the dimensions of injury law that were making their mark in and through the physical injuries that accompanied the railroad's expansion. The Captain's personal financial sacrifice is all the more remarkable, for example, given his industry's "drawing in" of "its horns" with regard to the recognition and recompense of the injuries of its laborers. The Captain's stature grows in light of his demand that his former employees are offered recompense, even though he declines to demand repayment for his own personal injuries, financial and domestic.

Cather parallels the business injuries associated with the Denver bank failure with the personal and emotional injuries associated with marital infidelity; the novel recognizes the financial dangers of a growing American economy as well as its emotional costs. "Wage labor, intimacy labor," writes Laura Kipnis, "are you ever not on the clock?"[8] To underscore more fully the implications of the economy of injury, work-related and domestic, in Cather's novel, we must turn briefly to the historical accounts of the emergence of injury law. The nineteenth-century legal discourse about injury, a discourse manifest with particular rigor around the new laws designed to adjudicate it, provides a crucial context for understanding things named and unnamed in Cather's novel. According to accounts narrated by legal scholars, injury or tort law expanded in the United States in the middle of the nineteenth century in order to handle the mounting negligence claims for industrial accidents. With the rapid pace of industrialization, thanks especially to the railroad, injury became a common cost of economic production. Indeed the growing branch of tort law that met the demand made by these railroad cases would not be far from Captain Forrester's consciousness or Judge Pommeroy's. Yet the paradox of the expansion in tort law meant to address the injuries of railroad laborers was that as quickly as the law sprung up it was consequently curtailed. A good example is the 1842 fellow-servant rule, which prohibited workers from bringing suit against their employers for injuries caused by co-workers. The ruling by Justice Shaw in *Farwell v. Boston* made clear that the railroad and a number of other industries were legal bodies different from the bodies of its laborers seeking recompense for injuries. "He who engages in the employment . . . of specified duties and services, for compensation, takes upon himself the natural and ordinary risks and perils incident to the performance of such services, and in legal presumption, the compensation is adjusted accordingly," Shaw wrote.[9] For most railroad employees, the injuries that often accompanied this work were to be suffered silently; their pain, as Captain Forrester acknowledges, often remained legally unrecognized and hence uncompensated.[10] The case of *Farwell v. Boston* marked the triumph of what Horwitz calls "contractarian ideology," which assumed that the negotiation of wages would compensate for employee risk (in tort law it is called the "assumption of risk"), thus limiting the scope of employer liability for injury. Attending the transformation in tort law, according to Horwitz, was the crucial change in the relationship between employer and employee in the United States, from a measured paternalism to the impersonal relations governed by the market. As the Judge tells it in Cather's novel, the directors of the bank cared little for the working man trying to buy a house, take care of an ill relative, or send a child to school; the market does not accommodate but rather dictates the successes and failures of the depositors' investments.

Examining this changing relationship, scholars from Horwitz to Nan Goodman have argued that the subsequent introduction of legal doctrines into the expanding tort domain, doctrines such as the fellow-servant rule, negligence (which was interpreted loosely by the courts), and the assumption of risk meant that despite the apparent extension of legal remedies for injury, the new principles of tort and contract laws often made the recognition and compensation of injury unavailable to those who most suffered, namely industrial workers.[11] Moreover, as doctrines of negligence changed in the nineteenth century from strict liability (which attributed liability based solely on immediate causation without inquiry into fault or carelessness) to more modern theories of liability known as duty of care and universal liability (which sought to incorporate assignations of blameworthiness within its scope), industry felt threatened, and corporate risk taking appeared more dangerous. How would the economy continue to grow, industrialists and even judges asked, if the courts were crammed with disgruntled workers suing their employers? It seemed to the courts and to the marketplace that it would not, and hence as quickly as the expansion of injury law sprung up to compensate industrial laborers for their physical injuries so too was it consequently curtailed by the courts (Goodman, 7). Thus injury law may appear to have expanded in order to cope with the growing negligence claims for industrial accidents, particularly the escalating damages caused by the railroad and suffered by the working class, yet new legal principles also made the recognition and compensation of physical pains largely unavailable to those most afflicted. It is only men of honor like

Captain Forrester who even offer a "moment of silent recognition" for those who get nothing.

Within the public sphere of commercial law—a sphere that, as Judge Pommeroy reminds us, quickly became overwhelmingly favorable to business interests—the scope of damages and the domain of actionable injury became exceedingly narrow. What is important to note, however, is that the work-related injuries identified by these critics, injuries that increasingly were uncompensated in commercial injury law, were not the only injuries receiving a new legal and cultural definition in the middle to late nineteenth century. The corporate economic structure developing in the United States coincided with a psychic structure, also evident in the law and described in literature, in which men, regardless of their fiscal status, could potentially profit from their feelings and pains. What appeared to be the narrowing definition of injury excluding laborers from just compensation in the law courts, for example, did not discourage these same legal bodies from making awards for emotional injuries to plaintiffs in cases in which sexual relations or "private" marital relations—what Carol Pateman has called the "original" if unacknowledged contract—were at stake, as we have seen in Howells's divorce novel.[12] The unacknowledged and uncompensated injuries to masculine status in a modern industrial economy—from Daniel Forrester, the aging railroad pioneer who must suffer the new young bank directors looking "down their noses" at him, to the men who get "nothing in this world"—found voice in a compensatory domain, that of domestic relations, in which emotional distress was given literary as well as legal substance and, in turn, was heard.

Although little attention has been paid by some critics interested in the history of injury law to this so-called private sphere—to the home in Sweet Water that the railroad passes on its way into and out of town and to the boundaries of marital sexual relations—notions about injury often demanded a broader interpretive scope. As work relations were adjusting to the needs of a new national economy—one in which Forrester and his "hands" were left empty—and as marriage was increasingly seen as consensual and affectionate, it often became a wife's body and her lover's property that helped to constitute and to absorb male pain as an emerging legal category with increasing evidentiary weight. No longer a subjective cry of bodily harm, pain became a problem of compensation and evidentiary representation in the United States. If the laboring man could not beat the corporation at court, for instance, he might legally beat his wife, or, better, he could beat her lover out of his property (perhaps the gentleman was always already entitled to such a claim).[13] Even as tort law was defining itself as a measure of compensation for injuries largely economic in kind, attesting to the transformation of work and the depersonalization of labor relations, a depersonalization that Forrester fights so hard to fix, it was another category of harm that emerged in the public and private spheres of American life. This broad range of pains came to be known as "emotional injuries."

In Cather's novel, it is not only the emergence of the westward railroad aristocracy, but also the emergence of a corresponding economy, including an emotional economy between the sexes in Sweet Water, that marks the very primacy of injury in Captain Forrester's life. One of the crucial episodes of injury comes *after* the Captain learns that he is in financial trouble; the bank in which "railroad employés [sic], mechanics, and day laborers" had deposited their money, and in which he too had invested his savings, fails. Upon Judge Pommeroy's emotional retelling of the event, the Captain suffers a stroke (74). Although Niel reassures the reader that "a stroke could not finish a man like Daniel Forrester" (78), the loss of the Captain's name—a name that, because of his wife's affair, will soon become the subject of town gossips—very well could. When Niel, the novel's embodiment of what he himself calls "affection and guardianship" (69), later tries to protect the ailing Captain from finding evidence of Marian's affair by unsuccessfully hiding a letter addressed from Marian to Frank, Niel comes to understand that the Captain, whom he describes as a "wounded elephant," "knew everything; more than anyone else" already (78, 99). The Captain's financial failures, Niel's observation suggests, are no match for the silent wounds of infidelity. Indeed, Cather confirms this through the trajectory of Daniel Forrester's illness. Forrester suffers two strokes: the first is economic, and it immediately follows the retelling of his financial ruin; the second and deadly stroke is domestic. The Captain dies shortly after the night Marian Forrester's affair with Frank Ellinger becomes the subject of the town's gossips.

I want to turn to a moment earlier that night, when the bridge onto the Forresters' property floods and is nearly destroyed about the same time that Mrs. Forrester reads in a Denver paper that Frank has married Constance Ogden. The right-of-way that invites visitors to the property throughout the novel is washing away, and Marian Forrester must trudge through mud and rain "up to a horse's belly" to leave home for town (129). Mrs. Forrester makes her way to Niel's law office to have one last conversation with her lover. Niel cuts off the conversation by snapping the phone lines before their intercourse becomes too heated.

The criminal conversation that Niel perhaps unwittingly interrupts is an action understood by civil law as the equivalent of adultery; it enabled a husband to bring damages against a third party for the husband's loss of sexual relations with his wife.[14] In fact, criminal conversation, which is not within the domain of criminal law but rather injury law, allows a heavy financial burden to be placed upon a third party not only as punishment for the "trespass" on the property (the wife and on the marriage contract more generally); but, it is important to note, it also permits compensation for the injured feelings that may result. Crim. con. (its legal abbreviation) is "conversation" inasmuch as the boundaries that define the act of adultery are often constructed upon circumstantial evidence, reasonable speculations, hearsay, and the like, while its damages are assessed by virtue of successful accounts of pain and suffering.[15] Reparations for criminal conversation were meant to redress, at least in part, the apparent loss of reputation that would likely come with the conversation of neighbors, fellow workers, and others who learned of and gossiped about a spouse's "crime."

The lovers' last conversation is hardly the trespass it once was according to the civil law action of criminal conversation, if only because Niel is able to interrupt the stormy evidence of their affair just moments before it is exhibited over the phone lines for public hearing.[16] Niel takes it upon himself to disrupt the conversation between Marian Forrester and Frank Ellinger literally and figuratively in his law office ("It was time to stop her, but how?") by taking the "big shears left by the tinner and cut[ting] the insulated wire behind the desk" (114). He does this at the moment the lovers' indiscretion is in danger of discovery, as they begin to argue their need to "play it safe" (114). Niel conceals the evidence of the "crime" while he is managing the law office during the absence of his uncle, Judge Pommeroy; he reluctantly is participating in the profession that thrived on criminal conversation proceedings.[17] Yet when Niel should be studying his law books, he instead reads novels; when he should be mastering legal reasoning, he instead is busy constructing fictional "double-lives" (67). Thus Niel Herbert both knows (because he takes the protection of Marian Forrester's indiscretion upon himself) and does not "know" (because he does not understand, nor has he mastered the terms of law enforcement) the dimensions of the so-called crime he is witnessing. When earlier in the narrative he overhears Marian's "soft laughter" and Frank's "fat and lazy" laugh drifting through a bedroom window, it is neither his moral nor his legal authority but rather his aesthetic judgment that is offended, for he is not yet learned in the law (71). In fact, it is after the moment of his discovery of Marian and Frank's affair (he plays the spurned lover, tossing the bouquet of flowers he has picked for Mrs. Forrester in a ditch) that Niel cements his decision to ditch his legal career and pursue architecture in Boston. With this gesture, Niel refuses his apparent vocational inheritance as a lawyer; yet he also embraces his lay role as a potential spokesperson for injured men like Captain Forrester.

Despite Niel's guardianship, soon after the night that Marian has her last word with her former lover—a conversation that becomes a subject of gossip between Mrs. Beasley, the telephone operator, and Molly Tucker, the seamstress—Captain Forrester suffers the stroke that will end his life. "Soon afterward, when Captain Forrester had another stroke, Mrs. Beasley and Molly Tucker and their friends were perfectly agreed that it was a judgment upon his wife" (117). Whereas Niel attempts to protect Marian in his law office from disclosing what could be the costly evidence of her affair, he ultimately is unsuccessful in managing the gossip coming over the telephone lines, the same lines that will shortly bring "telegraphic news" of Captain Forrester's death (123). Quite apart from Mrs. Beasley's and Molly Tucker's judgment of Captain Forrester's condition, a judgment based on circumstantial and inferential evidence heard over telephone lines, the Forresters represent for Cather two different methods of managing their injuries. If Marian Forrester is able to find uneasy protection from Niel Herbert during her angry telephone conversation with Frank Ellinger, the Captain, perhaps the most congenial, certainly the least conversational figure in the novel, can only internalize his losses. The aging railroad pioneer finds no compensation for these injuries; subsequently, he dies. "Old settlers and farmer folk came from all over the county to follow the pioneer's body to the grave" (124).

It is important to note that the Captain's injuries and final death issue directly from his emotional losses rather than, as readers might initially expect, his financial distresses. This is the judgment of the townspeople, although none, according to Niel, "could have been crueler" (117). Even when Niel tries to prevent Marian from publicly disclosing her affair and thus bringing harm to the Captain and her both, it is most specifically the Captain to whom Niel repeatedly extends his narrative sympathies, and the Captain whom Niel most desires to protect. If Niel claims to admire Marian Forrester, for example, he also acknowledges again that her relations with Forrester "stamp her more than anything else" (65). Niel conveys for the novel's readers the Captain's dramatic demise: he is "like an old tree walking"; he is encumbered by his own bulk, and his features collapse "as when a wax face melts in the heat" (97, 23). This demise escalates in the face of Marian's disloyalty, at which point she immediately becomes "lost" for Niel (91). Niel's narrative offers the Captain up as a startling example of the potential scope of emotional damages that were beginning to gain acceptance in the latter half of the nineteenth century. Marian's criminal and quickly interrupted conversation is but a fictive instance of the factual cases (and numerous "heart-balm" actions might offer a similar analytic terrain) in which men like Captain Forrester were constructed as victims and were compensated for their suffering. In some such cases, men like Niel or the Captain might author narratives that spoke not of bodily physical harms but of interior emotional injuries. Niel Herbert's authority to unplug Marian Forrester's voice as it wavers injuries dangerously over the telephone lines is not only matched, but exceeded, by the power accorded to the Captain's unspoken reservoir of related emotional wounds.

If injury law defined itself economically, to recall Horwitz's and Friedman's accounts, criminal conversation suits allowed men to act as protagonists in narratives that issued in a broader range of crimes called emotional injuries.[18] Mrs. Forrester might have read, along with the marriage announcement of her former lover, scores of reports on divorce proceedings, criminal conversation, and alienation of affection suits that were filling the daily papers across the country. On any given day one might have found in a variety of newspapers an array of divorce cases in which the plaintiff names the third party as a cause for or party to the proceedings.[19] Because no-fault divorce was not possible in many states until well into the twentieth century, adultery remained a crucial cause of action for divorce; in addition, criminal conversation became a way to exact monetary compensation, punish one's erring spouse, and bring suit to end an unsuitable marriage.[20] Despite public exposure and lengthy trials, actions for criminal conversation were growing in popularity in the United States at the turn of the century; by the 1920s these cases were commanding huge settlements.[21] With the growing size of punitive damages awarded by juries, large sums of cash were meant to abate the "injured honor" of the husband, appease his "mental anguish," and compensate for his "damaged" goods.[22] Although the label of "conversation" would seem to presuppose two participants, the law, for many years, did not recognize the participation of women in the conversation: women did not initiate it, nor were they subject to it; they were by law the objects of the conversation. For a man bringing forward a criminal conversation case, however, the catalog of injury included "the deprived comfort, fellowship, society, and assistance of his wife in domestic affairs," stressing his loss of her services. Criminal conversation transformed material interests into "a more sophisticated notion of 'property' that included contractual entitlements to the labor of others."[23] Such injuries also included the husband's "dishonor and disgrace," language that draws quite forcefully from the realm of painful feeling rather than solely lost property.[24] These cases sought to compensate the husband who "has suffered great mental anguish and injured feelings," phrases that confirm the tort's focus on "intangible or dignitary interests," not only the economic or physical.[25]

Cather's play upon the tensions between fact and fiction—the growing incidence of compensable emotional wounds in the United States set against the "bare . . . play of [masculine] emotions" in her novel—asks readers to reconsider the meaning of men's emotional wounds. They are not merely examples of patriarchal property rights; they also counter the insistent story disavowing masculine emotions. This aspect of the novel's work is especially important given the dominant cultural suspicion of "emotive" narratives, which were attributed, most often, to women. Despite women's presumed historical embodiment of emotion, their stereotyped status as purveyors of the private affective sphere, and their supposed representativeness as subjects of and audience for the "sentimental" in the nineteenth-century United States, the early emergence of actionable injuries such as criminal conversation suggests that women often found themselves given a limited emotive voice as men narrated their more capacious rights in just this regard. Legally compensable emotional injuries were lost to women.

For men, emotional injury—and the legal history of crim. con. is representative in this regard—is fraught with slips between literary melodrama and legal procedure. As criminal conversation trials began to attract more attention from a public seeking sensationalism and vicarious sexual stimulation, newspapers and law reports presented numerous detailed accounts of adulteries, and by the eighteenth century a genre of legal narratives had emerged in England that rivaled the novel for readers' attentions. L. Simond, a Franco-American tourist traveling in England in the early nineteenth century, wrote home in disbelief about the prevalence of such actions: "I have heard of 10,000 Sterling awarded in some cases, which is certainly rather dear for a *conversation*! The husband pockets this money without shame, because he has the laugh on his side. . . . The publicity which such prosecutions necessarily occasion, and all the details and proofs of the intrigue, are highly indelicate and scandalous."[26] The intrigue surrounding the proliferation of criminal conversation cases (as well as the courts' increasing inability to discern fictitious cases) led to its repeal in England with the 1857 Matrimonial Causes Act.[27]

The heyday of criminal conversation did not arrive in the United States until the 1875 trial *Theodore Tilton v. Henry Ward Beecher*, the nation's most infamous case. In it, Theodore Tilton accused America's beloved preacher Henry Ward Beecher of committing adultery with Tilton's wife, Elizabeth. Although the jury deadlocked in its decision about the crime and its compensation, the cultural denouement was decisive: the trial and its cause of action captivated the public. In fact, Cather's novel recalls the salacious reporting and storybook constructions about marital infidelities that were filling the newspapers and law courts. Niel relates a story about Marian Forrester's first fiancé, Ned Montgomery, who we learn was the victim of the cuckold's unwritten law, a "law" that allowed the injured husband to reap direct and immediate return injury against a seducer, including murder. "When Marian Ormsby was nineteen, she was engaged to Ned Montgomery, a gaudy young millionaire of the Gold Coast. A few weeks before the date set for their marriage, Montgomery was shot and killed in the lobby of a San Francisco hotel by the husband of another woman. The subsequent trial involved a great deal of publicity, and Marian was hurried away from curious eyes and sent up into the mountains until the affair should blow over" (141). In the mountains she meets and subsequently marries the widower Captain Forrester, and the "affair" blows over for a time. Like her former fiancé, however, Marian Forrester will eventually break the written law of sexual conduct.

What makes criminal conversation especially interesting in the context of Cather's novel is not only the way in which it threatens to materialize masculine emotions by "furnishing" them in new and, for Cather, often unsettling ways, but also the way in which the action claims for itself an allegedly transparent narrativity—there are no things not named

—when it comes to sexuality. For example, Mrs. Forrester's affair with Frank Ellinger might read like a summary judgment for the legal action of criminal conversation, yet neither the narrative nor witnesses within the narrative actually describe or see the adulterous act. As a conversation might suggest, both Niel and one of the adolescent boys from town named Adolph Blum overhear the voices of Frank Ellinger and Marian Forrester in apparent collusion.[28] The literary fiction, a fiction that encourages its readers to understand that something sexual has taken place between Marian and Frank, resonates in the legal reasoning that quite often permits the law to attribute substance to the "sexual," although it begs the question, Where does the evidentiary authority to make discriminations concerning what constitutes sexual acts reside? In the legal example of criminal conversation, it is, ironically, in Cather's things not named (in this case, the sexual activity that is not described) that is understood by virtue of its capacity to name merely the genders of those involved and the boundaries that encompass them. In other words, a woman and man may have engaged in "deviate" sexual activity (defined in this case as nonmarital) when they spend private time together, when they find themselves alone: the unspeakable then is spoken.[29]

What was regarded as evidentiary in the law in the nineteenth and early twentieth century often depended upon the construction of narratives whose claims to produce sexual "proofs" shared many of the fictive conventions in literature, conventions that were, in turn, shared by many of the symptomatic readings of sexuality that were also producing proofs in contemporary fields from biology to sexology.[30] In the space between the naming of the legal action of criminal conversation and the sexual action that the legal terminology was meant to name was a broad range of meanings, many of which were scrutinized and, quite often, named with rigor at the turn of the century. Criminal conversation cases, for example, appeared to work upon the law's assumption that sexuality could be unproblematically represented, although literary representations of sexual acts were challenging the very extent of the law's claims to narrative transparency. For instance, the legal construction of narratives about sexuality was often founded upon the conspicuous absence about what sexuality entailed. In criminal conversation the designation of the "crime" of sexual trespass was itself inspired by the techniques of the literary in that it asked its litigants continually to imagine and to act upon offenses that were sometimes matters of allusion and representation.[31] If in a criminal conversation proceeding there were no eyewitnesses who saw the crime being committed firsthand, for example, testimony took the form of a narrative that reconstructed certain events, bits of conversation, and other forms of circumstantial evidence that were finally constructed by a skillful attorney, journalist, or novelist to appear "convincing."[32]

Witness the scene of transgression between Marian Forrester and Frank Ellinger. Marian and Frank make off for the river and surrounding forest to "cut cedar boughs for Christmas" (50). They stop and make their way into the thicket; the novel does not describe for its readers the details of their action within the forest path. Cather continues, "When the blue shadows of approaching dusk were beginning to fall over the snow, one of the Blum boys slipped into the timber" where he presently heard voices moving near. Frank Ellinger and Marian Forrester emerge from the wood arm in arm, carrying the robes from the coach on which they lay, but no cedar boughs. (The narrator's conscious omission of the cedar boughs is, of course, only of relevance to the reader, as Adolph Blum would not have known the excuse for their foray.) After a long, amorous embrace, Frank lifts Marian into the coach and asks, "What about those damned cedar boughs?"(55). Marian responds, "It doesn't matter," but Frank, ever thoughtful about the appearance of such things, goes back to fetch the evergreens. The Blum boy, who followed their tracks toward the coach, hides behind it where "Mrs. Forrester had been waiting . . . with her eyes closed, feeling so safe, he could almost have touched her with his hand" (55). He hears her breathing, her eyes fluttering, her "soft shivers" as she sits waiting for Frank's return. The Blum boy overhears, but does not fully see, the intercourse between the two. From his vantage point, which is both partial (he is hidden from view), and dependent upon circumstances about which he has no knowledge (the evergreens), whatever crimes may have been committed in the "eye of the law," crimes that have not been seen but may be suspected, the narrator tells us, are "safe" with Adolf Blum (56). Indeed, the evidentiary ambiguities that may be enough to warrant proof of conduct in case law are felt by Blum as little more than shivers of reminiscence.

Cather's use of the word "safe" with reference to Adolf Blum, like the safety referred to in Marian Forrester's conversation with Frank Ellinger, is meant to invoke precisely its opposite: the potential dangers of misused and misplaced narrative authority. If this misuse is merely threatened with Adolf Blum, it is substantiated with Niel Herbert, who intends to protect Marian but who repeatedly passes judgment on her actions. Niel, unlike Adolf, is an unsafe witness; he finds, as do the courts in case after case of criminal conversation, that "the conduct of these parties might lead thinking right-minded people to but one conclusion. . . . 'There was something wrong'"; such feelings, according to the courts, were actionable regardless of whether the charges of adultery were vehemently denied or whether there was any direct proof (*Wheeler v. Abbott*, 1911). In the state of Nebraska, for example, the state in which the action of *A Lost Lady* unfolds, "direct proof" of adultery in criminal conversation cases was unnecessary. The case that served as precedent in a number of crim. con. actions in that state found: "It was not indispensable to a recovery that the acts of sexual intercourse should have been established by the testimony of a disinterested eye-witness. Adultery would be very difficult of proof if such were the rule; but it may, like any other fact, be established by circumstantial evidence."[33] Establishing an actionable criminal conversation claim meant that the circumstances involved must, according to the law, be "convincing."[34] "Secret meetings (particularly at night), telephone calls, displays of 'playfulness' or affection, exchanging 'love letters' or notes . . . are all factors a plaintiff should emphasize."[35] Such scenes of narration, all of which appear in Cather's novel under the watchful eye of Niel Herbert, could be enough to intimate that a conversation had taken place (although one might not be able to establish that genital intercourse had occurred). Adolf Blum's lack of ocular evidence, in other words, could still be interpreted to mean that injurious activity had taken place in the eye of the law.

Given the view that the law maintained as to its workings, a view that perceived itself as impartial and gender blind, literary fictions like Willa Cather's make visible just how dependent the law may be upon the partial glimpses of human eyes and emotions for its details. It is the literary domain that allows readers to see the residual spaces in which the emotional, the sexual, the injurious, and their accompanying evidentiary ambiguities are something other than self-evident. Indeed, this is the lesson that the novel's narrator, Niel Herbert, eventually learns, emotionally painful as it seems to him throughout his narrative. Against his intended profession in the law, in which actions like criminal conversation speak what is often "unspeakable," Niel pursues a "double life" of literature "with all its guilty enjoyments" (67). It is this double life, in fact, that encourages Niel to abandon his study of the law in favor of a career in architecture. While his uncle's law books surround him with their "solemn" weight, the literature books that Niel devours surreptitiously become for him "living creatures, caught in the very behaviour of living" (25, 67). Rather than his "dull" law studies, literature "influence[s] [Niel's] conception of the people about him" and forces him to reconsider the complexities of interpersonal relationships (66, 67). Literature allows him to glimpse the irreducible. Yet literature does not wholly rescue Niel from his urge to do precisely this, to reduce those people and relationships to their easiest digestible parts: Frank the "coarse worldling," Marian the festering "bloom," the Captain, a "wounded elephant," and so on. Despite the world that Niel reads about, the world that "sumptuously sinned long before little Western towns were dreamed of," Niel often remains incapable of what he calls "long perspective" (67). The reader he becomes, rapt with the incongruities of lives lived and lives recorded in "form and phrase," is also the narrator with little capacity to appreciate the double lives of those around him. Neil, as a narrator, is quick to judge; indeed, it is Neil Herbert, not Adolf Blum, to recall Marian's and Frank's scene in the woods, who threatens to name what he thinks he sees. Niel's reaction to events, glimpsed, like Adolf Blum, behind a veil of thicket, is one of "blind anger" and disgust (71). Cather reminds readers of the danger of unsafe, short perspective when the narrative asks the question, "[What] if it had been Thad Grimes who lay behind that log, now, or Ivy Peters?"

Marian and Frank's secret rendezvous in the woods is followed soon after by another scene in which it is Niel who "lay behind that log," although for Niel the log is more appropriately French windows, and the thicket is a "prickly bunch of wild roses" (71). While the Captain is away in Denver warding off financial disaster, Niel, awash in his impulse of "affection and guardianship" rises early to "make a bouquet for a lovely lady" (69, 71). At the moment he stoops beneath Marian's shuttered bedroom window to place flowers on her sill, however, he overhears a strange man's "fat and lazy" laugh, a laugh that he thinks can come only from Frank Ellinger, whose name Niel was "annoyed" to find on the hotel register the day before (69). Unlike Marian's eyes that close in safety near the sleigh in the woods, Neil's eyes are "blind with anger" at the thought of Marian with Frank. "In that instant between stooping to the window-sill and rising, he had lost one of the most beautiful things in his life. Before the dew dried, the morning had been wrecked for him; and all subsequent mornings, he told himself bitterly" (71–72). Consumed with acrimony and self-pity, Niel decides to leave Sweet Water; he leaves not with "long perspective" or, like Adolf Blum, with shivers of reminiscence, but rather with "weary contempt for [Marian Forrester] in his heart" (67, 145).

Niel's account of the Forresters and Sweet Water is punctuated by the series of emotional injuries and psychological losses that he himself suffers. Niel's narrative rather than the Captain's will, for example, basks in the emotional harm of criminal conversations; if the Captain is unwilling to capitalize on the potential injuries caused by his wife's adultery, Niel's narrative makes the case against Marian Forrester itself. It is a case not made on behalf of the Captain, who accepts Marian the way she is, but on Niel's own behalf. His image of Marian, like all his mornings after his initial discovery, is "wrecked" by his belief that there is something "coarse and concealed" beneath her "brilliancy" (72). Marian's flawless exterior is sullied, her surface brilliance dimmed in Niel's eyes. It is important to note that much of Niel's attraction to Marian is to this surface: the "loveliest smile," skin with the "fragrant crystalline whiteness of white lilacs," eyes "full of light"; in a word, he is "bewitch[ed]" by his vision of her (83, 26). Marian is described most often as a jewel to be viewed and appreciated; in fact, Niel repeatedly records the moments in which Marian is duly "valued" as a jewel by her husband and, by association, by Niel: "A man bought [jewels] for his wife in acknowledgement of things he could not gracefully utter. They must be costly; they must show that he was able to buy them, and that she was worthy to wear them" (122, 42). Although Niel gently suggests that this is an "archaic" view (about jewels, not about women), he returns to Marian's charms and subtly queries whether she is worthy of their cost.

The novel repeatedly frames intimacy voyeuristically, whether it be through the display of jewels, a stolen moment in the woods witnessed by a young man, or a laugh or touch heard or seen through an open window. Cather parallels Niel's first bitter loss, which prompts him to ditch otherwise "defenseless" flowers, his legal studies, and Sweet Water, with a similar scene later in the novel. Shortly after the Captain's death, Niel, who had returned to town to help the ailing Captain after his second and final stroke, once again stops outside Marian's window, this time a dining-room window, again to appreciate flowers on the Forresters' property. As Niel stands in the shadows, he glimpses Ivy Peters putting his "arms around [Marian], his hands meeting over her breast" (145). Unlike the scene of intimacy that Adolf Blum serenely witnesses in which Frank holds Marian "crushed up against his breast" as he helps her into the sled, Niel immediately recoils in anger at the sight of

Ivy's embrace (145). Like Niel's visceral reaction to Frank's "fat and lazy laugh," the look of Ivy's proprietary hands draped around Marian's body sends Niel scurrying away from the house and down the road for "the last time" (142).

The theatrical framing of Niel's recurrent episodes of loss confirms that his emotional attachments are inseparable from his possessive gaze. Even from the earliest moments of the novel, when Niel is a boy of twelve, readers see that Niel's vision is proprietary. After an accidental fall (trying to catch a blinded woodpecker to put it out of his misery, forecasting Niel's own pain and blindness), Niel's eyes open and he finds himself in a stately room, curtained, wood paneled, and he thinks to himself "that he would probably never be in so nice a place again" (21). When Niel becomes a regular guest at the Forresters' home, he recognizes that their home lessens the pain of his own economic and domestic decay. Niel's home "was not a pleasant place to go to," he thinks; it is "a frail egg-shell house, set off on the edge of prairie where people of no consequence lived" (21). Niel continually contrasts his home with the Forresters', their stately rooms, idyllic meadows, and seemingly serene shelter of dignified companionship; through his association with the Forresters, Niel feels that he gains consequence and self-respect. When he thinks about his own home and family, he feels what he calls "an air of failure and defeat" (22). Readers learn, for example, that Niel's family, much like the Forresters, suffers when the railroad "draws in its horns." Niel's father and not the Captain, moreover, is "one of the first failures to be crowded to the wall" (22). It is against economic and domestic disaster that Niel first embraces the law; he remains in Sweet Water to study under his uncle after Niel's father packs up for an office job in Denver. Yet later, even after this initial urgency passes and Niel abandons the practice of law, he continues to embody the sentiment that the law conveys. His emotional well-being is indivisible from his material sensibilities; this correspondence drives his possessive resentments.

What Niel most holds against Mrs. Forrester is her refusal to be possessed. Neither Frank, Ivy, Neil, nor even the Captain can contain her; she is "not willing to immolate herself, like the widow of . . . great men [like Captain Forrester], and die with the pioneer period to which she belonged; . . . She prefer[s] life on any terms" (145). Marian never conforms to Niel's expectations: she takes lovers, she makes business decisions that Niel deems unscrupulous, and she "feel[s] the power to live" despite her husband's death. In fact, after this death, it is "years . . . before Niel [can] think of [Marian] without chagrin" (146). Niel must lose his emotional and material attachment to Marian in order to find her again. He accomplishes this one evening in Chicago, when Niel meets another lost friend from the past: Ed Elliot. Ed relates his encounter with Marian Forrester, subsequently Marian Collins, in a hotel in Buenos Aires. Ed first recognized Marian by her laugh, which, he says, "hadn't changed a particle" (148). Neither had much else, Ed recalls. Marian asked Ed about Niel and the other boys from Sweet Water, but she especially wanted Niel to know that "things have turned out well" and that she "think[s] of him" often (149). It is important that Marian returns to Niel not in the flesh but rather as what he describes as a "bright impersonal memory" (147). Although Niel's first impulse at this information is to contemplate "mak[ing] the trip to see her," Ed also relays the news of Marian's death. With her physical death, Niel can let Marian go, free of anger or judgment. He is in fact happy to hear that "she was well cared for, to the very end" (150). Ed Elliot is "warm" with pleasure at Niel's response.

In this final scene of the novel, Niel embraces Marian, like the Captain's "idle" meadow, in and for herself. Niel finds himself reclaiming her memory by dissolving his long-held possessive resentments. He allows Marian to "suggest things much lovelier than herself" (147). The singular "power" of the suggestion of Marian, her ability to call up "thing[s] not named," as the "perfume of a single flower may call up the whole sweetness of spring," becomes "compensatory" for Niel in his final catalog of memories of "his long lost lady" (147). "He came to be very glad that he had known her, and that she had had a hand in breaking him in to life" (147). Niel finally embraces Cather's own narrative quest: to reclaim memories and to honor the past without succumbing to a certain kind of nostalgia, one that objectifies women and encourages a newly modern impulse to commodify and "overwrite" men's emotions. The novel ends with Niel able to emulate his "hero" Captain Forrester, to remember Marian without needing to calculate and speak her "cost." In his final gesture toward Marian's memory, Niel's impulse for attachment and possession give way to his appreciation of aura and art.

A certain wounded feeling had taken possession of me.
—*Henry James*, Notes of a Son and Brother *(1914)*

four

On Personal Quantity

Psychic Injury in Henry James's *The Golden Bowl*

Sacred Wounds

In the first book of *The Golden Bowl*, Maggie Verver, concerned that her recent marriage to Prince Amerigo has unbalanced the "symmetry" of her personal relationships, approaches her father, Adam Verver, with the hope of stirring his special "interest" in her friend Charlotte Stant. Maggie concludes that her father must acquire a wife in order to lend "equanimity" to the delicate relations between him, his daughter, and his son-in-law. To Maggie, Charlotte appears the perfect fit: Charlotte is "courageous" and "clever," and, as Maggie tells her father, she is "*interesting*—which plenty of other people with plenty of other merits never are a bit."[1] What makes Charlotte "interesting" personally to Maggie and potentially to her father is Charlotte's "fineness" in light of her apparent failure on the marriage market. Charlotte is "great," yet she remains unclaimed (134). Adam immediately wants to know what attempts have been made, what prospective buyers/bidders there are, and how many—for it is in the language of "acquisition" that Charlotte is most often referred to in the novel—but Maggie, beyond revealing that Charlotte has "loved" and "lost," resists this enumeration (137). Adam, however, is unwilling to yield; he must know the provenance of the object of inquiry, and he feigns disbelief that Charlotte can be so "credit[ed]" by Maggie without the proper accumulation and assessment of such detail. Although

Adam listens to Maggie, who "had never come so near telling [Adam] what he should take it from her to believe" about Charlotte's "value," he repeats on several occasions his "need of some basis on which . . . his bounty" can be "firm" (137). Toward this end, Adam decides to shift the exchange with his daughter over Charlotte's merits from the language of economy and collecting to what he presumes will be a more fluent language for his daughter, the language of disclosure, the language of feeling. "Don't young women tell?" Adam asks, expecting that the language of the female heart naturally betrays its secrets. Maggie, however, curtly retorts, "Do young men tell?" a reply to which Adam laughs, exclaiming, "How do I know, my dear, what young men do?" Although Maggie and her father both assume degrees of ignorance over the revelation of feeling, it is during this exchange, the only such instance in the novel, that Maggie grows "sharp" with her father (138). The telling of feeling, she insists, is what "vulgar girls do" (138). Concerned that she has reacted "odiously" with her father, that by allowing her composure to be ruffled she has demonstrated the very vulgarity that she would distance herself from, Maggie tries to explain her position. "'Such wounds and shames are dreadful: at least,' she added, catching herself up, 'I suppose they are; for what, as I say, do I know of them?'" (138).

This exchange between father and daughter is memorable on several accounts. It introduces the crucial vocabulary of "balance" into the novel's relationships; Maggie is certain that a fourth body, Charlotte's, will reestablish relational "equilibrium." This exchange also reiterates the economic imperative that drives Adam Verver; material and human acquisitions are applied "the same measure of value" (145). Also introduced into the equation is another kind of measure, a measure of feeling that is cast as a uniquely unknown quantity. Maggie knows that she, unlike Charlotte, has "never had the least blow" (138); her statement is an ominous foreshadowing of events to come. Maggie's contrast with Charlotte is not the only imbalance that bears weight in this passage, however. As Charlotte is defined by her suffering and Maggie by its absence, so too is the prince's "knowledge" (the prince is the unnamed party in the transaction) set against Adam's ignorance. The prince is the young man who does what Adam does not know, and despite Adam's easy laugh at such a thought, his statement "How do I know, my dear, what young men do" shares with his daughter's the element of foreboding. Both will discover how the very currency they are reluctant to "tell"—that of emotional injury—will become the most powerful "basis" and "bounty" among the four characters.

It seems particularly important that Maggie's only cross words with her father in the entire novel are on precisely these grounds, the disclosure of wounded feelings. Maggie describes such "wounds" at first as "dreadful," but then she suggests that they also are "sacred" and require protection: "One can always, for safety, be kind. . . . [O]ne feels when that's right" (138). Maggie's call for "safety" anticipates her reaction to her own "blow" and "sorrow" narrated through the lens of her consciousness in book 2. Here in book 1, the prince's book as it were, they seem but a momentary lapse in a larger design: that of "symmetry," "balance," and "safety" against damage to the surfaces of the novel's relationships (286, 13, 138). In book 1, the discourses of aesthetics and anesthetics appear to go hand in hand: what accompanies flawless beauty—of objects, human acquisitions, furniture, or marital arrangements—is freedom from pain. Critical debate often describes *The Golden Bowl* precisely in this manner, as a novel obsessed with *not* wounding. Daniel Brudney, for example, has argued that James's characters demonstrate a unique form of consciousness: "They treat each other as sentient creatures, and indeed as creatures who are sentient as only human beings—perhaps only these human beings—can be: creatures of extraordinary subtlety who can be caused intense pain by the slightest untoward vibration. Everyone's exertions go toward preventing such pain, toward keeping the air still."[2] In book 1, the prevention of pain is closely aligned with the characters' embrace of the "beauty of the furniture." Each guarantees the other's "flawless surface." Yet this equation, this delicate balance, is impossible to maintain; stronger and more painful air blows by the second half of the novel.

This chapter examines a crucial change in James's novel; it involves the rejection of the characters' original agreement, with their investment in the prevention of injury, to their recognition and calculus of mental and psychic pain; the novel shifts, in other words, from the prevention of wounds to the proliferation of them. Like the books explored in earlier chapters of this book, *The Golden Bowl* examines how emotional wounds, particularly male emotional wounds, become a valuable currency. Maggie Verver calls this currency a "market of misery"; it is a market that encourages the cultivation of wounds at once "dreadful" and "sacred." Squire Gaylord in William Dean Howells's *A Modern Instance*, we may recall, commands a courtroom of pain; he "out-feels" his daughter and wins his legal dispute (for and against her). Willa Cather's Niel Herbert also recounts a detailed melodrama of male affect, one in which Niel's suffering outstrips the wounded subjects that his narrative alleges to recount. In these narratives, men capitalize upon their wounds, be it those stemming from divorce or those issuing from marital infidelity. In fact, the young Henry James's household also valorized the marketplace of misery; claims of pain and injury, which Tom Lutz has called in his study of the Jameses "the politics of invalidism," precipitated Henry's first trip to Europe.

Like the male protagonists in earlier chapters, Prince Amerigo is envisioned as an injured subject; through his perceptions of his deep feelings and their accompanying wounds, he initiates a challenge to the delicate balance of power and pain among the characters in the novel. The prince's investments in injured feelings make possible what is tactfully called the novel's "readjustment of relations." It is a readjustment, I argue, that ends in his favor: his "personal quantity" is reassessed; his wife's interest in him is renewed; Maggie's money and the principino remain with him in Europe; and Adam and Charlotte Verver effectively are banished to America. The prince, insisting on his "personal systems" throughout the first book and creating the conditions for the flourishing of emotional harm, precipitates a reinterpretation of the relations of power and pain in the novel. In so doing, the prince, like Howells's and Cather's wounded men, embodies and advances new categories of mental sentience that were emerging in fields like psychology and law at the turn of the twentieth century.

Shortly before Henry James would begin to write *The Golden Bowl*, his former Harvard classmates Samuel Warren and Louis Brandeis urgently proclaimed in their now-famous 1890 *Harvard Law Review* article "The Right to Privacy" that the constitutive structure of injury—what the Ververs initially try to protect themselves from, injury to property and person, as well as its corresponding legal measures of protection within injury law—required amplification. Like the prince's pressures for "readjustment," their article aimed to "define anew the exact nature and extent of such protection" (193). For Warren and Brandeis, "The Right to Privacy" mounted a substantial challenge to what they saw as the legal disavowal of psychic life, demonstrating that not merely property (the Ververs' valuable surfaces) but also the emotive (what Amerigo claims are his hidden depths) should become a barometer of compensable harm (196). The legal recognition of a citizen's "emotional life" was based, in large part, on literary work and on the authorial relationship to writing. In fact, Warren and Brandeis invoked literary art as the most appropriate medium through which to measure the legal status of emotions: "The protection afforded to thoughts, sentiments, and emotions, expressed through the medium of writing or of the arts . . . is merely an instance of the enforcement of the more general right of the individual to be left alone" and is "in reality not the principle of private property, but that of an inviolate personality."[3] Warren and Brandeis conceived of what they called "inviolate personality" as a necessary measure of protection for the individual against the "modern enterprise and invention" that accompanied capitalism. "The development of the law was inevitable," they argued. "The intense intellectual and emotional life, and the heightening of sensations which came with the advance of civilization, made it clear to men that only a part of the pain, pleasure, and profit of life lay in physical things. *Thoughts, emotions, and sensations demanded legal recognition*" (my emphasis) (195). Against the threats of the capitalist marketplace, in which people like Charlotte and Amerigo become mere fetishized commodities, Warren and Brandeis urged the inalienability of thoughts, emotions, and sensations. Their cultural logic mirrored the therapeutic culture's "invention" of the psychological as an antidote to forms of personal alienability associated with capitalism. The right to privacy, which sought to expand the domain of injury law—an ambition that arguably cast it within the very marketplace that it proclaimed to contest—took works of literature and their authors as its most exquisite examples of its announced resistance to "modern enterprise."

Early in James's novel, Prince Amerigo embraces the inviolability of his thoughts, emotions, and sensations. I will argue, however, that Warren and Brandeis's legal theory provides a crucial context for reading *The Golden Bowl* precisely for the ways in which James's novel resists the logic of his peers. *The Golden Bowl* does not exhibit (as Warren and Brandeis contend literary works and their authors do) the inalienability of emotions; on the contrary, James's novel shows how emotions are an intimate and negotiable part of the marketplace, a matter of privilege and of power. Adam Verver, in the passage with which this chapter begins, demands that Charlotte's stories of emotional harm be part of his exchange and "bargain" with his daughter; to Adam, Charlotte is "alienable" from the start. Maggie, however, resists such an appropriation, capitalizing not on the disclosure of Charlotte's personal stories themselves but rather on the value of their rightful withdrawal from the exchange. The Ververs' transaction anticipates a narrative arena that readers see develop over the course of the novel in which the psyche becomes marketable, material, and compensable. Even Amerigo, who early on in the novel embraces the language of the "personal" and insists on its withdrawal from the exchange with which *The Golden Bowl* begins, uses his "personal quantity" as a commodity in his marital renegotiation at the novel's end. The characters' actions cast themselves quite differently from the logic of the right to privacy, which, as critics have argued, was "invented" in order "to counter the problem of the alienability of personhood that emerged with modern capitalism, in order to keep stories about the self from circulating in the market and hence to resist the risk of appropriation by the market."[4] Against the discursive construction of privacy in the law, which is dependent upon a "natural" interiority that demands legal protections, James's novel presents the powerful and the protected as those who develop and control the discourse on interiority; the characters' emotional harms that require "protection" are very much manifest within a marketplace of sentient materiality, from bodies and bowls to the novel itself.

Although the legal example is one to which I will return later in the chapter, I briefly want to turn to the arena of psychology, the extraliterary discourse with which James is most often linked. James has been memorialized by his readers and his critics as the great master of the psychological novel; indeed, critics often have read the psychological realism in his novels such as *Portrait of a Lady* (1881), *The Bostonians* (1886), and *The Golden Bowl* (1904) as operating within the conceptual universe imagined by Warren and Brandeis, as offering a unique site for the expression of the inalienable psyche. By the late nineteenth century, at the same time that Warren and Brandeis wrote in favor of the cultural protection of thoughts, emotions, and sensations, a relatively new field like psychology also turned attention inward to focus on the mind's troubles, articulating, analyzing, and in some cases, compensating the suffering soul. Rather than insisting on its own formal integrity when it came to human emotions, psychology, like the law, looked outward beyond its immediate frames of reference. It became commonplace to assume the correlation between psychology and literature; as Judith Ryan suggests, "psychology, it was widely assumed, studied how human emotions functioned and could be best pursued by examining great writers and the way they present the feelings and actions of their characters."[5] In fact, this cross-disciplinary correspondence has fueled much of the Freudian criticism on James (6). James's novels continue to be described by critics as obsessed with interiority, and they often are read as particularly rich instances of female interiority, a description that contributed to James's feminization in critical circles at an early date.

James did not merely embrace an emergent cultural vocabulary about emotion, interiority, and the human capacity for psychic injury; he added a unique voice to a growing debate about the very texture of emotional wounds. *The Golden Bowl* contests readings of feeling as a model for the deep structure of human (and especially female) consciousness; as we shall see, Amerigo's "personal quantity" trumps Maggie's "personal nature" at several important points in the novel. The novel illuminates how psychological wounding at the turn of the twentieth century became a crucial matter of public commerce, its novelization neither a domain of indiscernible "interiority" nor a promise of shared and systemic female suffering. Literary fictions like *The Golden Bowl* illuminate how emotional depth and psychic pain were inflicted, owned, and compensated. For James's protagonists, who at the start of the novel firmly believe that their private agreements are to keep each other free from harm, fictions of commensurability are too delicate to maintain, and the emotional damage that ensues among the four characters becomes quite measurable.

It is important that Maggie, in the exchange with her father with which this chapter begins, reacts with "vehemence" against Adam's implicit suggestion that women are more likely than men to cultivate an arena of wounded feelings. James not only writes against the cultural logic of "inviolate" emotion that began to solicit cultural favor outside his novel, he makes the prince and his "personal systems" the spokesperson for a new economic imperative. The prince's "inward voice" leads Maggie to "speak in a new tone," one that rearranges economic acquisitions as well as personal feelings and relationships in the novel (299). Although Adam Verver is described as the "economically constructed" man, Prince Amerigo, the discoverer, becomes the master of a different currency, that of senses, depth, and feeling. The prince privileges this language and medium; it is the prince upon whom Maggie models her "conscious repossession" in the second half of the novel (305). As Maggie ultimately declares, the prince is the "master of her fate" (313).

In reading *The Golden Bowl*'s discursive engagement with injury, especially its illumination of a cultural shift from the protection against material injuries to the proliferation of emotional wounds, I argue that this engagement must be placed in the context of masculinity. As Leland Person has argued, critical emphasis on "Maggie Verver's controlling role" in the novel, "obscures one of James's most complex male-to-male relationships."[6] Homoerotic elements underpin the relationship between Adam and Amerigo, as Person argues. But more important for our purpose here, Adam and Amerigo represent at first glance competing yet ultimately complementary economies of goods and of feelings, and it is the latter's masterful manipulation of the "empire" of the "personal," as this chapter will show, that ultimately prevails. The prince remakes his personal anxieties about his "place" into an affirmation of his personal power; he turns "emotional turmoil" into "subjective potency," and situational "ambivalence" into "psychological capital."[7]

Amerigo, like Adam, works with a seemingly "invisible hand"; we repeatedly are told in the novel that he does nothing. Both Adam and Amerigo gain power in their seeming passivity, a power that Mark Seltzer and Person have noted especially with regard to Adam (Person, 163). It is Amerigo and not Adam, however, who performs a kind of "sympathetic" introspection that confers him status; he remakes what Adam Smith called "moral sentiments" into economic virtues.[8] While Adam certainly allows Maggie at various points in the novel to "supervise" the Ververs' material economy through acquisitions and arrangements, Amerigo appears to confer Maggie even more power by encouraging her to ventriloquize his "sovereign personal power" (James, qtd. in Person, 168). Amerigo puts Maggie in touch with her "personal nature," which in book 2 she eagerly claims and capitalizes upon despite her reluctance to acknowledge Amerigo's power or her "nature" in the first half of the novel (381). Maggie, in the second book, manifests the sentiments, the feelings, and the wounds that she once disavowed, and she becomes the prince's vehicle for renegotiating the economic and familial relationships in his favor. Despite the prince's feminized appearance early on in the novel—in his role as a "precious object" in the Ververs' economy and in his role as the spokesperson for "interiority," what the narrative calls the prince's "private subtlety"—he is able to efface his power, to displace his feminization, and to deploy Maggie as an agent in his "readjustment of relations" (326). In fact, the prince's disguise of his power is the "culture of feeling" writ small in James's novel, in which women are assumed to manifest "submarine depths" of feeling while men's relation to and power derived from this vehicle is conveniently mystified (329). The prince not only basks in mystery but also in superior judgment both aesthetic and anesthetic throughout the novel; he alone recognizes the crack in the golden bowl, and he uses its rupture to secure his ends.

Precious Objects

The narrative of *The Golden Bowl* begins as Amerigo leaves the offices of the lawyers who have fixed the terms of his impending marriage. Although we are never told quite what the document entails, we do know that it involves an American collector, his daughter, and a man with "history," indeed, volumes of history that can be read and in which the collector and his daughter have seen fit to invest. *The Golden Bowl* begins with a bargain: Mr. Verver's millions for Prince Amerigo's name. To that marital bargain each party brings expectations: "It was in face, content as he was with his engagement and charming as he thought his affianced bride, his view of that furniture that mainly constituted our young man's 'romance' that he was intelligent enough to feel. He was intelligent enough to feel quite humble, to wish not to be in the least hard or voracious, not to insist on his own side of the bargain, to warn himself in short against arrogance and greed" (12). If Amerigo is clearly "romanced" by money, Maggie makes clear to Amerigo just how he is valued by her father: "'You're at any rate a part of his collection,' she had explained—'one of the things that can only be got over here. You're a rarity, an object of beauty, an object of price'" (10). The prince corresponds knowingly that he is "to constitute a possession" (18). Marriage in *The Golden Bowl* is presented as a calculatingly contractual and apparently cost-effective alliance, as were many such mergers of wealth and title not only in the James oeuvre but also in representative works by novelists from Trollope to Wharton.

For Maggie and Adam, however, "human acquisitions" and "fine piece(s)" of art also are an aesthetic barrier against harm; father and daughter live by what they call the "superstition of not 'hurting'" (145, 118). This "superstition" propels the characters' actions. When, for example, father and daughter recognize that Maggie's marriage to the prince will disrupt their paternal "union," both design to obtain Charlotte (each for the other) as "security" against the pain of their separation (99). Adam is quite forthright with Charlotte in his intentions: "'To put her [Maggie] at peace is therefore,' he explained, 'what I'm trying, with you, to do. I can't do it alone, but I can do it with your help'" (165). "I was to be with you," Charlotte concurs, "for her security" (166). (The past tense here, anomalous in the passage, implies that the terms of the agreement may change.) James presents each of his characters as entering the social contract for mutual security: Maggie for title, Adam for Maggie, Charlotte and Amerigo for need. Indeed, the terms of this contract are based upon the "superstition of not causing harm," the belief in the necessity, if not the fear of failing in their designs to be free from injury (although as a superstition may suggest, the need for maintaining such a freedom may lie within the realm of the irrational). Not causing harm repeatedly is introduced into the novel as the condition upon which all relationships, particularly the marital relations, are to be managed. Even as friend and confidant Fanny Assingham relates to her husband an account of Charlotte and Amerigo's previous relationship, she maintains that Maggie would be "in her strange little way, so hurt. . . . She must never know it" (59).

It may be useful here to recollect an earlier account of what the introduction called the etymology of injury: the story of the social contract, which depended from its origins on political philosophies that recount the necessities for freedom from harm. It is certainly not an unusual notion, given the trajectory of Western political thought, for a novelist like James to invest his characters with the belief that their freedom from causing injury creates a morally sound basis upon which to contract relationships with others. The prevention of injury has been the essence of modern notions of the nation-state, the paternal family, and the individual body. In James's novel, the three seem intertwined. Amerigo's quest for sexual and economic "security" at its most intimate (which leads to his marriage to Maggie), is an intimacy that seems to preclude it from concerns of the state; yet as Mark Seltzer has suggested in another context, this quest also should be read in terms of a national mission: "The figure of Amerigo and his lineage [as well as] the allusions to Adam Verver's conquistadorial position . . . make reference to the origins of Western imperialism."[9] Although Amerigo in this assessment is an antiquated precursor to Adam's more modern conquests, Amerigo discovers a new uncolonized territory through which to assert his power: those once "dreadful," now "sacred" wounds. Despite Adam Verver's "conquistadorial position" at the start of the novel, the prince's "sovereign" terrain renavigates the very site and substance of conquest. Where once protections against injury, the repeatedly conceptualized and oft repeated reason behind civic community in many of the seminal texts of early political philosophy—and the raison d'être in the Ververs' households—took their substance, particularly in Locke, from their extensions in material property, these extensions are different from the more modern conceptions of harm, which, like the prince's conceptions, begin to gain cultural favor.[10] James's novel maps the transformation of notions about injury from its manipulations of property to its manifestations of mind. In the etymology of injury, Adam's conquistadorial gestures are but a precursor to the prince's own.

At the novel's start, the susceptibility for injury of Charlotte, Amerigo, Adam, and even Maggie is repeatedly grounded in the characters' conceptions of what constitutes valuable property, including the properties of their bodies themselves. Bodies being in the right place, in the proper configuration, is the narrative key that locks the surface of the relationships together. Maggie's demand for equanimity in her relations (her gesture of sympathy with Amerigo is also to declare herself an "object of price") and the Ververs' horror of "hurting" condones Amerigo and Charlotte's affair: what is equitable for father and daughter must be so for son-in-law and mother-in-law. The external term understood by all in the two marriages is to not harm, thus the constitutive value of such a status, remaining unharmed, requires the facilitation of the relation between father and daughter "at any cost" (117). According to the terms negotiated by father and daughter, their spouses' affair would appear to fall within just bounds. Amerigo and Charlotte confide to each other that it is to shield Maggie from "bruises" that they take the pledge that resumes their affair, acknowledging that they must protect Maggie from injury: "I can't put myself into Maggie's skin—I can't, as I say. It's not my fit—I shouldn't be able, as I see it, to breathe in it. But I can feel that I'd do anything to shield it from a bruise" (228). It seems fitting that Charlotte would adapt a metaphor about the body, specifically the skin, in order to express her desire not to hurt Maggie: Charlotte is the warm body meant to shield Maggie from the pain of worry about her father. Even in Maggie's talk of the "license and privilege" of marriage, which she notes is her most common topic of conversation with Amerigo, she morosely imagines a disagreement with her husband: "Should he some day get drunk and beat [her], the spectacle of him . . . the exhibition of him that most deeply moved her, [would] suffice to bring her round" (no doubt a troubling response to domestic violence, real or imaginary) (122). For Maggie, as for Charlotte, the nature of wounds tends to be imagined and manifest on the body; hence, Charlotte's seductive body commands interest in the novel.[11] Notably, on the eve of his marriage to Maggie,

Amerigo recalls his own holdings in Charlotte in just such terms: "It was, strangely, as a cluster of possessions of his own that these things, in Charlotte Stant, now affected him; items in a full list, items recognised, each of them, as if, for the long interval, they had been 'stored'—wrapped up, numbered, put away in a cabinet" (35). What follows this reclamation is a detailed inventory of Charlotte's comely features. Although one might argue, indeed rightly, that such a display is representative of the way in which women are bound in patriarchal cultures by their bodies, with the matter of Amerigo's "exhibition" of himself and the currency of his person James arguably prohibits such a strict gender distinction. Rather, the fragility of the very surface of things, of all objects and of all bodies, becomes the distinct measure of all of the characters' need to "protect" in the first half of the novel; it is also why, with the breaking of one of those objects, the golden bowl, other ruptures ensue.

It may come as no surprise that the elaborate lengths that are taken to protect one another from injury might be considered by Charlotte and Amerigo as just cause for their affair; sex between them functions, as they claim, to maintain a flawless and undamaged surface. Indeed, the sacred vow that seals Charlotte and Amerigo's affair becomes the novel's most extraordinary measure of the characters' need to protect each other against injury. "It's Sacred, she breathed back to him. They vowed it, gave it out and took it in, drawn by their intensity, more closely together. . . . Their lips sought their lips, their pressure their response and their response their pressure; with a violence that had sighed itself the next moment to the longest and deepest of stillnesses they passionately sealed their pledge" (228). James meticulously constructs the irony of this moment: the only overtly sexual contact in the novel is over a pledge not to harm; their "sovereign law would be the vigilance of 'care,' would be never rashly to forget and never consciously to wound" (239). It is a pledge initiating what is certain to be considered by some a very harmful affair. Of course, Fanny Assingham notices the irony of this from the start: "The dear man married to ease his daughter off, and . . . by extraordinary perversity, . . . the very opposite effect was produced" (284).

Readers certainly have considered what the Ververs (Maggie and Adam) call "not hurting . . . at any cost" among the costliest and most painful things (118). For some of these readers, the transfer of desires at the end of the novel has been considered a victory both for Maggie and for James, whose representations of marriage in his many works has been anything but celebratory. (One need only think of the poor prognosis for

Basil and Verena in the last line of *The Bostonians*: "It is to be feared that with the union, so far from brilliant, into which she was about to enter, these were not the last [tears] she was destined to shed.")[12] Indeed, if the marriage between Maggie and Amerigo is not the culmination of "normative" development (in a Freudian sense), but rather both marriages are entered into to promote "unnatural" desires (father for daughter, and later, by the law of familial relations, mother-in-law for son-in-law), then by the end of the novel, as Jean-Christophe Agnew has argued, the "unnatural" attachment of implicit incest and implicit adultery are sacrificed to the "normal," "natural" attachments of marriage (91). The reestablishment of "normative" marital relations in *The Golden Bowl* might appear to be a valorization of a "private sphere"—a space in which marriage is reaffirmed, "privacy" seldom ruptured, and apparently no one unjustly harmed. Indeed, Maggie's "buried" face, unlike Verena Tarant's in *The Bostonians*, has frequently been interpreted to mask a smile rather than tears.[13] The novel, however, problematizes several of its apparent constitutive conditions: the psychological depth upon which the structure of harm is articulated, the boundaries of privacy that protect the marital relations, and the nature of pain through which these relations are felt.

Personal Quantity

Although the prince's "capture" of Maggie crowns his pursuit, James's first chapter in the first book of the novel follows a restless prince not quite content in his "success"; he repeatedly is described as "more serious than gay" (4). It appears early on that the prince's book may become a tale of abjection (of the kind that Maggie fears for herself: "I might, at all events, for all I know, be abject under a blow") (138). The prince relays a sense of lost manhood: he obediently "accept[s] the 'social limitations' of [their] life" and does not miss "what [they] don't give him" (130). Adam, by contrast, seems more "manly" because he can buy and sell goods and, through great wealth, people; Adam is the master of commerce in conventional capitalist terms. The prince seems nothing but a hired hand in Adam's patriarchal economy; in fact, Leland Person suggests that the question James poses about Amerigo is whether he can "retain his manly integrity while hiring himself out to another man" (Person, 159). His prospects for doing so appear doubtful after the transaction with which the book begins; the prince is left with "nothing to do as yet further, but feel what one had done" (4). Left feeling rather than doing (and, in terms of Adam's early assumptions, in the feminine position), he feels and contemplates his place in Adam Verver's "principle of reciprocity" (4). This principle allocates the Verver millions for the prince's name, a name that both Adam and Maggie are romanced by from the start (60). In the spirit of reciprocity, however, the prince wishes to be not only a name but also a voice, to "converse properly, on equal terms as it were, with Mr. Verver" (5). Despite the prince's practice of fluency in English, he notes that he and Adam continue to speak different languages. The prince's sense of his "difference," especially from Adam, characterizes much of the first book (5).

The prince images this difference, for example, by describing himself and Adam to Maggie as if they were not men but chickens: Adam Verver is the "natural fowl" still in control of his "movements, his sounds," not yet caught, feathered, and cooked, while the prince is "chopped up and smothered in sauce . . . with half the parts left out" (6). It is not Adam who makes out best by being freely seen and heard, however. Amerigo tells Maggie that he is "eating [her] father alive—which," he claims, "is the only way to taste him" (6). Leland Person reads this extended metaphor as an example of Amerigo's "destabilize[ed] . . . gendered and sexual self" (158). The prince, Person argues, turns "homoerotic desire into emulation" (158). Yet "eating" Adam also means ingesting his magnificence and power; for this reason Amerigo finds Adam "tasty." Amerigo declares that Adam is "simply the best man I've ever seen in my life," and Maggie agrees, noting that it is his "American way" (6). The prince, also consuming this notion, "practic[es] his American"; he desires to use his relation with Adam to create something different yet again of himself (5).

As Adam is devoted to economic principles, the prince is beholden to what he prizes as his "particular self" (7). The prince invests in psychological capital, which, as Raymond Williams has argued, gained its cultural authority precisely in relation to the dominance of the economic principles of industrial and corporate capitalism.[14] The prince carves his place at the corporate family table by preparing a wholly different dish from Adam, not one of material objects but of what the prince calls "personal quantity" (7). As the prince mixes metaphors varying from free-range chicken and haute cuisine to books, he reveals to Maggie that the best part of any dish *is* that which is left out: "There are two parts of me. . . . One is made up of the history, the doings, the marriages, the crimes, the follies, the boundless *bêtises* of other people. . . . Those things are written—literally in rows of volumes, in libraries; are as public as they're abominable. Everybody can get at them, and you've both of you wonderfully looked them in the face. But there's another part, very much smaller doubtless, which, such as it is, represents my single self, the unknown, unimportant—unimportant save to you—personal quantity. About this you've found out nothing" (7). Maggie, of course, replies that she isn't interested in the prince's "unknown quantity, [his] particular self"; rather, it is his archive—"the generations behind you, the follies and the crimes, the plunder and the waste"—that is most important. "Where," she asks, "without your archives, annals, infamies, would you have been?" (8). Maggie reiterates for the prince that he is an "object of price" and not a subject of interest, but the prince is not content to leave it at that. The prince gleans from Maggie that in the Ververs' assessment of value the "finest objects are often the smallest"; the "finest," he implies, may even be the least visible (11). Although Amerigo is conscious not to appear "arrogant or greedy" in his conversation with Maggie, reminding himself again of "his own side of the bargain," ultimately he designs to "redress the balance of his being so differently considered" (13).

The prince incessantly refers to his "difference," not merely in terms of language, nationality, or monetary worth; he thinks of difference as that between his outer "value" and his inward possession. In a conversation with Fanny Assingham, Amerigo asks Fanny to help him see himself through his wife and his father-in-law's eyes: "Through them I wish to look" (23). Amerigo believes that Fanny has the "sense" through which he can execute this design. Fanny replies, in one of her strongest compliments to Amerigo, "I should be interested to see some sense you don't possess" (24). The prince, Fanny exclaims, is a virtual "Machiavelli" of sense, implying that through his senses the prince commands power (24). Readers are told that the prince's outward appearances and his inner senses make "a contrast that he was intelligent enough to feel" (12). This contrast leaves the prince consumed with what he describes as "dangers from within" (12). In his exterior form, however, Amerigo seems resigned to his place: he "desire(s) to proceed, taking everything into account and making no mistake that may possibly injure" (28). This resignation is surprising to Adam Verver, who wonders at the prince's ability to show "no visibility of transition . . . no violence of adjustment" (100). The prince, Adam declares, has succeeded in "remaining solidly a feature," while ceasing "to be, at all ominously, a block" (2). Maggie's dismissal of the prince's "personal quantity" in favor of his appearance, and Adam's wonder at the prince's amiable compliance, suggest something different and more complicated at work. Adam even calls this difference forth: "If the prince could only strike something to which he hadn't! This wouldn't, it seemed to him, ruffle the smoothness, and yet might, a little add to the interest" (117). The ambiguous pronoun "he" in the first sentence is telling. Adam, the "first" male, looks to Amerigo, the discoverer, to "strike" out to new territory. This is precisely what the prince intends to do: "The prince was saving up, for some very mysterious but very fine eventual purpose, all the wisdom, all the answers to his questions, all the impressions and generalizations, he gathered; putting them away and packing them down because he wanted his great gun to be loaded to the brim on the day he should decide to let it off. He wanted to make sure of the whole of the subject that was unrolling itself before him; after which the innumerable facts he had collected would find their use" (121). The prince is "putting . . . away" and "packing . . . down" all the "impressions and generalizations" he gathers for future employ. They all form part of an unknown "quantity," which Maggie is quick to reject, but whose possibility Adam embraces without ever directly invoking it as such.

Even though Amerigo is referred to at various points in the narrative as a "domesticated lamb" and as one who is "magnificent" in his seeming acquiescence, he represents more than an emblem of acquisition for Adam (119, 130). The prince satisfies that which Adam lacks, and not just in name, physical stature, youth, and sexual potency (the narrative reminds us that Adam is short, balding, not so young, and possibly impotent); the prince also is in command of territory that Adam often yearns for but is alienated by: sovereign personal power. In one of the novel's more detailed passages about Adam, the narrative compares two houses: the house of art and the house of the mind. In the first house, Adam stands as its master; he has "designed [the house] as a gift," one which he "set down by his hands as a house on a rock—a house from whose open doors and windows, open to grateful, to thirsty millions, the higher, the highest knowledge would shine out to bless the land" (107). Adam is confident in his ability to provide all the "treasures" necessary to sate the thirst of "millions," who, in turn, will be "grateful" (107). Adam is the giver of knowledge; he constructs this house of treasures with his own hands, and he is seemingly selfless in his desire to give it to his fellow citizens. This is the height of Adam's felicity. Within a few moments, however, Adam's thoughts turn to a different house, one in which he is not the master builder but virtually an unwanted guest: "His real friend, in all the business, was to have been his own mind, with which nobody had put him in relation. He had knocked at the door of that essentially private house, and his call, in truth, had not been immediately answered; so that when after waiting and coming back, he had at last got in, it was, twirling his hat, as an embarrassed stranger, or trying his keys, as a thief at night" (110). In the house of art, Adam is a glorious "founding father"; in the house of the mind, he is, at first, nothing less than a thief and an "embarrassed stranger." This distinction is crucial; whereas Adam's strength comes from the objects he is able to buy and house, the prince has a "personal system." For him "the illumination indeed was all for the mind"; he thrives in the house Adam truly wishes he had built (215).

Both Adam and Amerigo direct their attention beneath the surface in book 1; both men suggest that value lies not only in outward but also in inward capital, although Adam is less adept at this form of ownership. Adam, we will remember from the exchange with which this chapter began, knows nothing of what young men like the prince do or tell. Like Adam, who wonders at the prince's seeming indifference at being "placed," Amerigo finds it "remarkable" "to feel how everything else the master of the house consisted of, resources, possessions, facilities, and amiabilities . . . depended on no personal 'equation'" (237). Unlike Adam, whom the prince sees as lacking "personal 'equation,'" Amerigo, as Fanny Assingham relays to her husband, is, like his namesake, a "discoverer" (60). His "difference" and his "personal equation" become a means of conquest. Amerigo recognizes and capitalizes upon hidden potential: the unacknowledged feelings of harm that implode in the second half of the novel. Adam, meanwhile, blindly describes the prince as a "pure and perfect crystal" (102). He sees no crack in this crystal's superior appearance. Like Adam's mistaken estimation of Amerigo, the golden bowl, the novel's namesake, bears an invisible crack, and its exposure portends a change in the novel's relationships of power and value. With the discovery of the golden bowl's secrets, Maggie, who was once only interested in surface aesthetics, becomes supremely interested in "mental acts" and "sentient sel[ves]," the very substance of the prince's "difference" in the first book (308, 329).

The novel ends differently than it began. Where once the prince was left with "nothing to do but feel," he walks out of his later marital renegotiation with his wife, his son, their millions, and his own "sovereign self" intact. Maggie, on the other hand, has "sacrificed" her father; her father has given up his one "deep intimacy"; and Charlotte has lost the prince (214). Maggie confides in Fanny that in the end her plan has "saved" the very people that she and her father conspired to acquire for their own safety, while she and her father are "the ones who are lost . . . lost to each other" (541). Though Charlotte, as we shall see, hardly feels "saved," Amerigo notes that he has "gained more from women than he had ever lost by them"; he admits that at any given moment the women in his life "combine and conspire for his advantage" (257). Maggie's book plans and ultimately embodies the prince's "redress" (13).

Golden Rules

As Maggie presents Amerigo with the narrative of her purchase of the golden bowl, she is "ashamed" to say the price that she paid for it (444). Indeed, it is the high price she paid and the gift she was to make of the bowl to her father that "worked" on the proprietor of the shop, leading him to seek Maggie out to return to her a portion of her payment. "What had perhaps most moved him," Maggie recalls, "was the thought that she ignorantly should have gone in for a thing not good enough for other buyers," particularly buyers like Charlotte Stant and Prince Amerigo, customers, the shopkeeper learns upon his visit, with whom Maggie is intimate (462). Although readers of the novel from F. O. Mathiesson to Jean-Christophe Agnew have fully documented Maggie's and her father's "collecting" and, in turn, "aestheticizing" of their objects of interest, including their prospective spouses, this moment with the shopkeeper, like her father's mistaken appraisal of Amerigo, exposes the fallibility of Maggie's aesthetic. In fact, the shopkeeper's exposure of the flaw in Maggie's aesthetic pursuit is the novel's structural and symbolic center; like the flaw in the bowl itself, it invites the display of what the characters in the first half of the novel have labored so hard to deny: the apparatus of injury at work in the novel. James himself painstakingly describes the prince and Charlotte as costly items within this structure of injury because, as we have seen, for father and daughter the prevention of injury to each other is worth any expense. And while Maggie is unable to see the crack in the crystal, the damage that is already in the bowl dictates the rupture of what is perhaps the novel's most delicate provision: the Ververs' design of not "hurting." It is the moments prior to the smashing of the bowl that break both the aesthetic condition (the idea that the Ververs are consummate collectors) and the anesthetic condition (the corresponding belief that what accompanies flawless beauty is the freedom from pain). The shopkeeper's revelation to Maggie of the flaw in the bowl discloses the flaw in her own pursuit.

Though the shopkeeper's gesture of goodwill certainly humbles Maggie's aesthetic claim, he does substantiate her greater intimation when he recognizes Charlotte's and Amerigo's pictures and identifies them as the earlier customers interested in the same golden bowl. The shopkeeper finds himself strangely "moved" by Maggie, and he feels enough to unwittingly provide evidence justifying Maggie's suspicion that there is an undetected flaw in her own marital designs: Charlotte and Amerigo have hidden their prior relations (462). The value of the bowl comes to rest not in its price, therefore, but in the value of its "witness"; as Maggie says, "that cup there has turned witness—by the most wonderful of chances" (419). Although Maggie is shamed by her inability to calculate properly the aesthetic quality and monetary value of the object of her interest, it is its prior history, relayed by the shopkeeper, which for her justifies its price. The bowl for Maggie, as for Charlotte and Adam before her, is what Elaine Scarry would call "sentient."[15] It becomes the extension of the characters' feelings; it contains unspoken knowledge and holds the pleasure and the pain for each. For Amerigo, shopping with Charlotte on the day before his wedding to Maggie, the bowl is an ill omen, and he rejects it as a gift at the novel's start. Charlotte, however, later recalls the bowl as an expansion and projection of her feelings for Amerigo, "I feel the day like a great gold cup that we must somehow drain together. I feel it, as you always make me feel everything, just as you do; so that I know ten miles off how you feel!" (263). For Maggie the bowl is neither a witness to passion nor, as she was to make of it, a gift to her father, but rather a vessel that corroborates her suspicions. Indeed, as she less humbly claims, its value for her is in the secrets it has so surreptitiously hidden. What that cup turns witness to, therefore, is not solely contained by the fiscal value that has tended to accrue around the novel's aesthetic objects (including the prince and Charlotte); rather, it comes to embody the cost of feeling.

Maggie's simultaneous humbling and hubris in the shape of the golden bowl introduces an even more precious measure than the prevention of injury into the familial economy; it introduces the calculus of emotional pain into the novel. The breaking of the bowl and the various kinds of feelings it unleashes initiates a different configuration of aesthetic and anesthetic value, value measured by the price of suffering and the claim to pain. Indeed, not only the aestheticizing of the Ververs' spouses, but also the anesthetizing of all the relations in the novel comes, if not to an abrupt end, then to redefinition in the moment described above. The storekeeper feels for Maggie, whose feelings of suspicion have been substantiated into feelings of betrayal; she feels and wants to feel Amerigo "writhing in his pain" (441). With the breaking of the bowl, one of the objects of price in the novel, it is the properties of emotion and the ownership of injury that begin to accrue value for the subjects of the novel. "To feel him," Maggie fancies about Amerigo, "to think of his feeling himself, her adversary": the bowl becomes the vessel by which this commerce, competition, and consciousness about feeling functions (403).

Book 2 begins with Maggie listening to an "inward voice" that speaks "a new tone" (299). Like Amerigo in the first book, Maggie becomes consumed with the "deeper need to know where she really [is]" (340). She speaks with no one but Fanny Assingham about her "insurmountable feeling[s]," and Fanny, rather than express alarm over her friend's "torment," praises this new Maggie (384, 395, 384). "Here you are indeed, as you say—such a deep little person!" (380). Fanny recalls the prince's personal language from the first book. He "expect[s] [Maggie], desire[s] her to have character; his wife should have it, and he wasn't afraid of her having too much" (15). Fanny repeats this sentiment: "I've always been conscious of your having concealed about you somewhere no small amount of character" (381). Fanny calls this "new tone" the expression of Maggie's "precious little innermost . . . little golden, personal nature . . . blest by a greater power" (381). With the recognition of Amerigo and Charlotte's deceit, Maggie is called upon to respond to the very "blow" that earlier in her exchange with her father she avowed no knowledge of. Rather than "be abject," however, Maggie declares herself, again echoing Amerigo, "different"; she will now use these "dreadful" and "sacred" wounds as a "great moment" for "conscious repossession" (305). This includes not only repossession of the prince but "command" of his vocabulary as well; Maggie, who once disavowed the prince's "personal quantity," now declares herself absorbed with her own "personal nature" (381). If this "conscious repossession" is cast, at first, competitively with Amerigo ("quantity" against "nature"), Maggie acknowledges quickly that whatever Amerigo desired, "he would always absolutely bring . . . off" (313). Maggie "naturally" performs Amerigo's designs.

Within James's novel, personal nature is made powerful not by withdrawing it from the marketplace or casting it with privileged inalienable status, James's novel demonstrates how psychic injury becomes a new currency and means of power. Perhaps it is no wonder then that Samuel Warren and Louis Brandeis invoked literary work as the most appropriate medium through which to measure the legal status of the mind. Their desire to move away from property as a measurement of the right to protection to nonmaterial categories of emotion was a transformative moment within legal reasoning. According to Warren and Brandeis, the basis for the recognition that thoughts and emotions could constitute a domain of protection, in fact, the structure for the argument, lay in part in the work of writing. It was the example of literary art, they argued, that enabled the creation of a separate category for the protection of "emotional life," a life that was necessarily separate from the protection and extensions of property. By analyzing a series of copyright cases involving unpublished manuscripts, Warren and Brandeis challenged what they called the "fiction of property" in the literary text, building an evidentiary narrative in which a literary author is granted "the right to be left alone," the right to withhold his or her manuscript from the public by denying publication. Writing, they argued, should be understood as a measure of an author's emotional and private life, a life separate and discreet, a life that must be protected from the public. Not to provide such protections to the sanctity of an author's narrative would be a violation of the author's dignity, there being "no basis if discerned upon which the right to restrain publications and reproduction of such so-called literary and artistic works can be rested, except the right to privacy, as part of the more general right to the immunity of the person—the right to one's personality" (207). Warren and Brandeis's model of authorship, a model that privileges the inviolate and literary self, became a model through which to extend "immunity" to all humanity against the suffering and the pain of intrusions to one's privacy. The literary imagination of interior lives, the aesthetic presentation of thoughts, feelings, and emotions, and the corresponding belief that such imaginings were the inalienable expression of their author mandated the need for protections that the category of privacy (what was to be the numbing anesthetic against the public world) would ensure.[16]

That the protection of aesthetic productions might expand into a kind of cultural semantics in which the freedom from injury (and the maintenance of the inviolate) is at issue is the very equation upon which James's characters in *The Golden Bowl*, if not the novel itself, originally depend. Readers can see the concepts propounded by Warren and Brandeis exquisitely at work in James's novel. For example, the prince early on in *The Golden Bowl* appears to embody a belief in what Warren and Brandeis call the private emotional life when he adamantly claims to withdraw some part of himself from the original marriage agreement. If the prince is to be a warm body or a lucrative name in his legal agreement with the Ververs, he believes that he has reserved out of the bargain his most sacred part, what he deems to be priceless and not for sale, his "personal quantity" (7). The public property of the written book is instrumental in the value that the Ververs place upon the prince; if this book is not the archetype of "the private," as perhaps the prince originally might hope, the prince's narrative that he claims to withdraw from circulation constitutes, just as Brandeis and Warren would have it, his private "right." The prince has his story, which can and has been read; it is public and material. But there is also, as he claims, the unexaminable, the private, the "interior," and to the invasion of this he is "immune."

Despite his belief in "immunity," Amerigo also repeatedly professes his psychic injury (injury as a measure of his lost dignity and failed authorship; the rights to read him, in part, are on display and a fit subject for investment) for a good portion of his narrative in the first book. He frequently belies the discomfort he feels in Maggie's "domestic detachment" (231); he recognizes that father and daughter want "to be together—at any cost" (188). The cost to Maggie and presumably to her father would be Amerigo's infidelity, the ultimate refusal of his "place." For the prince, his pathos seems to derive from his having been managed and arranged, from his being possessed, much like the bowl, as an object of value, an object that will afford Maggie and Adam their "safety." In the prince's estimation, he has been "reduced" to a "not quite glorious substitute" (259). It is, as we have seen, his own painful self-definition as an object in the Ververs' exchange that is instrumental in his sexual bargain with Charlotte. Amerigo's feelings as "[an] outsider, a foreigner, and even as a mere representative husband and son-in-law" (258) lead most clearly to his justification of his affair: "Over and above the pleasure itself, [the] scruple would certainly gratify both Mr. Verver and Maggie" (255). By calling the decision to revive the affair with Charlotte his "scruple," he intends to count his actions within the moral economy of the novel: the decision is within the bounds of what the prince and others consider not wounding "at any cost." We learn fairly early on in the novel, however, that although each character struggles to present an injury-free exterior, each secretly suffers: Adam for Maggie, Maggie for Adam, Charlotte for Amerigo, and Amerigo for his unacknowledged "sovereign self." (They suffer to the exclusion of the other characters but not to the exclusion of the reader; it is a secret only partially kept.) Unlike Maggie, who suffers the pain of her improper aesthetic judgment and the subsequent pain of deceit, the prince appears humbled in his "place" as fine title and little else. His humiliation issues not only in his sense of duress, but also in his sense of just deserts.

It may be this paradigm of suffering (the sexual in alliance with the economic) that many of James's men could be said to be victim of (Lambert Strether, Merton Densher, Hyacinth Robinson, John Marcher, and Basil Ransom, among them). Although he is a prince, Amerigo's title is all he has left in a world where monetary accumulation measures worth and where failure and humiliation are omnipresent. This masculine economy of pain is not appropriated uncritically or purely sympathetically within James's novels, however. In *The Bostonians*, for instance, Basil wins Verena, a conquest after his self-professed failures as an author and the loss of his status as a "southern gentleman" (and his failure as a lawyer), although his failures are wounds that feel quite numb in comparison with Olive Chancellor's tortured emotions. If we were to read the novel as a competition for the recognition of feeling rather than the "rights" to Verena, Olive's pain overwhelms Basil's capacity for suffering. Likewise, in *The Golden Bowl* it appears that at the moment the golden bowl is smashed, a face of pain different from the prince's own discloses itself, and Maggie bears its features. The narrative division in James's novel, the first half from the prince's perspective, the second half from Maggie's, makes its readers consciously aware of the question of authorship and the gendered claims to immunity from suffering by placing Amerigo and Maggie in competition to substantiate their stories, stories that offer "different" developments in their own protection from harm. The status of injury, which in the first half of the novel is quelled by the manifestations and manipulations of bodies and property, withdraws into a commerce of psychic wounds in the novel's second half. Amerigo crucially anticipates this change when he declares himself early on in the novel flush with "dangers from within" (12).

The novel's troubled maintenance of good bodies who will not wound and of suffering souls who keep their interior lives hidden from view may be attributable to what James's readers have come to credit him with creating, psychological realism: characters who live the life of the mind and who exhibit the painful emotion of the soul. For many of James's readers, as for Warren and Brandeis, who build their claim of privacy upon what they perceive to be a transparency between an author and his work, these interior wounds are indicative of a kind of metaphysical depth of character and author, a depth that simultaneously necessitates and manifests what Warren and Brandeis have called "the immunity of the person" (207). Unlike the prince, who suffers himself "differently considered" in the first half of the novel, Maggie suffers in the second half of the novel not as she originally imagined she would, the pain of body with body, but rather the pain of "deceit" (445). Amerigo again "prepares" Maggie for such pains by insisting early in their marriage that she acknowledge his constitutional incapacity to "lie, dissemble, or deceive" (12). Maggie is uncomfortable with Amerigo's "intensity" of discussion; she thinks to herself that "duplicity, like 'love,' had to be joked about. It couldn't be 'gone into'"(12). Even four years later, Maggie has difficulty speaking of these matters. Rather than display her knowledge of the affair in words, Maggie allows only her "inner" voice to betray her feeling, "the horror of the thing hideously *behind*, behind so much trusted, so much pretended" (471). It is the horror of the unsaid, the uncovered, and the unexposed inside that at this moment of reckoning becomes the most injurious to Maggie. That the surface of things has a dark underside was not at all part of the original bargain (neither, we might remember, was the prince's "personal quantity"). It is not this inside or model of depth, however, that the novel confirms. The characters' sufferings do not enable them to emerge deeper or richer into wedlock; nor is Maggie's psychic injury an example of an "exquisite" "internalized consciousness," although such declarations have been made and celebrated elsewhere.[17] Feelings in *The Golden Bowl*, as I have been arguing, are not a model for the deep structure of human consciousness; they become, rather, a question of commerce. James's literary fiction illuminates how psychic injury is enforced, possessed, and recompensed.

If Warren and Brandeis take literary work as evidence upon which to build their case for the right to privacy, James's novel resists this cultural logic not by fictionalizing the "natural" "inviolability" of the self but rather by imagining the growing marketplace for such a status. In *The Golden Bowl*, Maggie and Amerigo come to trade on claims to interiority. The prince's petition to the "personal" is in the language of measurement, for example; it is deemed by him in terms of quantity, not, as readers might expect, quality. James also makes clear at the start of the novel that despite the prince's insistence on quantity, it is merely the illusion that there is something not quantifiable that gives the prince comfort in his current status. Although he is "invested with attributes" and an object of "appreciation," the notion that a second part of him—the single, unknown, and personal—is brought into the bargain in an effort to be left out of it constitutes his claim to interiority and simultaneously belies his claim from the start. Reflecting upon Amerigo's investments in his "unwritten" book, James makes clear that authorship is not only an already public relation, it is one that demands the appearance of interiority, depth, and immunity when nothing and no one is immune. The model of authorship offered by Warren and Brandeis in "The Right to Privacy" is flawed when it comes to James's own understanding of the work of fiction. Brook Thomas makes this point in his reading of *The Bostonians:* "For James a work is not, as it is for Warren and Brandeis, coextensive with its creator until he alienates it as a piece of property to the public" ("The Construction of Privacy," 738). Authorship, whether the prince's or James's own, has constitutive value only in its public consumption.

Maggie takes the prince's illusion about his personal quantity and gives it currency by invoking it as part of their marital renegotiation. Though Maggie and Amerigo's marriage appears to preserve the possibility for Amerigo's self-professed "unknown" to remain just that, marriage also occasions the commodification and materialization of deep feeling. In fact, Maggie turns the prince's discourse on depth and interiority into a marketable commodity by strongly inflecting it with the language of injury. Amerigo's investment in privacy, in the privilege of an interior inaccessible self that he believes he has hidden from his investors, anticipates the claims that Maggie will make in their marital renegotiation, claims that also invest in "depth" while conceptualizing interiority as injured feelings and casting those feelings in distinctly transactional terms. When Maggie reminds Amerigo of his previous assertions (to the single self, the unknown, the personal) in their private renegotiation of their marriage contract by offering up the seemingly equivocal "You're so deep," it is this very entitlement to depth that becomes the marital renegotiation's most valued currency (446). While emotional depth, according to Warren and Brandeis, is manifest in the act of protecting the inviolable, Maggie secures her own deep feeling just as she demands Amerigo and, later, Charlotte, to "arrange yourself to suffer least" (434). Indeed, the prince seems to lose his claims to depth along with his authorial voice the moment that Maggie asserts her own claims in this regard.

Amerigo does not suffer under the terms, the end of his relations with Charlotte, that Maggie imagines, however. The novel repeatedly suggests that Amerigo's affair with Charlotte is just "play" (293). Fanny Assingham quips that he "doesn't care for Charlotte. . . . [M]en don't, when it has all been too easy. That's how, in nine cases out of ten a woman is treated who has risked her life. You asked me just now how [the prince] works . . . but you might better perhaps have asked me how he plays" (287, 293). For the prince, Charlotte's "loss" has little effect on his "personal system" (152). In "Maggie's book," Amerigo takes frequent trips to London, becomes an avid book collector, and ultimately decides where he and his wife travel and live. If the first book suggests the illusory nature of the prince's "personal quantity," the second book leaves Maggie with the constant wonder about precisely its substance. Maggie is confounded by Amerigo's thoughts and designs. She admits that she truly has "found out nothing" about Amerigo's "single self," while Amerigo, true to Maggie's demand, does appear "to suffer least" among the four characters (7).

To Amerigo, women "combine and conspire for his advantage," while his sole "recompense" is to "make love to them" (257, 17). Lovemaking is little "recompense" to Maggie, however, who begins her marital renegotiation "by asking herself how she [Maggie] could make him [Amerigo] think more of her" (545). Just as the prince envisions Charlotte as a series of comely features, we learn that Maggie too represents a series of acquisitions to him and not quite the other way around; she "really hasn't had him," declares Fanny Assingham, "never" (281). The prince, throughout the first book, is far more interested in Adam; he thinks of himself as a far better son-in-law than husband, and he endlessly is intrigued by the difference in values between him and Adam (102). For Maggie to command the prince's attention, readers learn that her "sense will have to open" (280). She must not solely be "awake" to her husband's affair, she must be conscious too of her own "difference" (295). The crack in the golden bowl and the sexual secrets it unleashes become the occasion for such an opening, although her success in such a project has been the subject of continuing critical debate.[18] Fanny, thinking of her own personal stake in the renegotiation, desires to script Maggie's victory when she declares, "Your husband has never, never, never . . . never been half so interested in you as he is now. But don't you, my dear, really feel it?" (430).

What Maggie feels is less certain than Fanny's declarations suggest. Departing from her intentions at the novel's start, Maggie now wants to provide her father with safety against the knowledge of what "young men do"; she schemes to "tax Charlotte's art" and, most of all, to exact recompense from the prince—not physical recompense but one based on the acknowledgment and value of her "sentient self" (283, 400, 329). Amerigo, at a pivotal point in the marital renegotiation, capitalizes on Maggie's new interest in "personal quantity"; he presents his recompense to Maggie in just this currency of the personal: "It's you, *cara*, who are deep" (447). Although at the end of the novel Maggie appears to command authority, psychological and relational, Amerigo relishes in just such appearances; they repeatedly enable him throughout the novel to have "after his fashion, the last word in their exchange" (11). Maggie, recognizing Amerigo as always "having planned for the last word . . . saw him enjoying it. It was almost as if—in the strangest way in the world—he were paying her back" (347). The prince does not "pay [Maggie] back" in the way readers might initially imagine, by conceding his defeat and "making it up" to his wife in the manner best suited to his physical prowess, sexually. He does so by appearing to grant Maggie her most valued currency: her privileged feelings of "depth." At the same time, however, he surreptitiously produces in her what she acknowledges is a "small pang . . . a new uneasiness" (347).

The Golden Bowl ends as it begins, with a marital negotiation, but rather than storming the British Museum to delight in her investment in the prince's open book, Maggie acknowledges and protects the prince's personal quantity, which true to his earliest statements are those about which Maggie has found out nothing (7). The novel returns to the legal contract with a different bargaining measure: it is the prince, not solely Adam, who now retains what Leland Person calls "capitalist privilege" by seeing Maggie "work on his behalf" (Person, 154). Maggie legitimizes the prince's personal system; she speaks in the prince's voice while allowing him conveniently to disappear, and she gives credence to the prince's search for an equivalent to Adam's economy by giving the prince's psychic "difference" distinct (marriage) market value.

For Maggie, the protection of her interests means not only her (re)-possession of the prince, but also his recognition of her difference, her deep feeling, even though this recognition, despite earlier "superstitions" to the contrary, will wound. Just as Maggie ventriloquizes the prince's interests, Charlotte enables Maggie to feel a form of psychological mastery in the face of her emotional wounds. In the exchange between father and daughter with which this chapter begins, readers learn that Charlotte's greatness is manifest in the very depth of her wounds, wounds that Maggie claims only surface knowledge of. Maggie gravely declares to her father that Charlotte "has suffered" (137). When Maggie sees fit to decry her own "blow" and her own "insurmountable feeling," however, Charlotte is required to appear the "least distorted and disfigured" (137, 395, 434). Charlotte must hide her wounds, which once the currency of value has changed in the relationships from the "magnificence" of appearances to the power and depths of emotional injuries, reiterates once again Charlotte's status as nonprivate and nonsacrosanct. Despite Maggie's mandate for Charlotte to hide her feelings, the most overt display of pain in the novel remains Charlotte's own. "She had turned suddenly to crying, or was at least on the point of it—the lighted square before her all blurred and dim. The high voice went on; its quaver was doubtless for conscious ears only, but there were verily thirty seconds which it sounded, for our young woman, like the shriek of a soul in pain. Kept up a minute longer, it would break and collapse—so that Maggie felt herself, the next thing, turn with a start to her father. 'Can't she be stopped? Hasn't she done enough?'" (512). Although hearing Charlotte's cry is anathema to Maggie, the "quaver . . . for conscious ears only," Maggie uses each detail in her own expanding arsenal of wounds to dismiss Charlotte and to exact the substance of her own suffering. "[Maggie] might . . . have yearned for . . . a range of feelings which for many women would have meant so much, but which for *her* husband's wife, for *her* father's daughter, figured nothing nearer to experience than a wild eastern caravan" (470–71). Instead of plunging into what for some people, but certainly not for Maggie, would be the raw pleasure of feeling pain (like Charlotte's "soul in pain"), Maggie exacts another method of compensation.

Maggie turns the intangible, the immune, the affectional, if not the equivocal, into standard juridical claims. Maggie's justice, "the law of her attitude" (418), is carried out as if by legal design. She collects what she perceives to be "evidence" (397); she "cross-examin[es]" witnesses, and she builds her "case" (460, 445). She even claims that to renegotiate the terms of their new marital contract, the prince must "suffer arrest from her now" (445). Maggie turns to the dominant language of the law to give feeling authority, and with this gesture, she once again legitimates the prince's investments in personal quantity; he suffers "arrest" from her, while she remakes his intangible quantities into a matter of recompense. Indeed, Maggie's law is carried out with such precision that in one of the earliest reviews of the novel the fictional story is perceived and metaphorized as coextensive with legal narrative. A 1904 review in *The Nation* describes *The Golden Bowl* as if it were a court trial. "He [James] doesn't literally tell the story: he only examines witnesses, comments on testimony, infers and speculates prodigiously, leaving us free to make what we can of the case, to grasp or miss its facts and its wide significance, according to our capacity for independent mental operations."[19]

Emotional Law

Grasping the newly emerging status of emotional wounds in law courts at the turn of the century often depended upon the ability of courts to admit and respond to studies carried out in medicine or psychology. Although Warren and Brandeis invoked literature as a means of effecting legal change, scholars more often looked to psychology in questioning the admissibility of evidence for assessing legal liability, especially in cases involving emotional injuries. Tort scholars such as Calvert Magruder, a professor at Harvard Law School and subsequently a judge on the U.S. Court of Appeals, presented studies such as those by psychologist Walter B. Cannon as expert evidence. Cannon argued, as it turned out in grave error, that the diabetic could trace the origins of his physical disease from his internal feelings of pain and "great emotions."[20] Not surprisingly, the emotional pain of sexual betrayal was read as one of the most potent impetuses for physical disease in many of these legal opinions. Cannon cites an 1898 study that traces the onset of diabetes in a man "directly after his wife was discovered in adultery" (67). Sexual relations, relations like those presented by means of a broken bowl in James's novel, often became some of the most conspicuous cases for damage to the psyche.[21] More important, these cases of forbidden sexual relations reoriented the cultural psyche to a quite tangible field of emotion. Although Warren and Brandeis maintained that privacy was a necessary "right" by disengaging "independent mental operations" from the world of property, the work on the manifestation of feelings of pain and rage on the body in diseaselike symptoms, work produced by Cannon and, notably, Henry James's brother William, led law courts to immediately reassess their perceptions about the nature of harm by challenging the strict distinction between interiority and physiology.

Like Henry, who was suspicious of the postulation of an idea of consciousness that was "behind" (to use Maggie's term) or "deep" (to use Amerigo's) and thus immune from circulation, William James set out to prove the untenability of the inviolable. In "What Is an Emotion?," an essay published in *Mind* in 1884, six years before Warren and Brandeis's attempt to define privacy from a new category of emotion found in the art of writing, William James challenged the relationship between bodily functions and the way the mind perceives feeling: "If our hypothesis is true, it makes us realize more deeply than ever how much our mental life is knit up with our corporeal frame, in the strictest sense of the term. Rapture, love, ambition, indignation, and pride, considered as feelings, are fruits of the same soul with the grossest bodily sensations of pleasure and of pain" (188–205). What for Brandeis and Warren was a distinct category of rights—rights defined by emotional intangibility and inviolability—was for William James very much inextricable from materiality, from the body and its properties. Emotions could not be isolated or alone protected because mental sentience was always enwrapped in a corporeal frame. "All our pains, moreover, are local, and we are always free to speak of them in objective as well as in subjective terms," James argued in his 1905 essay "The Place of Affectional Facts in a World of Pure Experience" (273). For William James, the material and immaterial are of the same substance; it is the vocabulary used to describe them that changes according to need: "With the affectional experiences . . . no urgent need has yet arisen for deciding whether to treat them as rigorously mental or as rigorously physical facts. So they remain equivocal; and, as the world goes, their equivocality is one of their great conveniences" (274). Contrast this with *The Golden Bowl*, in which the unequivocal language of pain and the stratagems devised in an effort to be free from it (in the novel there is a "great need" to discern "affectional facts") structure all the early relations in the novel. As these strategies change, and the characters embrace the proliferation of emotional wounds, their wounds are like the affectional facts that William James describes: objective and subjective, equivocal and indisputable at the same time. As William James alters the climate of opinion about the correspondence between the emotional and the corporeal through his theory of affectional facts, in which the division between the physical and the psychic depends upon the distribution of descriptive language, Henry James's novel makes this alteration material.

Both William and Henry treat affectional facts as an object of analysis in their work; this is in part an effect of both brothers' own experiences with psychic duress. Both suffered from a disease at the turn of the century labeled "neurasthenia." Indeed, pain and its operations, the "manipulative politics of invalidism," measured the degree of entitlements in the James household: the more claim to illness, the more entitled to benefit and treatment one was.[22] In fact, one might argue that *The Golden Bowl*, a novel written at James's emergence from one of these attacks later in his career, is an account of just such a playing field, one that might aptly be called the "manipulative politics of pain." Although the manipulative politics against pain in *The Golden Bowl* originally makes the proper configuration of bodies (like that of the furniture) the primary grounds of consent in the contracts between the characters, it is proven an illusory means of damage control. The wounding of nobody, the fragile pact upon which all the relations in *The Golden Bowl* appear to depend, cannot finally suffice. In a growing culture of pain, psychic injury in the hands of men like Amerigo becomes a forcible ground for recognition, protection, and power.

The last twenty years have produced an incessant fluctuation of opinion, both as to what a work of fiction should be, and as to how it should be written. If there has been one thing constant in this critical upheaval it is the conviction of the reviewers that they can enlighten novelists on both these points.

—Edith Wharton, "A Cycle of Reviewing," Spectator *(1928)*

five

The Science of Affect

Professionals Reading and the Case of *Ethan Frome*

In an early review of *Ethan Frome* (1911), critic Edwin Bjorkman described Edith Wharton's novel as "so overwhelming that the modern mind rebels against it as a typical specimen of human experience."[1] The pain it produces in its reader, he suggested, is so profound that the reader must read it as something other than itself; she must abstract the experience of the characters into a larger social critique. "If it had no social side," Bjorkman wrote, "if it implied only what it brought of suffering and sorrow to the partakers in it, then we could do little but cry out in self-protective impatience: 'Sweep off the shambles and let us pass on!'" (296). It is similar concerns with the feelings of pain and suffering produced in the novel's readers, indeed, displayed in the novel itself, that led Lionel Trilling some forty years later to dismiss the then widely popular novel by saying, "I am quite unable to overcome my belief that *Ethan Frome* enjoys its high reputation because it still satisfies our modern snobbishness about tragedy and pain."[2] Trilling rejected the novel's public and critical acclaim, at once acknowledging its acute rendering of pain but nonetheless remaining unhappy with its effect: "It is terrible to contemplate, it is unforgettable, but the mind can do nothing with it, can only endure it" (139). Like Trilling, Irving Howe maintained that *Ethan Frome* was a "severe depiction of gratuitous human suffering in a New England village"; he called the novel a "work meant to shock and depress," one that often had been received "wrongly [as] being so successfully the tour de force Mrs. Wharton meant it to be—that is, for leaving [its readers] with a sense of admiration for the visible rigor of its mechanics and a sense of pain because of its total assault upon our emotions."[3] While the novel garnered praise by some early critics for its narrative technique, its style, its "mechanics," the most urgent concerns to emerge from the novel's reception immediately following its publication into the first fifty years of critical dialogue about it had to do with the problems of suffering that the novel not only witnessed but also produced. What was the *purpose* of this emotional "assault," critics repeatedly asked, and what end were readers to draw from it?

When Edith Wharton wrote in 1905 to Dr. Morgan Dix that no "novel worth anything can be anything but a 'novel with a purpose,'" her words, given the above queries, seemed virtually prescient. Like William Dean Howells, who urged that novelists must "cease to lie about life," Wharton began writing about the unseemly "motives" and thwarted "passions" of "common folk." Her efforts led to what was to become widely regarded as her most tragic work of fiction. The narrative of *Ethan Frome* unfolds in a bleak New England town appropriately called Starkfield and tells the story of three of its inhabitants: Zeena and Ethan Frome and Zeena's cousin Mattie. The narrator, an engineer held up in Starkfield because of a factory strike, sets about to uncover Ethan's story when he becomes intrigued by what appears to him to be the "contrast" between Ethan's "outer situation and his inner needs" (6). Although the reticent townspeople tell the narrator little about Frome's outer or inner condition, the narrator pieces together a tale that largely unfolded twenty-four years earlier, one that details Ethan's growing love for Mattie, who has come to live with the Fromes in order to help the hypochondriacal and mean-spirited Zeena with the housework on the farm. As Zeena comes to suspect Ethan and Mattie's mutual affection, she arranges for Mattie's abrupt dismissal. With their separation imminent, Ethan and Mattie make a failed suicide attempt that leaves both of them disabled and under the watchful "care" of Zeena. By the time the narrator meets Ethan, these events have turned the previously sweet Mattie "sour" and provide some explanation for the "dead" look in Ethan's face (6). Although this bleak tale is Wharton's narrative of "men and women as they are," to invoke Howells's prescription for realistic literature, Wharton's realism was met at its publication with puzzlement and dismay for its apparent lack of "purpose." Whereas *A Modern Instance* was praised for its accuracy and acumen regarding the contentious issue of divorce, for example, Wharton's account of unattainable love so wounded the sensibilities of its contemporary readers that critics decried, "to what end?"

Critical responses shortly following the novel's publication anticipated the broad discomfort that influential literary critics of the mid-twentieth century such as Trilling and Howe would later voice: what, these critics asked, is the effect of pain and suffering in a literary work? Although Bjorkman lavished some praise on the novel, exclaiming, "Mrs. Wharton has passed from individual to social art; from the art that excites to that which incites" (299), other reviewers were less receptive. In the *Bookman*, Frederic Taber Cooper cautioned: "It is hard to forgive Mrs. Wharton for the utter remorselessness of her latest volume, *Ethan Frome*, for nowhere has she done anything more hopelessly, endlessly gray with blank despair." Taro, foreshadowing Trilling, questioned the end to which the novel's portrayal of suffering is put, finally concluding that "art for art's sake is the one justification of a piece of work as perfect in technique as it is relentless in substance."[4] A critic for the *North American Review* was more sympathetic, if not with the novel than with Wharton herself, and speculated that "there is a certain inexorableness about Mrs. Wharton, as if she herself were constitutionally opposed to happiness, as if she were somewhat compelled to interpret life in terms of pain."[5]

The difficulty of representing and interpreting emotional pain had been a problem for literary criticism before *Ethan Frome*. We need only recall the beleaguered Civil War soldier who could convey the facts and figures of battle wounds in his letters, diaries, and memoirs, but more rarely, as critics lamented, the emotional complexity of their experiences. Or Howells, who bemoaned the plethora of harms that the mid-nineteenth-century novel seemed to occasion and so rewrote the subjects and objects of injury, giving them new shape, texture, and methods of redress. As Lionel Trilling suggested in the mid-twentieth century, pain is quintessential literary subject matter. More recently, Elaine Scarry in *The Body in Pain* (1985) has described what she takes to be the intimate relation between pain and the imagination: "Pain and imagining are the 'framing events' within whose boundaries all other perceptual, somatic, and emotional events occur; thus, between the two extremes can be mapped the whole terrain of the human psyche."[6] If the novel may be considered one terrain in which pain dwells, perhaps literary criticism should be described as a mapping of this landscape. One could trace a cartography of critical response to pain and artistic production at least back to Aristotle, for whom the enjoyment of tragedy and the paradox of suffering rendered "pleasurable" was a central question.[7] Indeed, the problem posed by Aristotle became, in manifold guises and to differing degrees, the issue posed again and again for those seeking to explain the centrality of pain in art, from Edmund Burke and Friedrich Nietzsche to Wharton's colleagues William Dean Howells and Henry James through her most vocal mid-twentieth-century critics, Lionel Trilling and Irving Howe. Perhaps questions about pain and the imagination, questions posed by a long history of writers, philosophers, and theorists, might be summed up by what now seems a familiar observation, one offered by a critic in *The Nation* who declared of Wharton's *Ethan Frome*, "The wonder is that the spectacle of so much pain can be made to yield so much beauty."[8]

Interpreting emotional pain became a matter of increasing cultural debate at the turn of the century, and novel reading played a significant part in that debate. As inquiries about the spectacle of pain flourished well beyond an Aristotelian philosophical tradition, such concerns defined the discipline of literary scholarship shortly before the publication of *Ethan Frome*. The critical reception of Wharton's novel, which puzzled over the function of emotional pain, especially male emotional pain, followed upon a heated dispute within a growing profession of male readers who questioned the extent and place of the critic's engagement with the emotions. Early literary critics such as Bliss Perry, who wrote one of the first full-length studies of American literature, and Calvin Thomas, an early president of the Modern Language Association (MLA), argued over the role the contemporary novel might play in departments of literature. Does the novel have a social function, these critics asked, and if so, what is the critics' role with regard to it? The bewildered responses to Wharton's novel are representative of a process by which critics inside the academy and without began to articulate just what the role of the contemporary novel and its readers would be. Literature, many of these critics argued, provided an eye onto the world of emotion at a time of increasing cultural demands to expand understandings of the emotive realm. In fact, for literary critics under institutional pressure to claim a social function in a university culture that, as Christopher Newfield describes, "evolved within an industrial capitalism that was ponderously, aggressively, even anxiously, instrumental," their self-proclaimed expertise at reading pain and emotion became a way to defend their professional authority.[9] As literature and its emotional effects increasingly became an object of professional literary study in the university by century's end, a subject with which this chapter itself ends, emotion came to be treated by an emerging group of male literary professionals as a new science built upon the necessity of reading. The discourse on emotion within departments of literature and within the university served a crucial function: it became the groundwork for "blending" the "apparent opposites of autonomy and manageability" central to the production of what later would become known as the "knowledge worker" (Newfield, 93). To read emotional pain and to make sense of it became part of a cultural drive toward the quantification of emotion, a cultural imperative that, as we have seen in prior chapters, flourished across disciplines.

This chapter begins with the critical debate that emerged just after the publication of Wharton's novel, and it ends by examining how that debate is reflected in the early professionalization of criticism and the making of a discipline of professional readers. This chapter argues that the unmet critical expectations for Wharton's novel—pain to what end?—suggest that *Ethan Frome* may trouble the dream of emotional manageability that the new scientists of affect, male literary critics, appeared to court. The pages that follow examine the presentation of emotional pain in *Ethan Frome* not only as a crucial departure from the explanatory paths of the sentimental novel—in which suffering often denotes a path toward redemption—but also as a resistance against contemporary cultural pressures, met in part by male literary critics, to read pain in a compensatory way. Wharton's novel refuses the science of affect by the manner in which it remakes the role of the sympathizing intermediary, the way it articulates not only the necessity of understanding pain but the duplicities of judgment about it. These qualities play an important role within the novel itself and in the increasingly impersonal world beyond its borders. *Ethan Frome* thematizes new problems of sympathetic mediation for the reader, for whom reading was no longer simply a physical act to take place in leisure but also a skill that relied upon the ability to extend, to project, and to imagine—to navigate a delicate balance of fact and affect; this way of reading was at once announcing itself as a challenge for male literary critics and as a mandate for contemporary readers across cultural texts.

There can be little doubt that Wharton, at least in part, perceives herself as a moderator of sympathy in *Ethan Frome*; in her preface, the first she was ever to write, she refers to herself in just these terms, as a "sympathizing intermediary." "If he [the author] is capable of seeing all around him, no violence is done to probability in allowing him to exercise this faculty: it is natural enough that he should act as the sympathizing intermediary between his rudimentary characters and the more complicated minds to whom he is trying to present them" (viii). It does not seem particularly unusual, given Wharton's assessment, to assert the power of the novel in navigating strong feeling; indeed, the notion of "sympathy" was a successful rhetorical strategy even before the popularity of the sentimental novel in the United States. By the time Wharton wrote *Ethan Frome*, a novelist's role as "sympathizing intermediary" had become a common idiom in U.S. literature and culture. Critics might even argue that the problem of emotional pain presented in *Ethan Frome* is merely a legacy of its most immediate forebear, the sentimental novel, which made suffering intelligible and pain visible to a mass culture in the United States at midcentury.[10] If Lionel Trilling's criticisms are reliant upon an Aristotelian tradition of catharsis, for example, his criticisms also adapt the teachings of the sentimental tradition, a tradition in the United States that took a decidedly moral rather than purely aesthetic stance with regard to the presentation of pain. Though Trilling and other critics in the mid-twentieth century did not turn their attentions to the sentimental novel of the mid-nineteenth, sentimental literature provided the most direct connection to what Trilling longed for: a causal link between the "artistic" presentation of pain and its affective relations. Such novels, written primarily by women authors, deliberately sought to develop empathy in their readers, to point readers beyond the confines of the novel, and to instruct their readers on how to live and lead moral lives. Since Ann Douglas's well-known critique, *The Feminization of American Culture* (1977), sentimentalism has been a source of extensive critical debate concerning the agency, effect, and influence of these authors and their novels, although it is beyond the scope of this chapter to chart all the turns this debate has since taken.[11] Certainly the connection between sentimental literature and its "cultural work" has been scrutinized not for its lack of "effect" (the criticism Trilling levels at Wharton) but precisely because of its extensive efficacy in American culture, from its influence in the abolition movement to its contributions to the consumer marketplace. A sentimental novel like *Uncle Tom's Cabin* (1852), for instance, could elicit sympathy for suffering slaves and call its readers into the joint enterprise of feeling (feeling that might result in action). At the very least, the sentimental novel helped to demonize bodily pain and punishment to slave or master in the cultural psyche. Richard Brodhead has argued persuasively in "Sparing the Rod," for example, that the sentimental novel functioned to instill what he calls "disciplinary intimacy" in its readers; reading novels restrained and trained readers in the place of physical punishment.[12]

The wide emotive scope envisioned by a novel like *Ethan Frome*, in which not only the male body but also male feeling and its expression comes to be central, certainly owes a debt to the emotive landscape of the sentimental novel. The novel's presentation of irresolvable emotional pain is manifest through Wharton's interest in the sentimentalized and disabled body, for example; Ethan's disfigurement is the navigating tool through which the novel begins its presentation of suffering. Although "but the ruin of a man," Ethan's disabled body initiates the narrator's inquiry (and in turn ours) into the dimensions, the conditions, and the domain of pain. Bodily difference is the object of curiosity from the novel's start: Ethan's "lameness check[ed] each step like the jerk of a chain."[13] That body also drops away as a reference point when the story flashes back twenty-four years earlier, as we follow young Ethan hasten "at a quick pace" to meet his wife's cousin, Mattie Silver (11). Readers discover that the elder Ethan's wounded limbs are not the primary source of his pain. Harmon Gow, a neighbor, early on tells the narrator that "sickness and trouble" have filled Ethan's plate "since the very first helping" (5). Ethan's wounded limbs are but the perpetual symbol of his wounded feelings, and the problem of long-dormant feeling is at the heart of Ethan's troubles.

Readers who were trained in empathy from the pages of the sentimental novel, who first saw others experience pain—indeed, who cried on its very pages—were being asked to acquire faculties by which to read pain differently in a novel like *Ethan Frome*. Though the sentimental novel presented bodily suffering as undeserved and often cruel, pain was always explicable to the novels' readers with recourse to religion and the figure of ultimate suffering, Jesus. If the recompense for suffering in the sentimental tradition was eternal bliss, what accompanied the secularization of suffering, suffering given shape and substance in a realistic novel like Wharton's, must be a new method of recompense, if not a new structure for the justification of pain. Whereas the sentimental novel actively solicited readers' feelings, feelings that had clearly defined objects and subjects for expression, in *Ethan Frome* both illicit relations and complex feelings are hidden. The novel, therefore, relies upon the sentimental tradition and departs from it, offering a different kind of engagement for the reader of feeling. This is evident in the novel's bewildered critical reception. *Ethan Frome* refuses to contain the pain it presents in a safe moralized sense; pain and suffering in the novel are not paths toward redemption, and there is no clear moral authority at work. That Wharton does not create a narrator whose moral voice is well-known to the community and does not choose to have the tale told by a character whose intentions are seemingly self-evident indicates a shift in the framework through which to read the novel. If her narrator had been a pastor, as he is in the most contemporary film version of Wharton's novel, for instance, we might read the novel as a warning, however unsolicited, against illicit desire. The difficulty in *Ethan Frome* comes from the recognition that pain, particularly the male pain that the novel imagines, must be theorized and acted upon in a new way. Wharton, by secularizing her tale of suffering, takes the issues of psychic pain, lust, and revenge outside the more predictable paths of explanation and accountability. Different from the novel's association with the domestic sphere of female sympathies, and different from the redemptive tale, the story of Ethan's emotional wounds evokes a cognitive crisis, one that requires a new structure of justification for emotional pain and in light of which a whole set of "cures" concurrently emerged across the culture outside the novel in order to relieve it, from psychology to tort law to literary criticism itself. Wharton's early readers were forced to interpret the secularization of suffering in a growing culture of pain.

When we first meet Ethan Frome, we are told he seems "part of the mute melancholy landscape, an incarnation of its frozen woe, with all that was warm and sentient in him fast bound below the surface" (5). The novel bears witness to Ethan's struggle to find a path for sentience to resurface. Every time Ethan tries to express his feelings, however, words seem to betray him; in fact, when he nears some method of realizing his emotion, all that comes out is a gruff and unsophisticated mumble. We see this for the first time when Ethan picks Mattie up after the dance and surprises her by remaining hidden while she "rejects" a ride from Dennis Eady. "Ethan had the sense of having done something arch and ingenious. To prolong the effect he groped for a dazzling phrase, and brought out, in a growl of rapture: 'Come along'" (19). Ethan often feels himself on "the brink of eloquence," and although the reader continually sees him struggling for an effective line to convey his feeling, he always falls short. During Mattie and Ethan's dinner together, their long-awaited time alone, his words never reach beyond the mundane: "At last, after casing about for an effective opening, he took a long gulp of tea, cleared his throat, and said: 'looks as if there'd be more snow'" (34). Through Ethan's relations with Mattie, however, he first learns the possibility for expression of what is described as his "bliss of feeling" (14). Mattie seems to speak what Ethan feels; her words become his: "Words at last had been found to utter his secret soul" (14). But this shared feeling of pleasure is limited to their few long walks in the snow, for, as we learn, within the Frome household the relation between Ethan and Zeena is plagued by painful silence: "Within a year of their marriage she [Zeena] developed the 'sickliness' which had since made her notable even in a community rich in pathological instances. . . . Then she too fell silent" (30). The problem of the novel for Zeena, and most acutely for Ethan himself, is how feeling is rendered.

Unlike Ethan, who struggles with deeply submerged emotions, Zeena's feelings are continually manifest upon her body; the neglect and anger that the narrative suggests she harbors readily present themselves in her medical symptomology. Likewise, Zeena has a medical vocabulary available to her; it comes through the mail from manufacturers of "patent medicine," and it allows Zeena to be, in Harmon Gow's words, "the greatest hand at doctoring in the country" (5). Being "wholly absorbed in her health" becomes a social occasion for Zeena (26). She visits Aunt Martha Pierce in Bettsbridge, and she confers with friend Eliza Spears about the skill of certain doctors. Recalling the symptomology of the hysteric, Zeena's body speaks; it speaks for a seeming want of sympathy, or perhaps for a deep wound in her unconscious. Her physical pain is a measure of her mental suffering.[14] For Ethan, the attention paid to his wounded body at the beginning and at the end of Wharton's novel is a framing device; it is one meant to draw the reader into an axis of pain and measure of feeling unconfined by the dimensions of his body. The narrator directs the reader inward early on: "Though all had conceded that Ethan Frome's [troubles] had been beyond the common measure, no one gave me an explanation of the look in his face which, as I persisted in thinking, neither poverty nor physical suffering could have put there" (4). Ethan requires a vocabulary different from Zeena's to present and account for his suffering; in fact, he is not even cognizant of his feelings until Mattie seems to speak the words that he discovers have been muffled deep within.

Wharton dramatizes a struggle over the nature and very texture of pain, particularly through the distinctions continually drawn between the "facts" of Zeena's physical ailments and Ethan's affective struggles: his emotional awakening. In the manner the narrator presents the tale to us, the novel assigns to its readers the difficult task of discerning "true" pain from "false" pain by focusing on a competition of suffering—a competitive structure of injury—that ensues between Ethan and Zeena. Zeena, as the model of the hysteric who too readily and too easily suffers—who, in fact, quantifies her suffering—is contrasted with Ethan, the martyr of silent suffering. "All I know," Zeena cautions, "is I can't go on the way I am much longer. The pains are clear way down to my ankles now" (27). Zeena is presented in the narrative as vocal and demanding about her physical illness, while Ethan is silent and succumbs to his emotional pain. Although the narrative suggests that Ethan's incapacity to express his pain is at its source a problem, his silent suffering, his disaffection from the excesses of language, also is presented as ennobling, particularly in the face of what is described as Zeena's "faultfinding" and her obsessive devotion to "complex ailments" (25). Zeena's pain is a means of getting attention, and when she fails to receive it from Ethan upon her return to Starkfield, she becomes determined to dismiss Mattie (27). Indeed, Zeena's pain-ridden body becomes both the cause and the remedy when Zeena wants to turn Mattie out of the house. Mattie must go so that Zeena can have a "hired girl." But more than that, Mattie must go so that Zeena can once again command her household and Ethan's attentions, so that he may feel, as she feels, the full scope of her suffering.

The problem of judging who may be the novel's most tragic victim is further dramatized by the secondary characters in the novel, who describe the Fromes differently and from whom we have opposing interpretations of the novel's final "accident" and its outcome. According to

Harmon Gow, it is Ethan who always has been caretaker in the Frome house: "I guess it's always Ethan done the caring" (2). At the end of the novel, Mrs. Hale, in a keenly ironic moment, claims that it is Zeena who has taken on the burden of care: "Zeena's done for her [Mattie] and done for Ethan as good as she could. It was a miracle, considering how sick she was—but she seemed to be raised right up just when the call came to her. . . . [S]he's had the strength given her to care for those two for over twenty years, and before the accident came she thought she couldn't even care for herself" (76). Of course, the narrator reminds the reader that what appears to Mrs. Hale as Zeena's sympathy and goodwill some twenty years later is never quite as it seems: the reader is told that before the "smash-up" "the one pleasure left," for Zeena "was to inflict pain" on Ethan (56). The opposing interpretations of the "accident" and of the Fromes' subsequent claims to suffering and injury further serve to complicate our discernment. Readers are finally left contemplating the extent to which Zeena's miraculous recovery rubs pain into Ethan's never-healing wounds, enabling an eternity of querulousness rather than what Mattie and Ethan sought in their suicide attempt, an eternity of peaceful silence.

The narrator, the readers' teller of secrets, becomes obsessed with uncovering the love triangle and its tragic sufferers. As a model for the reader and a stranger to the town of Starkfield, the narrator must piece together a puzzle. He must reconstruct the story of Ethan's "ruin" from reticent strangers, collecting "the facts" of the case, although, as he warns his listeners, these "facts" may not come easily: "Though Harmon Gow developed the tale as far as his mental and moral reach permitted there were perceptible gaps between his facts, and I had a sense that the deeper meaning of the story was in the gaps" (2). Staying at Mrs. Ned Hale's house, the lawyer's wife, from whom he hoped to acquire some evidence about Ethan Frome, he muses, "I had great hopes of getting from her the missing facts of Ethan Frome's story, or rather such a key to his character as should coordinate the facts I knew" (2). What the narrator finds, however, is that "her mind was a store-house of innocuous anecdote and any question about her acquaintances brought forth a volume of detail; but on the question of Ethan Frome" she is "unexpectedly reticent" (4). Ethan Frome inspires silence. The narrator's interest increases not only as a kind of fact-finding mission, but also as a response to the seemingly inexplicable spaces of storytelling by the townspeople; it drives him to find out why Ethan looks as if he suffers so. Yet as readers learn, the significance of Ethan's story is also in his own silences. In what appears to be a culture of complaint and narcissism, in which Mrs. Hale is more than willing to speak on any other subject, and of which Zeena Frome would seem to be Starkfield's most stunning example, Ethan's silence and the silence about him is mysterious and seductive. It is this silence that intrigues and, consequently, entangles the narrator, who notes that Ethan "lived in a depth of moral isolation too remote for casual access" (5). Indeed, Ethan's feeling, like the facts of his case, is buried: "Emotion had remained in him as a silent ache" (14). What we learn as the story unfolds is that Ethan's silent suffering is not merely a condition of a stifling winter burial in snow but a condition of relative permanence if not continual struggle. The narrator is deeply mystified by Ethan's woundedness. In light of the pain apparent in Ethan's face, the narrator becomes obsessed with its naming. Only when the narrator accompanies Ethan home after a snowstorm threatens to bury both men in its wake does he believe he has found "the clue to Ethan Frome" (10).

Like Wharton's early reviewers who wanted to read pain and to make sense of it, the narrator searches for explanations in the face of Ethan's silence. Unlike the narrator, for whom the mystery of the wounded male is partially satisfied by the sighting of querulous women, the early readers' repeated expectations for understanding pain found its purpose endlessly deferred. Because the early critical debate about *Ethan Frome* focused on the effects of pain and suffering (how it radiates beyond Starkfield and what it reverberates back), little has been written about the method by which pain is materialized in the novel. Much has been made of the circumstances—a simple farmer caught in his forbidden passion for his wife's cousin—but less often have critics analyzed the path that suffering takes. Cynthia Griffin Wolff, one of a handful of contemporary critical voices on *Ethan Frome*, describes the novel as a reimagination of Wharton's own troubled romantic relationships told in a different voice, setting, and gender.[15] Indeed, Wharton locates sympathy in a rather unlikely subject: a stout, burly, and unsophisticated male farmer. To suggest that Ethan as a protagonist might be a displacement of Edith herself, or that the site of sentiment is gendered from female to male, still doesn't fully address how pain is manifest. This is a matter over which Wharton worries in her preface: "Any attempt to elaborate and complicate [my protagonists'] sentiments would necessarily have falsified the whole" (vii). Zeena, as I have suggested, wears her emotional pain on her body; Ethan buries his feelings in silence, although his disabled body is the object of curiosity encouraging the narrator and, in turn, the reader, to learn more.

Bodies in the novel repeatedly are presented as receptacles and registries for the expression of emotion and feelings of deep hurt; this dynamic is its most vivid after the sledding accident toward the end of the novel: "The stillness was so profound that he heard a little animal twittering somewhere near by under the snow. It made a small frightened cheep like a field mouse, and he wondered languidly if it were hurt. Then he understood that it must be in pain: pain so excruciating that he seemed, mysteriously, to feel it shooting through his own body" (72–73). In the most striking and tragic moment after Mattie and Ethan's suicide attempt, Ethan feels his own pain through the "excruciating" noise of what he believes to be a field mouse but soon learns is Mattie. He tries "in vain to roll over in the direction of the sound," and he stretches "his left arm out across the snow" with little success (73). The sound of the "animal's suffering" is "intolerable" to him (73). His pain upon hearing her pain is given substance; it becomes real (73). Mattie and Ethan lie buried in the snow as yet unaware that their plans have failed; they have failed to "fetch" the tree that was to bring an end to their separation, their suffering—an end, Ethan thinks, to "feeling" itself (70, 71). *Ethan Frome* as a novel basks in this failure, in which buried feeling, like Ethan's and Mattie's buried bodies, is so intense it can only wound, and these wounds are most painfully self-inflicted. Trapped like his weighted body after the fall and trapped by his inability to act upon his feelings, Ethan struggles to find a recourse, an outlet for his desires and his emotions. Indeed, the inability of Ethan and Mattie to realize their passion for each other leads to their failed suicide attempt and to the moment of futile recognition emerging from Ethan's perception of his own pain. Yet the manner by which Ethan comes to know his own injury and understands that it must be pain—by thinking he hears a field mouse, by listening and recognizing that it is Mattie—is a central condition in the novel. It is certainly the most excruciating instance of the kinds of displacements that the novel presents: feeling made real and given substance, as in this final scene, through the body, voice, or pain of another.

If language is unable to be a path for the conveyance of feeling for Ethan, is there, we are encouraged to ask, another vehicle? The body, as we have seen in previous chapters, often defined cultural measures of feeling, particularly feelings of pain and injury; it was bodily injury that most often was recognized and, within the parameters of tort law, remedied, in a postbellum nation. More than the structure of physicality or even emotionality that are mediums for understanding and experiencing harm in the novel, what often manages to carry feeling, to convey its structure and to fill the silences and the gaps in the novel, is the material of the everyday. For example, it is Mattie and Ethan's inability to connect more than the brief touch of two ends of thread that weaves through and makes material each painful moment in the novel: "She sat silent, her hands clasped on her work, and it seemed to him that a warm current flowed toward him along the strip of stuff that still lay unrolled between them. Cautiously he slid his hand palm-downward along the table till his finger tips touched the end of the stuff. A faint vibration of her lashes seemed to show that she was aware of his gesture, and that it had sent a counter-current back to her; and she let her hands lie motionless on the other end of the strip" (40). Ethan and Mattie, alone together in the house for the first time, sit down in front of the stove after they have finished their evening chores. "'I've been in a dream,' Ethan thinks, 'this is the only evening we'll have together.' The return to reality was as painful as the return to consciousness after taking an anesthetic. His body and brain ached with indescribable weariness, and he could think of nothing to say or to do that should arrest the mad flight of the moments" (40). It is just then that Ethan sees Mattie's hand grasping her work "as if it were a part of herself" (40). He too reaches out to her sewing thread as if it could feel his touch, as if it could respond in kind; he thinks he feels his desires acknowledged and reciprocated through the "stuff that still lay unrolled between them" (40). Ethan and Mattie are bound by two ends of thread, a thin "strip" that acts as a conduit for their feelings. Although Ethan realizes at the end of the evening that he has not even managed to lay his hand or his lips on Mattie's own, he understands that what has passed between them through Mattie's sewing threads is enough.

This form of mediation permeates several other moments in the narrative as well. When Ethan picks Mattie up at a dance, he thinks nothing would be better than to "stoop his cheek and rub it against her scarf" (19). The scarf, like the sewing threads, absorbs his emotions. The climax of this form of mediation comes when Mattie reveals her feelings for Ethan by retrieving Zeena's pickle plate from storage in an effort to make the dinner table pretty. When Mattie inadvertently breaks the pickle plate, it becomes the symbolic disclosure of secret desires between Mattie and Ethan. Its use is a confirmation of Mattie's love for Ethan, the unspoken object that locates their passions. Likewise, the broken pickle plate confirms for Zeena Mattie's and Ethan's desire for each other. It is a measure of their feeling, as it becomes for Zeena an estimate of their betrayal. Indeed, Zeena, learning that the pickle plate is broken, is more animated than we have ever seen her; she is described as having "lips twitching with anger, a flush of excitement on her sallow face" (53). With this broken plate, Zeena helps seal Mattie's and Ethan's fates: "I tried to keep my things where you couldn't get at 'em—and now you've took from me the one I cared for most of all" (54). In Zeena's fury, the pickle plate and Ethan become one; if the broken pickle plate is a measure of Mattie and Ethan's relationship, so too is it a full indication of Zeena's loss. The displacement of feeling in *Ethan Frome*, the manner by which sentience resurfaces in the stuff of the everyday, is not only a literary device; it is also a critique and exploration of the extent to which suffering in a secular idiom could be and, indeed, was taken to be primarily cognizable in material terms. The narrative suggests that the personal relations among subjects within the novel, which are often mediated by material objects, are symptomatic of a struggle at the heart of how cultural fictions constitute subjecthood not only around desire but through the categories of pain, injury, and the recognition and compensation of distress.

For Zeena, pain is a weapon. She measures her illness by what she is given or begrudged to relieve her suffering; more than that, Zeena insists that her sickness is proportionate to her labor. She tells Ethan that she gave up her good health to care for his mother and that her demands for money and, later, for a "hired girl" are thus due her: "I'd 'a' been ashamed to tell *him* that you grudged me the money to get back my health, when I lost it nursing your own mother!" (48). Zeena demands a kind of workers' compensation for her household labor; she strikes, refusing to participate in household chores because she perceives herself not adequately compensated. "My folks all told me at the time you couldn't do no less than marry me after" (48). She talks about what she is "owed," and readily acquiesces to "exacting a compensation" from Mattie (29, 25). Zeena's strategy, her domestic walkout, is a method of recognition, if not a strategy for recompense, which should not be far from the reader's mind. As we learn early on in the novel, the narrator's stay in Starkfield also is a result of a labor strike: "I had been sent up by my employers on a job connected with the big power-house at Corbury Junction, and a long-drawn carpenter's strike had so delayed the work that I found myself anchored at Starkfield—the nearest habitable spot—for the best part of the winter" (3). Wharton's novel fictionalizes what perhaps could be read as a more radical version of the labor crisis that occasions the narrative, radical because delineated in a domestic setting in which work was not yet conceived of in these terms. Rather than expand upon the difficult transition between public and private labor in which women's work became naturalized within the home, however, I want to highlight the issues concerning work to make a broader point about the subject and context for the novel. Accompanying the problem of discerning the dimensions of emotional pain and physical suffering in the novel is the question of how to understand the "labor pains" in which Wharton grounds each disclosure, event, and character.

That Wharton's vehicle for storytelling in the novel is neither a striking laborer nor employer/owner, and that the narrator's managerial experience with labor unrest frames the narrative, provides a vocabulary upon which the Fromes' sad history is disclosed. The narrator, in other words, is not only a model for the reader in her judgment of the characters' suffering, but also a vehicle for introducing its administration and compensation. He initiates the terms and helps to connote the arenas—labor and, as we shall see, law—in which pain is coming to be quantified, and it is the notion of quantification that permeates his and other townspeople's assessments of the Frome tragedy. From the moment readers meet Ethan, for example, we are told of his perpetual labor on the farm and its meager compensations: "That Frome farm was always 'bout as bare's a milkpan when the cat's been round; and you know what one of them old water-mills is wuth nowadays. When Ethan could sweat over 'em both from sun-up to dark he kinder choked a living out of 'em; but his folks ate up most everything, even then, and I don't see how he makes out now" (5). Ethan meets the narrator only because he needs the extra money that driving him to the station can provide, although we get the sense that it is also a much-needed respite from a home and farm that are failing. Ethan perceives himself a "prisoner for life" (57) to the farm, and when Mattie, his "one ray of light," is to be "extinguished," he seeks to put a permanent end to his labors. Like Ethan, Mattie's work in the house is a constant subject for scrutiny in the novel; Mattie, according to Zeena, does not work hard enough, which leads to Zeena's excuse for dismissing her, leaving her cruelly without compensation and in the very condition for which Zeena accuses Ethan. With very few prospects for work in town, and with her inevitable separation from Ethan, Mattie too decides to quit life.

It is important to note that Mattie's and Ethan's desire to "quit" life, like Zeena's domestic walkout, is a form of refusal not unlike the labor strike that occasions the narrative. Given that the story is told through the voice of a narrator whose presence in Starkfield is the result of a labor dispute, it is no wonder that the narrative emphasizes the characters' labor pains; all are "alienated" in Marxian terms, whether from their labor on the farm, their work in the home, or their status in a deadening marriage. The novel engages with the difficulties, the disappointments, and the disaffections of labor. Despite the characters' agony over their failed labors, the matter-of-fact tone of the narrator concerning the reasons for his stay in Starkfield, what he conveys as the seemingly common character of the labor strike that occasions his story, is indicative of the increasing presence and power of labor at the turn of the century. As Wharton would well know, the towns near Starkfield were mill towns such as Everett and Lawrence, which by 1906 had chartered the National Industrial Union of Textile Workers. In 1911, the year of *Ethan Frome's* publication, the union gained momentum for the recognition of work-related injuries by conducting slowdowns and, in one case, holding a four-month strike of cotton workers at a local mill.[16] Whether factory hands or builders of the railroads, women and men sought enhanced rights and recompense for the dangerous and often deadly work they performed. While I do not want to suggest that this context for Wharton's novel demands that she be reconsidered as a voice of labor, I do want to acknowledge the unusual importance in *Ethan Frome* (a noted departure from Wharton's other work) of the narrative's concern with labor pains and their recompense.[17] Wharton is especially interested in male pain; she intimately describes Ethan's suffocation both in his marriage and in his work. Ethan is strangled in Starkfield not only by rural poverty, but also, in a larger sense, by the increasing anonymity of the industrial United States. Like the striking workers who populate the borders of Starkfield and the narrative, Ethan, to restate Marx, is forced to "face with sober senses his real conditions of life, and his relations with his kind."[18] When Ethan's small recompense, Mattie, is taken from him, his "senses" do not "sober," they deaden.

If the narrator's stay in Starkfield reminds us of the "conditions" and "relations" of Ethan's life of labor, the narrative also foregrounds the underlying tensions between agrarian and industrial America, from the failing farm that Ethan struggles to keep afloat, a failure presented in and against the success of merchants like Dennis Eady and Ned Hale, to

Ethan's own missed chance at becoming a professional engineer. So too is the railroad that passes in and out of town a barometer of technological advance and, more important, of psychological decline in the novel. Ethan notes that with the coming of the railroad when he was a young man, the local traffic of friends and neighbors ceased. Townspeople no longer passed by his house, paying visit to his mother when she was immobilized with rheumatism. It is the isolation inflicted by the mechanism meant to collapse the distance between people that causes Mrs. Frome to turn "queer": "After the trains began running nobody ever come by here to speak of, and mother never could get it through her head what happened, and it preyed on her right along till she died" (8). Ethan's cousin Zeena, called in to care for his mother, traveled to the Fromes by that same railroad from a village larger and "nearer to the railway" than Starkfield (29). Soon after his mother's death, when Ethan and Zeena decide to marry, he thinks she will be eager to move to a larger town; but purchasers for the farm are "slow in coming," and Ethan learns that "in the greater cities which attracted Ethan," Zeena "would have suffered a complete loss of identity" (30). Within a year, the reader is told, Zeena fell ill (30). In a gesture against anonymity, Ethan and Zeena do not leave Starkfield with the rest of those who boarded the railroad out. Indeed, the railroad and the transforming technological world that once offered Ethan passage from his dreary circumstances come to plague Ethan, as his mother, and, subsequently, Zeena, are estranged in this world, while Ethan himself loses the skills he needs to participate in it. The novel enters this alienation and explores one of the repercussions and manifestations of its transforming technologies: injuries to the psyche.

If the presentation of psychic pain had been a problem for male literary critics reading the novel *Ethan Frome*, for a growing public of readers the discernment of pain became central; readers were asked to extend their capacity for acknowledging feeling in an ever more anonymous and impersonal world. Judging and quantifying pain became fundamental to the development of an industrial nation. Not only literary critics, but also psychologists, lawyers, judges, and others were asked to accommodate and account for the seeming proliferation of pain. Wai Chee Dimock calls this "quantify[ing] sentience"; there was great cultural need, beginning in the nineteenth century, "to come up with something like a calculus of pain" (141). Edith Wharton writes *Ethan Frome* precisely within this calculus, at a time when literary critics, law courts, and corporations alike questioned whether lay persons could expand their capacity to understand suffering and to compensate injuries to body and mind. In 1910, for example, the year before Wharton published her novel, workmen's compensation legislation was passed in the United States; this legislation confirmed the public's commitment to extending the cultural "calculus of pain." I do not wish to assert a mere homology between the problems accorded industrial expansion and the tightening grip around Starkfield or Ethan Frome; rather, I would emphasize that discourses about injury crucially mark the narrator's work as well as Ethan's wounded body and psyche. Moreover, to be sufficient readers and interpreters of pain, one quantified sentience. This was not merely a female sentimental literary strategy or a male professional disciplinary practice; it was a growing cultural skill.[19]

For Trilling and other earlier readers of Wharton's novel who were perplexed by its rendering of pain, the questions they repeatedly asked were framed precisely in terms of quantification; suffering and injury, they demanded, *to what end and at what cost*? For an early literary critic like Bjorkman, for example, if the pain presented in Wharton's novel was not *worth* something, "we should pass on"; indeed, we might recall that the problem Trilling had reading Wharton's novel was that for him the pain the story presented was *worth nothing*. This language of cost accounting was shared by literary critics and nonliterary professionals alike. If the novelist's task, as Wharton acknowledges in her preface, is to render feelings, and the critics' task, occasionally to their chagrin, is to discern their meaning, the social sciences, for example, often saw themselves as honing their ability to repair the pain that accompanied them. In fact, literary criticism and legal reasoning seemed to inspire a similar question: How was the lay public to read, listen to, and judge pain in an expanded market not only of literature but also of feeling? *Ethan Frome*, we will recall, poses this very question by giving its readers the complicated task of discerning "true" pain from "false" pain; the novel presents a competition of suffering among its main characters.

Readers of fiction, as the narrator's role in *Ethan Frome* suggests, are both jurors of facts as well as readers of affect in a growing marketplace of pain. This reader/juror was not embraced uncritically, however. Along with an expanding interest in a cultural calculus of pain was a growing distrustfulness in the public's capacity to make discriminations with regard to these very issues. What might even be called a crisis of reading pain was particularly intense not only for Wharton's early critics and readers, but also, for example, for lay persons in law courts who as jurors were charged with the public duty of quantifying pain.[20] The judiciary, given what appeared to be an expanded cultural capacity for feeling (represented by novels like Wharton's) if not compensation for feeling, increasingly doubted that the lay public could read pain properly in injury cases and submit just verdicts based upon their "beliefs and practices."[21] Legal scholars sounded like their contemporary literary counterparts when they claimed, as Charles Gregory concluded of the court's view of the jury process: "This is an evaluating process and in its nature is not much different from judging a beauty contest or a competition among musicians. The conclusion, whatever it be, is not a fact conclusion; it is a value judgment" (40–41). Gregory, who was an early advocate for a more expansive view of negligence in legal cases of pain and suffering, explained the court's reticence when it came jury decisions in this way: "If the jury were always permitted to pass on the negligence issue, there is no telling what factors might move it to bring in a verdict for the plaintiff."[22] Lay juries, unlike readers of literature, were intended solely to be triers of facts. Because they were perceived as having inadequate skills to satisfy the increasingly complicated demands of "subjective" judgment with regard to pain, they were received as a threat to the functioning of the judicial system.

Amid this threat, and in a concerted effort to rein in what he confirmed was the "lawlessness" of the reading public, early-twentieth-century literary critic Bliss Perry, who would go on to write one of the first full-length studies of American literature, published a *PMLA* article in which he promoted the study of contemporary fiction in universities. Perry wrote: "This lawless and inconsistent public, craving excitement at any price, journalized daily, neither knowing nor caring what should be the real aim and scope of the novel, has the casting vote, after all, upon great books and little books alike. From its ultimate verdict there is no appeal. It is therefore no small service to literature that the colleges perform, when they send into this public, to serve as laymen, men who know good work from bad, and to know why they know it" (76). The reading of contemporary fiction, with proper instruction, might rein in a lawless public and help create standards of judgment for laymen. For literary critics, feeling threatened, as we shall see, by the institutional prominence of the social sciences, and fearing, moreover, their own insignificance, it seemed that contemporary literature had a social function after all.

Early-twentieth-century literary critics, adapting the discourse of the social scientists, cultivated and reinvented themselves not merely as writers and reviewers of literature, but also as scientists of emotion: professionals who might best evaluate as well as train others in the reading of feeling. Just as Wharton's novel disquieted readers who sought the containment of emotional pain in a safe moralized sense, literary critics responded to cultural and institutional pressures to expand their understanding of just what emotion may be and to redefine their work in relation to it. This reconceptualization of the literary scholar's self-definition and purpose was not without its internal battles, however. In his well-known study *Professing Literature* (1987), Gerald Graff characterizes the institutional debate over the nature of literary study at the turn of the century as one between scholars who advocated a technical approach to literature (distinguished by its discernment of data) and an emerging group of critics who campaigned for aesthetics (the subjectively sentient).[23] The debate hinged on a perceived danger among university scholars in the humanities that criticism was moving away from the objective material of empirical fact into the wholly subjective and speculative domain of feeling. Rhetoric and grammar were being replaced by criticism and literature, a move that many literary scholars feared would prove fatal to the profession.

Literary critics at the same time found themselves struggling over their disciplinary definition and institutional recognition amid a new sea of scientific realism. Men like Charles Darwin and Herbert Spencer were proponents of the positivism of "facts," and their cultural influence and popularity quickly created what one commentator called a positive "mania." "'Fact-Worship,'" noted another observer, "is the popular worship of our times."[24] The scientific spirit would lead many people, as David Shi describes, "to equate belief in facts with the substance of belief itself" (72). The cultural mania for hard data was preceded by higher education's institutionalization of new disciplines of social science founded upon the scientific method, disciplines such as psychology, anthropology, and economics, which all rapidly gained influence in the universities. Many turn-of-the-century scholars and intellectuals thought that truth, like pain, had a "calculus" and could be quantified, and that social scientists, as opposed to scholars of English—those rarefied bearers of taste and outdated preservers of antiquities—were best equipped to discern it. Scholars of English, with their own specialized departments by the mid- to late nineteenth century, were challenged anew to define their institutional place and their cultural authority. The popular worship of facts accompanied a positive assault upon literary cultures: "Culture is not to be attained by writing essays about it, or by forming ever so clear a literary statement or mental conception of what it is," wrote William Graham Sumner in his book *The Forgotten Man and Other Essays* (1919). Education must shun a "superficial literary tradition" that otherwise "befog[s] . . . reason."[25] Edward Ross, a sociologist at Stanford University, called the literary haze of unfactual figures the "horror of the subjective."[26]

Literary scholars who properly failed to shun the "subjective" and venerate facts were threatened with the mark of effeminacy. Facts, as David Shi describes, were "supposedly 'masculine' in their objectivity and potency, [and] seemed to offer a formidable new weapon in the assault on 'feminine' idealism" (72). Like Oliver Wendell Holmes in chapter 1, who derided what he called the "squashy sentimentalism" of the female population, many agreed with the sentiments of the economist and former Union general Francis Amasa Waler, who scorned what he called the "bankruptcy" of the feminine: "Liberty," Waler proclaimed, should no longer be embodied as a female but as a "fact." In the post–Civil War years, the bearers of effeminacy must be shunned, only "facts" and the "stern duties of manhood remain" (qtd. Shi 72). The new scientific spirit appeared to spurn all that could not be subjected with assurance to empirical tests, and literary scholars were impelled to rewrite the assault upon their field of study as if upon their very manhood.

Quite often the mania for facts was less exact than its advocates might have assumed, however. As soldier's heart challenged the gaze of medicine with the elusiveness of the psyche, as we saw in chapter 1, and as legal domestic disputes, such as those discussed in chapters 2 and 3, expanded the range of actionable and often subjectively defined injuries, a vital component of professional reasoning became the ability to accommodate a domain of injury less visible to the empirical eye. Emotion was not only the stuff of university study or literary criticism, it also was the subject of extensive cross-disciplinary and often rigorously masculine debate at the turn of the century, from the trenches of labor activism to the benches of law courts. For male literary scholars, these subjects were an opportunity rather than a deficit. As theories about pain expanded beyond the body to recognize and, in some cases, compensate injuries to the mind and the emotions, male literary critics found a new calling. They found themselves remaking the sphere of the emotions—traditionally associated with effeminacy and sentimentality—to fit newly scientific conceptions of affect. Literary critics redefined themselves as scientists of affect, those who might best assess as well as instruct others in the reading of feeling. The importance of emotions was reassessed, and their uses remade by male literary critics for their own professional needs.

In his 1896 address as president of the MLA, Calvin Thomas, working to mediate arguments about literary study both within the discipline and without, strongly advocated a middle ground between fact worship and subjective judgment. His lecture titled "Literature and Personality" argued that it was not "a betrayal of the scientific spirit to use one's judgment," concluding that "literary criticism is rightly conceived . . . as the science of the emotional effects produced by literature."[27] Thomas and his supporters looked to reconcile what was perceived to be the scientific enterprise of the scholar with the aesthetic expertise of the critic. "Emotional reactions under the stimulus of literature," he continued, are "facts which have the same right as other facts, to be carefully recorded and studied for such instruction as they may be capable of yielding" (Thomas, 305).

It was something like the science of affect that Thomas argued the literary critic was becoming trained to discern. As scientists of affect, literary scholars, increasingly in competition with social scientists, could assert their own importance. Social scientists argued, for example, that a faith in facts eventually would help to ease the tensions of an industrial and diverse nation, relieving social ills and promoting social reform; many even welcomed scientific reasoning as a method to advance answers in theology and moral philosophy. No jurisdiction went untouched. Literature and science not only were in competition over authority for moral instruction, therefore, but also over which discipline would "define knowledge itself."[28] Although educators and university presidents like Charles William Eliot argued that a "healthy" "progressive" life in a "democracy" required an education of the spirit ("Nor will the professional and scientific school, however excellent in its kind, supply what is needed" [323]), literary scholars began to define their own discipline as a unique branch of this scientific school. "We might almost describe our critical science [literary criticism], then," suggested J. M. Robertson, "as the science of consistency in appreciation, since the science of that would involve the systematic study of all the causes—in ourselves, in a book, and in an author—which go to determine our individual judgments."[29]

Unlike the English scholar of old who was a "scientist" of antiquity, laboring over Latin grammar and other linguistic forms, the new literary critic took his role as a scientist of emotion, as one with a special ability to ask questions of the interior life and to render emotive issues visible.[30] For those literary critics advocating disciplinary redefinition, aesthetic questions ultimately affirmed an intimate connection between art, material, and, often, political life. James Taft Hatfield, president of the central division of the MLA, opened his talk at the 1901 conference by congratulating literary scholars as "citizens . . . united in harmonious and effective co-operation [with] a large majority of the real leaders in important fields of study." Literary scholars, he claimed, advanced the "progress of science as a whole."[31] Joel Elias Spingarn, professor of comparative literature at Columbia University, argued that an education in aesthetic thinking would provide both a "deep national insight" and a "wide international outlook."[32] Spingarn and Hatfield, representing the new direction of literary scholarship, suggested that literary criticism could offer something like a meeting ground for the subjectively sentient and the empirically evident, and it was upon these grounds, according to some of these early critics, that a "representative body" of scholars and, by extension, a nation of citizens could thrive. "I hold, then," concluded Hatfield's address, "that our first duty and highest function, even as an organization of linguistic specialists, is . . . political, and that this deep note should be the first sounded at every political gathering: we must place enlightened, trained intellect at the direct service of the state, as the only solvent of the problems of municipal misgovernment, corporate greed, and the tyranny of manual labor" (391). Literary "scientists" of affect, these scholars argued, could affect political life. Of course, not every member of the MLA felt this urgent political calling. For instance, Bliss Perry took a more moderate view about the political potential of "linguistic specialists," arguing in "Fiction as College Study" that as art records "conversations, thoughts and feelings," it inspires teachers of English, more modestly, to "bring [this] work into relation with life, to make it bear upon the actual."[33]

It is precisely in light of this newly emerging vision of literary critics themselves as mediators between the contemporary art of thoughts and feelings and their relation with sociopolitical life that debate about the critical difficulty of reading Edith Wharton's novel took shape.[34] For critics of *Ethan Frome*, the rendering of pain and the problem of discerning its ends became a perplexing puzzle. Whether or not Wharton's readers finally agree with Trilling's condemnation of the novel for what he called its advocacy of "the morality of inertia," its lack of agency for moral decision making, or subscribe to more recent psychoanalytic interpretations of the novel's dilemmas, the reading of emotional pain as a requisite strategy in the novel commands interest, and did so particularly at the time of its publication, when the reading of pain quickly became a substantive cultural skill. Wharton's novel *Ethan Frome* is an example of the anxiety that attended new cultural conditions of judgment and recompense. Ethan's suffering profligates in his inability to articulate his own pain, his seeming misjudgment of others'; yet this also appears to the reader to be an esteemed part of his character, particularly given what Zeena and other inhabitants of Starkfield seem to exemplify: a culture of complaint. His disaffection from language can be read as an indispensable relief in comparison with the querulousness at the end of the novel of both Mattie and Zeena. It is important to note that in *Ethan Frome* both impulses are present: the privileges of emotionally charged language as well as its excesses, the necessity for the compensation of injury and the withdrawal from the market of need. As a novel that seemed at one time to represent or even to occasion a desire for a "science" of affective relations among its professional male readers, it should not be regarded solely as a mainstream voice of a disciplinary culture. *Ethan Frome* stubbornly seems to resist all early efforts at pain management sought by its early critics; it is in what one critic labeled its relentlessness, its excesses, that *Ethan Frome* remains eternally irresolvable.

For literary critics in the early twentieth century who appeared on the verge of losing their claims to moral authority in a culture coming to revere scientific facts, reading the irresolvable was a highly public and manly practice, one that depended upon several faculties skillfully developed for use beyond the parlor or the classroom. As academic men worked to reassert their professional authority and, with that, their manliness, they also insisted that the reading of pain become a cultural requisite of civic duty. Close to a century later, the rhetoric of affect continues to be a crucial arena for scholarly inquiry.

Epilogue

In 1887 M. J. Head entered a Georgia courtroom to submit a $10,000 lawsuit against the Georgia Pacific Railway for his "great trouble" and "injured feelings" after his forcible (and wrongful) expulsion from a Louisiana-bound train. Ejected from a car filled with onlookers and delayed two days in reaching his final destination of New Orleans, Head sued the railroad not only for his lost time and expenses incurred, but also for his experience of intense humiliation and distress. In the superior court where the case was first heard, the presiding judge dismissed these latter claims and directed the jury that if it found for the plaintiff, it should do so only for "actual damages," namely his lost travel costs. Head appealed the lower court decision to the Supreme Court of Georgia, where Chief Justice Bleckley took a different view of the meaning of actual damage. "Wounding a man's feelings," the chief justice opined, "is as much actual damage as breaking his limbs."

Nineteenth- and early-twentieth-century cultural pressures to expand definitions of harm, to recognize, as Chief Justice Bleckley urged, that wounded feelings are as much actual damage as wounded limbs, crucially recalibrated the politics of emotion and feeling in U.S. culture. As the discourse about emotion altered in light of its newest associations with the language of injury, for instance, it unequivocally remapped, as surely as the railway lines themselves, the landscape of gender. Head, the aptly named plaintiff, was scarcely alone, either in his deep-felt complaint or in his sense of great trouble and injured feelings. We have seen men throughout this study demanding diverse forms of cultural compensation for their pains and injuries, an emotional numismatics, if you will, whose logic crucially transformed the politics of suffering and its avenues of redress.[1] As early as the Civil War, the rhetoric of injury subtended claims of cultural authority, as the physical injuries of suffering soldiers were refigured as the emotional and manly wounds of literary men. Not only the battlefield but also domestic disputes became an occasion to recast and to reclaim emotions from feminization and devaluation; in William Dean Howells's *A Modern Instance*, Bartley Hubbard and Squire Gaylord compete for emotional authority, while Prince Amerigo in Henry James's *The Golden Bowl* creates a new marketplace for private emotion. Male emotional pain became the groundwork for new strategies of cultural power.

Yet this power was denied to those men for whom physical injury and disability was a daily facet of life. Despite Head's emotional injury claim against the railroad company, a claim that signaled expanding definitions of harm, the pains suffered by the workmen building the railway system (and, more generally, the exploding injuries of an industrial economy) were coming to be understood by midcentury as the cost—most often to laborers—of a greater economic good for the nation. Like L. Lindquist, a railway wheel turner who lost partial sight when a piece of steel embedded in his right eye, the men building the railroads routinely suffered severe head injuries, mangled appendages, lost limbs, and worse on their journey to fulfill the nation's promise.[2] In his annual address delivered before the Mutual Aid and Benefit Association at Chicago on November 21, 1888, only a short time after Head's case was settled, E. H. Belknap tried to persuade railroad employees to buy insurance to protect them against the inevitability of physical disability: "Has sickness ever overtaken you? Has trouble ever crossed your path? Have trials and adversity ever been your guests? Has the hand of death ever brought you near the door?"[3] He knew, of course, that the answer would be a resounding yes for virtually all in his congregation of conductors. Not only was the need for protection against injury great; injured railway workers who became financially and physically dependent were roundly excluded from the brotherhood of men. Disabled trainmen were "objects of pity and lessons of failed manhood."[4]

The narrowing of culturally acceptable forms of physical difference, which pathologized physical disability, corresponded with the expanding recognition of pain and the "disabling" emotional distress of able-bodied white middle-class men. I want to take this correspondence as well as the occasion of this epilogue to cast the book's reading of emotional injury and masculinity in critical alliance with a discourse that has not been immediately within its purview in the preceding chapters. Disability studies scholars have written about the period from roughly the 1880s to the

1930s as a time of significant redefinition in their field: "Public policies and law; emerging medical, educational, and social-service professions; and the institutions those policies and professions created either questioned the competency of people with virtually all types of disabilities for full citizenship or declared them disqualified."[5] In fact, the concept of disability itself, as Douglas C. Baynton writes, was used to "justify discrimination" against women, African Americans, and immigrants by "attributing disability to them" (33). These groups were charged with "flaws" such as "irrationality, excessive emotionality, and physical weakness," which functioned as a "sign of and justification for" their inequality. The language of disability was used to deny rights to some, and yet the vocabulary of emotional injury seized by white middle-class men often qualified their emotional losses, their harms, as uniquely worthy of recompense. The threat of failed, disabled manhood surely coexisted with lessons of masculine emotional success.

Indeed, the characteristics that excluded some from the full rights of citizenship were adapted by others as the surest signs of their humanity: the masculine broken heart could transcend his broken body, making him that much more a man. Claims of men's emotional injuries reinforced, to some degree, what Rosemarie Garland Thomson has called the compensatory model, in which disability connotes "not physiological variation, but the violation of a primary state of putative wholeness."[6] Seen in this way, physical and emotional losses are repaired with economic compensation, while those who are excluded from the ideals of liberal individualism and its able-bodied standards of "independence, strength, control [and] self-mastery," namely women and persons with congenital disabilities among others, fall outside its logic.[7] Yet psychic injury also challenges minoritizing definitions of disability in that it demonstrates that the very men who embodied and maintained the liberal ideal also at times embraced its putative opposite: emotionalism. Moreover, economic reparation was just one way in which the men in this study capitalized on their emotional wounds for cultural and personal gain. William Dean Howells and Henry James heroized the Civil War soldier's shameful "heart" in order to remake the rhetoric of national manhood, and literary critics at the turn of the twentieth century used cultural anxieties about measuring emotional pain to defend their professional authority. Each endeavored to revise the meaning of pain and emotional "damage," making it the basis for new claims of cultural authority.

Wounded Hearts has examined occasions in which sentimental power accrues to masculine injuries precisely when those injuries are emotional. The male characters in this study see themselves as victims of humiliation and disgrace, of pain and suffering, although they demonstrate, just as disability studies have recognized, that discourses of victimization do not always assist the disempowered. It is significant that several of the characters in this study, while afflicted with forms of physically disfiguring, even disabling injuries, amass sympathy and power within their narratives from their emotional rather than their physical pains. Take, for example, Willa Cather's Daniel Forrester. The Captain, we will remember, suffers a fall that prevents him from pursuing his railroad work; his injury likens him to his railroad brothers, many of whom were disabled in industrial accidents. Yet neither this injury nor his later stroke accrues sympathy for this character within the novel. It is the emotional wounds he suffers after his wife's affair, when the town gossips publicize her indiscretions and his cuckoldry, that ultimately kills him. Edith Wharton also imagines her protagonist Ethan Frome as "lame" ("he walks like the jerk of a chain"), yet the small attention paid to his bodily difference is overwhelmed by the catalog of his emotional and deeply buried wounds. Similarly, William Dean Howells's Ben Halleck is described as scarred with a "piteous" "lame" leg, his disabled body only a marker for what the novel presents as his more substantive (and nonrelated) emotional injury. In so many of these instances the physical disability that otherwise might marginalize these male characters or signal their "character deformity" is displaced by their more palatable demonstration of emotional wounds.[8] Like Henry Fleming, whose "red badge" is an external wound necessary to valorize his internal conflict, for many of the men in this study, emotional woundedness is a marker of "exceptionality to be claimed and honored" rather than shunned (Thomson, 18).

It is notable that in the emotional injury case with which this epilogue began, the court describes Head's emotional state as being as disabled as a "broken limb"; the difference, the court surmises, is only that "one is internal, and the other external; one mental, the other physical"; in either case, the chief justice asserted, the damage is not "measurable with exactness." Yet it is precisely the problem of exact measurement, or, rather, immeasurability, that confronted law courts, which were increasingly asked to hear such cases of relational internal injuries, and that inspired the cross-disciplinary discourse on emotional wounds that this book describes. What this discourse shares with that of disability is its diversity: the meaning of injury is pliable, and its value is culturally fashioned. Although the court in the above example seemed to recognize that there could be a spectrum of disabling harms affecting body and mind in ways that defy precise measurement, this recognition was not put into practice. It is all the more significant that "the complete unblushing male" embraced his emotional wounds and through them controlled how his pains and his injuries would be culturally rendered.[9]

Notes

Introduction

1. Hawthorne, *Scarlet Letter*, 140, 136. Subsequent references will be cited in the text.

2. Howells, *Modern Instance* (Penguin edition), 440. Subsequent references will be cited in the text.

3. For the story of how "psychology became a science . . . and invented that most modern of concepts, the mind," see Reed, *From Soul to Mind*, 3, xv.

4. Foucault, "Nietzsche, Genealogy, History," 140. For an eloquent description of a genealogical project in relation to trauma theory, see Leys, "Introduction," *Trauma*, 8–9.

5. The study of sentiment also has been described as transactional, economic, and systemic, although this analysis takes place largely through women's literature. See Merish, *Sentimental Materialism*. For a good description of this body of work, see Ellison, *Cato's Tears*, 8.

6. Cvetkovich, *Mixed Feelings*, 31.

7. The contexts for expressing emotion, the subjects experiencing it, its gendering, and thus its shape and substance change, although the structures of change are sometimes rendered invisible: "Social groups that invent the 'psychological' are engaged in the production of social meanings that are made to appear natural and self-evident through a great range of practices and performances" (Pfister and Schnog, "Introduction," *Inventing the Psychological*, 24).

8. Berlant, "Subject of True Feeling."

9. Bederman, *Manliness and Civilization*, 11; Traister, "Academic Viagra," 299. For an analysis of men's claims of victimization in late-twentieth-century literature and culture, see Sally Robinson, *Marked Men*.

10. Bruckner, *Tears of the White Man*.

11. Elizabeth Barnes has argued in *States of Sympathy*, for example, that sympathy (often erroneously feminized) and a democratic state are mutually dependent, while Dana Nelson contends that the "affective foreclosures" of early national manhood have "haunted" the "democratic

imaginary" (*National Manhood*, x). As Lora Romero (*Home Fronts*) has challenged the strict binarisms that tend to congeal around the domestic, June Howard ("What Is Sentimentality?") has disputed the false dichotomy of the sentimental and the emotional itself. Other scholars such as Julie Ellison (*Cato's Tears*) and Glenn Hendler (*Public Sentiments* and "Structure of Sentimental Experience") have started to revise the above depictions of emotional gendering and its literary histories by reviving emotive men. See also Stern, *Plight of Feeling*, and Lewis and Stearns, *Emotional History*.

12. Ellison similarly foregrounds this question in her important transatlantic study *Cato's Tears*, affirming that in the "long preeminence of masculine tenderheartedness" a man could "both have his sensibility . . . and despise it too" (19–20).

13. Sedgwick and Frank, *Shame and Its Sisters*, 17.

14. See, for example, Chamallas, "Architecture of Bias," "Women, Mothers," and "Writing about Sexual Harassment"; and Howe, "Problem of Privatized Injuries."

15. G. Edward White, *Tort Law in America*, xx.

16. Chamallas, "Architecture of Bias," 520.

17. For a discussion of Locke's influence on the founders of the United States, see Huyler, *Locke in America*. The introduction to Huyler's book provides a useful overview of Locke scholarship over the past several decades.

18. Mill, *On Liberty*, 10–11. Of course, what constitutes harm has been the debate concerning this particular text by Mill. "Liberals inspired by Mill define the boundaries of public morality in terms of 'harms' (to others). Kantian liberals tend to restrict public morality to the morality of rights and justice" (Postema, "Public Faces—Private Places," 78).

19. See Sandel, *Liberalism and Its Critics*, 1–11.

20. For a good summary of this debate in relation to critical legal studies, rights theory, and law and economics, see Singer, "Legal Rights Debate," 467–543.

21. It is within this long history of injury that the scope of protection against harm has been gradually extended to include harms suffered by women. For a discussion of the expansion of injury law in the context of critical race theory, see Delgado, "Words That Wound." For a discussion of identity politics and the problems of redressing social injury, see Wendy Brown, *States of Injury*.

22. Shamir, "Hawthorne's Romance," 2.

23. See Livingston, *Pragmatism and the Political Economy*, xvii.

24. See Pfister and Schnog, *Inventing the Psychological*, 35.

25. For a valuable discussion of these critics and this literature, see Pfister and Schnog, *Inventing the Psychological*, 35–40. See also Lears, *No*

Place of Grace, on therapeutic culture: "References to salvation dropped from view; psychological well-being became—though often only implicitly—an entirely secular project" (55).

26. Roy Porter characterizes Foucault's descriptions of psychiatric control as "so much more thorough, silent, and less scandalous" ("Barely Touching," 71).

27. Habermas, *Transformation of the Public Sphere*, 43.

28. This reading of a marketplace of emotion seeks to historicize emotions that are less timeless and often less virtuous than those described in Nussbaum's capacious study *Upheavals of Thought*.

29. Judith Butler opposes critical race theory's pressure to legalize hate speech, arguing that linguistic "misappropriation" has the power to dissolve words of injurious force. It is more dangerous, in Butler's analysis, to try to fix meaning (as if, she rightly notes, this were even possible) than to "risk the security of linguistic life" and, one presumes, to occasionally navigate in a world of potential psychic wounds. See *Excitable Speech*, 2–41.

30. Wendy Brown argues that women's "expanding relationships" to state institutions not only "produce . . . active *political* subjects," but, more important, they also may "produce regulated, subordinated, and disciplined *state* subjects" (*States of Injury*, 173). For Foucault's description of the disciplinary methods of modernity, see *Discipline and Punish*. See also Berlant, "Poor Eliza," *Queen of America*, and "Subject of True Feeling." Subsequent references will be cited in the text.

Chapter One

1. Da Costa, "On Irritable Heart," 2. See also Nemiah, "Neurotic Disorders," 1483.

2. Thomas Lewis wrote a book by this name in 1919: "When the young manhood of a whole nation is placed suddenly under arms, its whole habit of life, its housing, dietary and clothing, its times of rest and work, the nature of its employment changed . . . manhood is submitted to a most drastic test. Who then can affect surprise if many men fail when so tested?" (*Soldier's Heart and the Effort Syndrome*, 7).

3. Freud's 1895 study "On the Grounds for Detaching a Particular Syndrome from Neurasthenia" argued that because anxiety was symptomatic of these cases, they should be given a place among the growing number of emotional disorders (90).

4. Quoted in Young, *Disarming the Nation*, 88. See also Burbick, *Healing the Republic*, 5. Burbick narrates the conflicting debates, prescriptions, and representations of the national body in the "quest for health" (5). For more discussion of the national body, see Sanchez-Eppler, *Touching Liberty*.

5. Scarry, *Body in Pain*, 67.

6. Young's analysis of gender often relies upon the "masculinized woman" or the "feminized man" (*Disarming the Nation*, 44). For more on the feminization of the war, see Fahs, *Imagined Civil War*.

7. In the hands of Mitchell and Beard, neurasthenia became a "respectable" disease, a disease not limited to the upper or middle classes, or to men or women in particular, but increasingly afflicting men in the working classes toward the turn of the century. See Sicherman, "Uses of Diagnosis."

8. "In the more than 50,000 books which have been written on the American Civil War over the past 130 years, the focus has usually been on great generals rather than on bleeding and bewildered soldiers. . . . Although more attention has been paid to the common soldier of the Civil War over the past forty years, this interest has tended to translate into a passion for reenactments rather than a focus on trauma, pain, and tragedy" (Dean, *Shook over Hell*, 4–5). For a brief overview of Civil War historiography, see also James M. McPherson's foreword to Clinton and Silber, *Divided Houses*, xiii–xvii.

9. I'm thinking here of Williams's use of "structures of feeling" in *Marxism and Literature*, 133–34. For Williams, structures of feeling are phases or processes of feeling that precede classification and categorization.

10. See Trachtenberg, "Albums of War," as well as *Civil War through the Camera*.

11. See Newman, "Wounds and Wounding." The goal of war, argues Scarry in *Body in Pain*, is to injure, not to free. Physical wounds are the visible side of war, although Scarry has argued that such wounds never reveal the political stakes, the ideological questions, the gains or losses, or the political predicament; wounds are wounds. Newman takes issue with this point, arguing that recordings of physical wounds were themselves deeply political. See also Sweet, "Photography and the Scene of History."

12. Oliver Wendell Holmes Sr., "Doings of the Sunbeam," 11. In Holmes's account, war is the "dread reality" of the "truthful sunbeam," his pet name for the photograph. Holmes's digression about wartime photography is a cautionary moment in an otherwise celebratory article about the wonders of photographic representation. "The ditch" where the dead are buried and their "fragments" and "tatters" provide, in Holmes's view, a "commentary on civilization such as a savage might well triumph to show its missionaries" (12).

13. For more on the Civil War's technological transformation, see Fite, *Social and Industrial Conditions*, 42; Chandler, "Organization of Manufacturing and Transportation"; and Jenks, "Railroads as an Economic Force." The breech-loading rifle with repeat fire was among the most substantial innovations in this regard (Fite, *Social and Industrial Conditions*, 102).

14. Bellard, *Gone for Soldier*. The overwhelming presence of wounds al-

ways is noted: "It was a sad spectacle, nearly all of them in the prime of life, their handsome manly forms and faces disfigured with scars and bruises, while, in most cases, a limb was lopped off. But we err: these wounds will yet be, as they are now, their proud decorations, and shall ever win from their countrymen the rewards they so well deserve" (*Report of Vincent Colyer*, 36).

15. Griffin, "Scar Texts," 61.

16. Horace Porter, "Philosophy of Courage," 246.

17. For a good discussion of masculine embodiment, see Bourke, *Dismembering the Male*, especially the introduction and first chapter.

18. "I have more than once seen alarming coughs simply vanish after a few nights in camp" (S. Weir Mitchell, *Nurse and Patient*, 49). For more on Mitchell, see Tuttle, "Empire of Sickness."

19. Among its sufferers were writers such as Howells, James, and Wharton, all of whom form part of this larger study. Called "brain workers," these men and women were considered victims of nervous overactivity, and many sought out S. Weir Mitchell for his "cure." See Tom Lutz, *American Nervousness*, and Gosling, *Before Freud*, 11.

20. See Journet, "Phantom Limbs and 'Body-Ego.'" Outside literary scholarship, Mitchell is better known for his work on wounded soldiers. See Rey, *History of Pain*, 122, 227–30. For literary biographies, see Rein, *S. Weir Mitchell as a Psychiatric Novelist*, and Burr, *Weir Mitchell: His Life and Letters.*

21. Hysteria has been described as the ultimate female malady of the nineteenth century and labeled the most conspicuous example of the fragile female psyche. See Herndl, *Invalid Women*. There have been more recent studies on male hysteria, particularly on the work of Charcot in France. See Micale, "Charcot and the Idea of Hysteria"; Rousseau, *Languages of the Psyche*; Showalter, *Hystories* and *Female Malady*; and S. Weir Mitchell, "Case of Uncomplicated Hysteria."

22. The medical interest in neurology owed much to the Civil War, as Theodore H. Weisenburg, president of the American Neurological Association, noted; all of the organization's thirty-five original members served during the war. S. Weir Mitchell was asked to preside as president of the ANA, but he was unable to accept. See Weisenburg's review of the early history of the association, which first met in New York City on June 2, 1875, "The Military History of the American Neurological Association," 1.

23. Quoted in Rein, *S. Weir Mitchell as a Psychiatric Novelist*, 19–20.

24. Ibid.

25. S. Weir Mitchell, "Case of George Dedlow," 8.

26. See S. Weir Mitchell, "Phantom Limbs," 563. For another reading of this story, see Goler, "Loss and the Persistence of Memory."

27. Virginia Woolf, "On Being Ill," quoted in Bending, *Representation of Bodily Pain*, 85.

28. *Medical and Surgical History*, vol. 2, part 1, 638–39.

29. Theodore Diller, "Traumatic Nervous Affections," quoted in Dean, *Shook over Hell*, 29.

30. The favored term for men was "lunatic." See Showalter, *Hystories*, 65. See also Gilman, *Hysteria beyond Freud*; Kahane, *Passions of the Voice*; Micale, *Approaching Hysteria* and "Charcot and the Idea of Hysteria"; and Herndle, *Invalid Women*. Mitchell did use the term "hysteria" to describe men in the decades following the war. In his book *Clinical Lessons on Nervous Diseases*, he details four case studies of men suffering from hysteric symptoms.

31. See Anderson and Anderson, "Nostalgia and Malingering," 157. See also Dean, *Shook over Hell*, 128–30.

32. Edward Ogden to Sallie Ogden, letter 13, Ogden Papers.

33. See Diffley, *Where My Heart Is Turning Ever.*

34. In "Nostalgia as a Disease of Field Service," Calhoun treats nostalgia in more detail: "Nostalgia is an affection of the mind. . . . Any influence that will tend to render the patient more manly will exercise a curative power. In boarding schools, as perhaps many of us will remember, ridicule is wholly relied upon, and will often be found effective in camp. . . . [T]he patient can often be laughed out of it by his comrades, or reasoned out of it by appeals to his manhood" (132).

35. Ibid.

36. Quoted in Rosen, "Nostalgia," 29.

37. Hammond and Lanza, *Tales of Eccentric Life*.

38. S. Weir Mitchell, *In War Time*. Subsequent references will be cited in the text. For Mitchell's "near indistinguishability of patient and physician," see Michaels, "Introduction," *Gold Standard*, 23–26.

39. For a discussion of female emotions and the discourse of medicine, see Cynthia Davis, *Bodily and Narrative Forms*, 49–88.

40. Weisenburg, "Military History of the American Neurological Association," 1. See also Mendelson, *Interfaces of Medicine and Law*, 94–96.

41. Ferenczi, *Psychoanalysis and the War Neuroses*, 6. See also Leys, *Trauma*, 173–75, 303–5.

42. Ferenczi, *Psychoanalysis and the War Neuroses*, 6–7. See also Bourke, *Dismembering the Male*, 76–123.

43. Freud, "Psychoanalysis and War Neurosis," 16. See also Dean, *Shook over Hell*, 30–36, for a discussion of shell shock and the attitudes toward casualties of the First World War. It is interesting to note that pension records (a domain in which compensatory language begins to emerge with vigor) show that during and after the Civil War most pensioners with mental disabilities needed the requisite physical wounds in order to receive

their pensions (see ibid., 134, 143–45). For the clinical battle that raged about the nature of shell shock, see Southward, *Shell-Shock and Other Neuropsychiatric Problems.*

44. Malingering was considered an acute problem during the Civil War, although "feigned diseases" were most often physical in nature. In *The Medical and Surgical Reporter* 10, no. 17 (Aug. 22, 1863), J. Theodore Calhoun, assistant surgeon in the Army Corps, notes several creative attempts at producing physical illness: "A very common deception is the production of simulated fever. A species of wild onion that grows abundantly in Virginia is used for that purpose. The bulb is peeled and introduced into the rectum. In about an hour a flushed face and accelerated pulse is said to be produced, which can easily be mistaken for febrile symptoms" (229). See also McMahon, "Nervous Disease and Malingering," 17, and Bourke, *Dismembering the Male*, 76–123.

45. The breakdown in representative language also resulted in a "failure in humanitarian action," according to Eiselein, *Literature and Humanitarian Reform*, 77. See also ibid., 78–114.

46. Howells, "Reviews and Literary Notices," 121.

47. Edmund Wilson, *Patriotic Gore*, xiii.

48. Quoted in Dew, "Rally Round the Flag."

49. Quoted in Aaron, *Unwritten War*, xvi; see also Thomas Leonard, *Above the Battle.*

50. For a good review of this literature, see Young, *Disarming the Nation*, 1–23.

51. Lundberg, "American Literature of War."

52. Literary critics like to mention Walt Whitman's early observation that "the real war will never get in the books" as evidence of the dearth of literary value in the numerous publications to suffuse the landscape after the war. See Whitman, *Specimen Days in America*, 120. For a brief explanation of this disposition, see Masur, "Preface," "*The Real War Will Never Get in the Books.*" Edmund Wilson, Aaron, and Thomas Leonard are among a tradition of scholars who, although interested in reading Civil War literature, also are inclined to reject its literariness.

53. Oliver Wendell Holmes Jr., *Touched with Fire*, 27.

54. Linderman, *Embattled Courage*, 25.

55. See Kasson, *Rudeness and Civility*, especially chapter 5. See also Hochschild, "Emotion Work," and Lewis and Stearns, *Emotional History.*

56. Quoted in Linderman, *Embattled Courage*, 28.

57. Kaplan, "Spectacle of War," 81.

58. Edmund Wilson, *Patriotic Gore*, 758–59.

59. Rowe, *At Emerson's Tomb*, 147.

60. See Chisholm, *Civil War Notebook*, 15–17.

61. Dawes, *Service with the Sixth Wisconsin Volunteers*, 287.

62. Victor E. Compte to wife, Elise, Apr. 20, 1864, and Joseph M. Rabb to sister, Feb. 7, 1864, quoted in Dean, *Shook over Hell*, 93.

63. Shaw, *Blue-Eyed Child of Fortune*, 185. Subsequent references will be cited in the text.

64. Christian Epperly to his wife, Mary, Epperly Letters.

65. Howells, quoted in Young, *Disarming the Nation*, 7.

66. See Hedrick, *Harriet Beecher Stowe*, 312.

67. See Diffley, *Where My Heart Is Turning Ever*, 627–58. Diffley discusses, in addition to the Old Homestead story, the reconstruction genre of Romance. For writers and warriors alike, suffering exceeded what restorative gestures could be applied within a domestic economy, as hearth and home, once a "haven in a heartless world," became one final hospital bed.

68. Rhodes, *All for Union*, 239. See Kaser, *Books and Libraries in Camp and Battle*, for a discussion of reading among Civil War soldiers.

69. Fisk, *Hard Marching Every Day*, 190–91.

70. Faller and Faller, *Dear Folks at Home*, 45–46.

71. Many of these titles, although often chosen by the editor of the collection, draw upon the language and sentiments of the writers themselves.

72. Holmes to Felix Frankfurter, quoted in Aichele, *Oliver Wendell Holmes Jr.*, 144. See also Shi, *Facing Facts*, 54.

73. See Young, *Disarming the Nation*, 8.

74. The language is from Seltzer, *Serial Killers*, 95.

75. Quoted in Linsom, *My Stephen Crane*, 37; also noted in Lee Clark Mitchell, "Introduction," *New Essays on "The Red Badge of Courage."*

76. Against Christopher Wilson's characterization of the literary marketplace remasculinized by a new "cultural style" of robust masculinity, I argue for its putative opposite, the emotional mind. See Wilson, *Labor of Words*, 2.

77. Henry James, "Most Extraordinary Case." Subsequent references will be cited in the text.

78. It was a "horrid even if an obscure hurt," from *Notes of a Son and Brother*, quoted in Edel, *Henry James*, 58.

79. See Shi, *Facing Facts*, 50. Although I agree that Howells and James were anxious about their own masculine status, I disagree with Shi when he contends that "the Civil War, whether experienced or avoided, helped steer some people toward a more 'masculine' posture and thereby buttressed the 'realistic' assault on 'feminine' sentimentalism and decorous idealism" (50). These realists did not eschew sentimentalism so much as they reworked its territory.

80. See Aaron, *Unwritten War*, 121–32. See also Fredrickson, *Inner Civil War*.

81. Edel, *Henry James*, 61–63.

82. Horace Porter, "Philosophy of Courage," 251.

83. Higginson, "Bit of War Photography," 35.

84. Crane, *Red Badge of Courage*, 40. Subsequent references will be cited in the text.

85. See Crane, "Sergeant's Private Madhouse," in *Wounds in the Rain*. Numerous tales in this collection are about "nerves."

Chapter Two

1. Blanton and Riley, "Shell Shocks of Family Life," 282.

2. Hazel and Lewis, *Divorce Mill*, 224.

3. Myerson, "Nervous Husband," 11.

4. Howells's letter to James R. Osgood, his agent and publisher, quoted in Bennett, "Introduction," xxix.

5. G. Edward White, *Tort Law in America*, xx.

6. Dimock, *Residues of Justice*, 151.

7. Goodman, *Shifting the Blame*, 8.

8. Kaplan, *Social Construction*, 20.

9. "Words hurt (cut) more than swords" (1523); Christopher Marlowe, *Tamburlaine the Great*, 1.1.74: "The words are swords" (c. 1590); Shakespeare, *Titus Andronicus*: "These words are razors to my wounded heart" (c. 1594) (quoted in *Oxford Dictionary of English Proverbs*, 915).

10. For more discussion of these issues, see Shamir, "Hawthorne's Romance," 758–59. Subsequent references will be cited in the text.

11. Reverend Samuel Miller, quoted in Cathy N. Davidson, *Revolution and the Word*, 46.

12. Ibid. See also Nina Baym, *Novels, Readers, and Reviewers*; Mailloux, "Rhetorical Use and Abuse of Fiction"; and Barnes, *States of Sympathy*, 41–71.

13. Cady, "Neuroticism of William Dean Howells."

14. Shi, *Facing Facts*, 104. See Shi for more on the "robust school of realist fiction." Most recently, Kimberly Freeman describes Howells's divorce novel as his attempt to "save and protect" a "youthful and feminized audience" from the "misleading romantic ideas of popular novels" ("'Enormous Fact,'" 66–67).

15. See Bell, *Problem of American Realism*, 6, 22.

16. "Mr. Howells on Divorce"; Howells, quoted in Bennett, "Introduction," xv. For a different reading of Howells's response to Stowe, see Cynthia J. Davis, *Bodily and Narrative Forms*, 105.

17. See Howells, *Rise of Silas Lapham*, 197.

18. Hochschild, in "Emotion Work," refers to emotion work as the "act of evoking or shaping . . . feeling in oneself" (563).

19. Howells, *Criticism and Fiction*, 46.

20. Howells, *Modern Instance* (Penguin edition), 282. Subsequent references will be cited in the text.

21. Seen in this way, "the [emotional] cripple," to rephrase Thomson, is "essential to the cultural project of American self-making" (*Extraordinary Bodies*, 5).

22. May, *Great Expectations*, 47.

23. See Michaels, "Contracted Heart," 523.

24. See Basch, "Emerging Legal History of Women," 106, and *Framing American Divorce*.

25. See also *Freeman v. Freeman*, 31 Wis. 235, for a case in which mental suffering is unaccompanied by physical injury.

26. For different readings of the Hubbards, see Arms, "Literary Background of Howells's Social Criticism," 260; Vanderbilt, "Marcia Gaylord's Electra Complex," 374; Girgus, "Bartley Hubbard," 315, and "New Age of Narcissism"; Wright, "Given Bartley, Given Marcia," 214; Prioleau, *Circle of Eros*; Kaplan, *Social Construction*, 15–43; and Freeman, "'Enormous Fact.'"

27. Letter to James R. Osgood, quoted in Bennett, "Introduction," xxix.

28. See Bennett, "Introduction," xix.

29. Abandonment could be considered by the court to be cruelty: "Desertion may take place under such circumstances as to be cruelty, as where the departure inflicts grievous mental suffering" (William T. Nelson, *Law of Divorce and Annulment*, 310). See also *Jones v. Jones*, 62 NH 463, and *Cannon v. Cannon*, 17 Mo., Ap. 390. An entire chapter in Nelson's book is devoted to cruelty cases brought against wives (*Law of Divorce and Annulment*, 332–37).

30. Griswold, "Divorce and the Redefinition of Victorian Manhood," 242.

31. See Cady, *Road to Realism*, and Crowley, *Black Heart's Truth*. For a sample of the critical reception to this Indiana divorce novel, see "Mr. Howells on Divorce"; Maurice Thompson, "Modern Instance of Criticism"; and Eichelberger, *Howells through 1920*.

32. See Friedman, *American Law*, 436–39.

33. Ibid., 438; see also Griswold, "Law, Sex, Cruelty, and Divorce," 721–40. For a brief summary of the divorce laws in several states prior to the year 1897, see Cassidy, *Legal Status of Women*, 55–85

34. Quoted in Blake, *Road to Reno*, 90.

35. Quoted in Barnett, *Divorce and the American Divorce Novel*, 23.

36. Bureau of the Census, *Marriage and Divorce, 1867–1906*, 148. For men in Indiana, adultery still continued to be the foremost cause of divorce in the late nineteenth century, although not by more than a few hundred cases.

37. Quoted in Fertig, "Maurice Thompson," 105. See Fertig for a discussion of Howells's interest in the Indiana Omnibus Clause.

38. *Graft v. Graft*, 76 Indiana 138 (1881).

39. Pound, *Law in Books*, 21.

40. Friedman, "Rights of Passage," 659.

41. Friedman maintains that cruelty became the most popular ground for divorce in the later nineteenth century. See "Rights of Passage," 654.

42. Griswold, "Law, Sex, Cruelty, and Divorce," 722. Griswold has published extensively on divorce in nineteenth-century America. See also his *Family and Divorce* and "Evolution of the Doctrine of Mental Cruelty," 127.

43. Bureau of the Census, *Marriage and Divorce, 1867–1906.*

44. Hindus and Withey, "Law of Husband and Wife."

45. Griswold, "Divorce and the Redefinition of Victorian Manhood," 242.

46. Stanton said of the masculine need to "protect" women against divorce: "It is clearly a work of supererogation, for learned men to demand 'more stringent laws for women's protection!'—protection such as the eagle gives the lamb he carries to his eyrie! Alas, for the wrongs that women have suffered under the specious plea of protection!" ("Need of Liberal Divorce Laws," 243).

47. Quoted in Bennett, "Introduction," xxi.

48. *Whitmore v. Whitmore*, 49 Michigan Law Rep. 417 (1882).

49. Browne, "Oral Cruelty," 82.

50. *Carpenter v. Carpenter*, 30 Kansas 744 (1883). See also *Gibbs v. Gibbs*, 18 Kansas 419; *Bennet v. Bennet*, 24 Mich. 482; and *Powelson v. Powelson*, 22 Cal. 358.

51. Bishop, *Commentaries on the Laws of Marriage and Divorce*, 648.

52. See Bennett, "Introduction," xxvii.

53. For more of this history, see Ferguson, *Law and Letters*, 23.

54. Maurice Thompson to William Dean Howells, Mar. 29, 1881, Thompson Letters. Excerpted in Fertig, "Maurice Thompson," 105. No letters from Howells to Thompson survive.

55. See Tanner, *Adultery in the Novel.*

56. William T. Nelson, *Law of Divorce and Annulment*, 300.

Chapter Three

1. Cather's historical awareness of contemporary problems in legal reasoning, as evidenced in the epigraph that opens this chapter, frames a methodology in which I attribute to Cather's novel a sophisticated consciousness of legal fictions. Certain practices affected the direction of tort law regardless of whether Cather or other novelists actually recognized the full dimensions of the issues they had posed for themselves. The au-

tonomy and parallel development of law and literature interest me in this chapter.

2. Cather, *Lost Lady*, 69. Subsequent references will be cited in the text.

3. The quote in full reads: "It is the inexplicable presence of the thing not named, of the overtone divined by the ear but not heard by it, the verbal mood, the emotional aura of the fact or the thing or the deed, that gives high quality to the novel" (Cather, "Novel Démeublé," in *Not under Forty*, 41–42). Subsequent references will be cited in the text.

4. Cather, *Not under Forty*, v.

5. "The thing not named" is Cather's own phrase. Critics invoke it to suggest her lesbianism. See, for instance, Carlin, *Cather, Canon, and the Politics of Reading*, and Goldberg, *Cather and Others*.

6. Crane, "Monster." See also Fried, *Realism, Writing, Disfiguration*, for a discussion of Crane's writing "via images of streetcars, elevated railways, ambulances and the like" (132, 195; cf. 45).

7. See Donovan, *Railroad in Literature*. This book lists more than 100 novels that highlight the railroads; this number is equaled if not exceeded by the number of published short stories, essays, and biographies. For an incisive account of the railroad in early silent cinema, see Kirby, *Parallel Tracks*.

8. Kipnis, "Adultery."

9. *Farwell v. Boston and Worcester Railroad Corporation*, 45 Mass. (4 Metc.) 49 (1842); see also Friedman and Ladinsky, "Social Change and the Law," 51–58, for a discussion of the fellow-servant rule.

10. Horwitz, *Transformation of American Law*, 201–10; Friedman, *American Law*, 409–27. See also G. Edward White, *Tort Law in America*.

11. "As soon as the universal duty of taking ordinary care was introduced in America, it was curtailed by four important legal doctrines. The first and most important of these was the doctrine of negligence under which the courts defined fault and assigned liability only in the absence of ordinary care which was, generally speaking, construed quite loosely in favor of the risk-taking entrepreneur" (Goodman, *Shifting the Blame*, 7).

12. See Pateman, *Sexual Contract*, 1–18.

13. Unlike in England, criminal conversation plaintiffs in the United States were not primarily from the upper classes. The principal plaintiffs came from a wide array of social circumstances. For a discussion of the class dynamics in English criminal conversation cases, see Staves, "Money for Honor."

14. Women were not permitted to bring this action until the early twentieth century. See *Nolin v. Pearson*, 191 Mass. 283 (1906); *Rott v. Goehring*, 33 N.D. 413 (1916); and *Frederick v. Morse*, 88 Vt. 126 (1912). For states that held that a woman could not bring forward a criminal conversation action,

see *Hodge v. Wetzler*, 69 N.J.L. 490, 55 Atl. 49 (1903), and *Kroessin v. Keller*, 60 Minn. 372, 27 L.R.A. 685 (1895), quoted in Annotation, *Wife's Right of Action for Criminal Conversation*, 4 ALR 569.

15. Literally, criminal conversation was defined as "'criminal' because it was an ecclesiastical crime; 'conversation' in the sense of intercourse" (Prosser, *Law of Torts*, 875 n. 75). The circumstantial nature of the evidence involved with the tort was a primary factor leading to its repeal in England. See Stone, *Road to Divorce*, 232–33. That criminal conversation, which is a tort and not a crime, continues to be named "criminal" announces its relation to the crimes of adultery, fornication, sodomy, and rape, in which the standard of proof (beyond a reasonable doubt) is much stricter than the civil standard (preponderance of the evidence). For a thorough discussion of the legal history of criminal conversation, see Korobkin, *Criminal Conversations*, 10–26.

16. In 3 Blackstone's Commentaries, 139, it is said: "Adultery or criminal conversation with a man's wife [is] a civil injury (and surely there can be no greater), the law gives a satisfaction to the husband for it by action of trespass vi et armis against the adulterer wherein the damages recovered are usually very large and exemplary" (quoted in Annotation, *Turner v. Heavrin*, 4 ALR 562 [1st series]). Its more current definition (after women were permitted by law to act as plaintiffs) is as follows: "Defilement of marriage bed . . . considered in its aspect of a civil injury to the husband or wife entitling him or her to damages; the tort of debauching or seducing a wife or husband" (*Black's Law Dictionary* 336 [5th ed., 1979]).

17. The growing popularity of criminal conversation cases seems to correspond to the repeal of statutes regulating lawyers' acceptance of contingency fees and attorney-client contracts for fees. Although New York was the first to enact the Field Code of 1848, repealing fee regulation, the American Bar Association did not approve contingency fees until 1908. For a discussion of retainer agreements, see Brickman, "Contingent Fees without Contingencies," 49, and Leubsdorf, "American Rule on Attorney Fee Recovery," 9–10.

18. This is not an argument for whether tort law should protect emotional or relational interests. For such a discussion, see Finley, "Break in the Silence," 41; Bender, "Lawyer's Primer," 3; and Delgado, "Words That Wound."

19. *New York Times Index* 21, 2nd ed., lists a variety of cases brought from such places as Waterbury, Connecticut, to Omaha, Nebraska.

20. See Friedman, "Rights of Passage," 649.

21. The settlements in cases were growing larger toward the turn of the century, a fact that prompted the law's repeal in many jurisdictions. See *Mohn v. Tingley*, 191 Cal. 470, 217 P. 733 (1923) (75,000 compensatory and

25,000 punitive); *Overton v. Overton*, 121 Okla. 1, 246 P. 1095 (1926) (150,000 reduced to 60,000); and *Woodhouse v. Woodhouse*, 99 Vt. 91, 130 A. 758 (1925) (465,000 reduced to 125,000). For a longer list of cases, including cases calling for the repeal of criminal conversation, see Weinstein, "Adultery, Law, and the State."

22. These words were frequently used to describe the suffering of the husband in a variety of criminal conversation and alienation of affections cases. Juries often sympathized with plaintiffs in such cases, awarding huge settlements that would bankrupt the third party.

23. Korobkin, *Criminal Conversations*, 51. Korobkin in *Criminal Conversations* and Fox in *Trials of Intimacy* frame their interventions in law and literature (Korobkin) and history (Fox) around this legal narrative of adultery. Korobkin's valuable study argues against readings of the law as a site of super-rationalism set against a world of emotion and experience outside it, but the study doesn't go far enough in explaining how sentimental narratives may become an unlikely site of power for those men who wield them deftly.

24. *Smith v. Meyers*, 52 Neb. 70, 71 N.W. 1006. For a discussion of similar rulings and an analysis of alienation of affection and criminal conversation cases and their histories, see Marshall Davidson, "Thief Goes Free," 629.

25. 41 C.J.S. Crim Con., § 249.

26. Quoted in Stone, *Road to Divorce*, 232.

27. Ibid. See also Cott, "Divorce and the Changing Status of Women," 600 n. 44. Cott cites three early cases of criminal conversation that were used as a means of obtaining a divorce.

28. This literary device has a long history in the adultery novel. See Tanner, *Adultery in the Novel.*

29. Model Penal Code, § 213 (1962). The code employs this word to make reference to a variety of sexual "transgressions": adultery, prostitution, "homosexual" activity, rape, and coercion among them.

30. For a discussion of the sexual evidence offered in the scientific community at this time, see Russett, *Sexual Science*. This period also saw the rise of sexologists and degeneracy theorists who were intent on establishing the "facts" of sexual identity. To name just a few: Nordau, *Degeneration*; Ellis, *Psychology of Sex* and *Man and Woman*; and Krafft-Ebing, *Psychopathia Sexualis.*

For more recent scholarship on sexual science at the turn of the century, see Tom Lutz, *American Nervousness*; Birken, *Consuming Desire*; and Haller and Haller, *Physician and Sexuality*. I might also note that Cather was not immune from the rage toward sexual definition. In her early years as a journalist reporting on the trials of Oscar Wilde, she labeled his situation "the beginning of a national expiation" and used the occasion to display her own revulsion against such "sins." See Cather, *Kingdom of Art*, 389. For readings of Cather's sexuality, see Sedgwick "Across Genders, Across Sexualities"; Butler, "'Dangerous Crossing'"; Lee, *Willa Cather: A Life Saved Up*; and O'Brien, *Willa Cather: The Emerging Voice*.

31. The *OED*, 2nd edition, traces the definition of *conversation* as "sexual intercourse or intimacy" back to Shakespeare's *Richard III* and "his Conversation with Shores Wife." I do not want to suggest that what was considered adultery did not happen, but rather that quite often what was counted as sex was never an objective given.

32. For a discussion of circumstantial evidence in law and literature, see Welsh, *Strong Representations*.

33. *Smith v. Meyers*, 52 Neb. 70, 71 N.W. 1006.

34. Ibid.

35. Marshall Davidson, "Thief Goes Free," 656.

Chapter Four

1. Henry James, *Golden Bowl*, 134. Subsequent references will be cited in the text.

2. Brudney, "Knowledge and Silence," 397. See also Nussbaum, "Flawed Crystals."

3. Warren and Brandeis, "Right to Privacy," 205. "The remedies for an invasion of the right of privacy are also suggested by those administered in the law of defamation, and in the law of literary and artistic property, namely: 1. An action of tort for damages in all cases. Even in the absence of special damages, substantial compensation could be allowed for injury to feelings as in the action of slander and libel" (219).

4. Shamir, "Hawthorne's Romance," 746–79.

5. Ryan, *Vanishing Subject*, 6.

6. Person, *Henry James and the Suspense of Masculinity*, 152.

7. Pfister and Schnog, "Introduction," *Inventing the Psychological*, 40. For more on James's "queer modernity," see Haralson, *Henry James and Queer Modernity*.

8. For more on Adam Smith and the "ends of economics," see Dupré and Gagnier's article by that title.

9. Seltzer, *Art of Power*, 72.

10. Bodily injury, not mental injury, is Locke's subject of protection; in James's novel it is not solely property but also feeling that is incessantly scrutinized and classified for protection.

11. Maggie's maternal body is seemingly transparent. The principino, a muted presence in the novel, is evidence of the consummation of her marriage to Amerigo; moreover, the presence of the principino secures Maggie and Adam their time together.

12. Henry James, *Bostonians*, 370. For a discussion of marriage in *The Golden Bowl*, see Alberti, "Economics of Love"; Boone, "Modernist Maneuverings"; and Stein, *After the Vows*, 140–58.

13. See Boone, "Modernist Maneuverings," 385, for a discussion of the ambiguities of the novel's ending; see also Yeazell, "Difficulty of Ending," 100–130.

14. Williams, *Marxism and Literature*, 128–29.

15. "A perception about human sentience is, through labor, projected into the freestanding artifact (chair, coat, poem, telescope, medical vaccine), and in turn the artifact refers back to human sentience, either directly extending its powers and acuity (poem, telescope) or indirectly extending its powers and acuity by eliminating its aversiveness (chair, vaccine). The first has no meaning without the second: the human act of projection assumes the artifact's consequent act of reciprocation" (Scarry, *Body in Pain*, 307).

16. The article was written in response to media gossip that Warren found personally intrusive. See Ernst and Schwartz, *Privacy*, and Brook Thomas, *American Literary Realism and the Failed Promise of Contract*, 56–62. For a discussion of copyright and literary property in the case upon which Warren and Brandeis built their own, see *Folsom v. Marsh*, Circuit Court, D. MA, Oct. Term (1841).

17. See Brooks and Gewirtz, *Melodramatic Imagination*, chapter 6, on James, and Stein, *After the Vows*, 156. For a discussion of James's authorial subjectivity, "determined less by the refinements of his consciousness than by the imperatives of his unconscious fantasy," see Silverman, *Male Subjectivities at the Margins*, 157–81.

18. See Brudney, "Knowledge and Silence"; Holland, *Expense of Vision*, 331–49; and Walton, *Disruption of the Feminine*.

19. Book review of *The Golden Bowl*, *Nation* 26 (Jan. 1905): 74.

20. See Cannon, *Bodily Changes*, 66–67; Magruder, "Mental and Emotional Disturbance," 1034–67; Goodrich, "Emotional Disturbance as Legal Damage," 497–513; and Harper and McNeely, "Basis for Liability."

21. Although the notion of the "written body" is seminal to psychoanalytic readings of texts, it was the work of empiricist psychologists, not Freud, that attracted the attention of writers at the turn of the century. See Ryan, *Vanishing Subject*, 1–20. It should come as no surprise, however, that sexual evidence and sexual damages were central to the culture's understanding of psychic injury. This was also the period of the rise of sexologists and degeneracy theorists, including Nordau, Ellis, and Krafft-Ebing.

22. Lutz, *American Nervousness*, 250. Lutz documents writers and thinkers at the turn of the century for whom psychic duress was a daily condition: Howells, Dreiser, Wharton, Roosevelt, Mitchell, Norris, Gilman, and Henry Adams, to name a few. Lutz argues that neurasthenia was

a way for its sufferers to transform their perceptions of their own social, personal, and cultural value. See also Posnock, *Trial of Curiosity*, for a valuable discussion of the James brothers. Griffin argues in her book *Historical Eye* that in James, "mental events cannot be understood apart from their complex personal contexts" (12). See also Holly, *Intensely Family*, chapter 2.

Chapter Five

1. Bjorkman, *Voices of Tomorrow*, 296
2. Trilling, "Morality of Inertia," 138.
3. Irving Howe, *Edith Wharton*, 5.
4. Cooper, "Review," 312.
5. *North American Review* 195 (Jan. 1912).
6. Scarry, *Body in Pain*, 164–65.
7. See Aristotle, *Poetics.*
8. Book review of *Ethan Frome*, *Nation* 93 (Oct. 26, 1911): 405. For a historical inquiry into spectacles of pain, see Halttunen "Humanitarianism and the Pornography of Pain," 303. For a discussion of the emotive in literature, see Oxenhandler, "Changing Concept of Literary Emotion."
9. Newfield, *Ivy and Industry*, 91.
10. The list of works on sympathy and sentiment are vast. To name just a few that have not yet been mentioned in the book: Mullan, *Sentiment and Sociability*; Barker-Benfield, *Culture of Sensibility*; Marshall, *Surprising Effects of Sympathy*; and Crain, *American Sympathy.*
11. Douglas argues in *Feminization of American Culture* that such novelists replaced clergy as the voices of moral authority in nineteenth-century America. It would be too long a footnote to detail all the twists the debate has taken since Douglas's characterization of this literature. Especially prominent voices in the debate shortly following the publication of Douglas's book were critics Nina Baym and Jane Tompkins. See Nina Baym, *American Women Writers,* and Tompkins, *Sensational Designs.*
12. See Brodhead, *Cultures of Letters*, 29.
13. Wharton, *Ethan Frome*, 1. Subsequent references will be cited in the text. See Thomson, *Extraordinary Bodies*, for a discussion of the characterization of disabled figures in literature.
14. Of course, hysteria has been considered the female malady of the nineteenth century. See Showalter, *Female Malady* and *Hystories*, and Kahane, *Passions of the Voice.*
15. Wolff, "Hot Ethan, Cold Ethan." For Wharton, imagining a change in the site of sentiment not only constitutes a self-willed autobiographical disguise (as Wolff suggests), but as Edwin Bjorkman's early review of the novel implies, it may also socially "incite." For more on masculinity and Wharton, see Farland, "*Ethan Frome* and the 'Springs' of Masculinity."
16. Lens, *Labor Wars*, 172.

17. Wharton would leave the United States for France. Although her biographers have little to say about the social milieu in the United States that may have encouraged Wharton's stay abroad, it is clear that the events that would become *Ethan Frome* were in her thoughts. Wolff explains that Wharton's first writing in French became the beginning of *Ethan Frome*. See Wolff, *Feast of Words*, 158–59. See also Benstock, *No Gifts from Chance*, for discussion of Wharton's life abroad.

18. Karl Marx, *Communist Manifesto*, 57–58.

19. Abel has called one form of the secularization of suffering, suffering that has come to require material compensation, a "market in sadomasochism" ("Critique of American Tort Law," 281). Scarry describes the product liability trial as materializing "the counterfactual by endowing it with the material form of compensation" (*Body in Pain*, 299).

20. This is not to suggest that distrust of the jury system was solely a recent phenomenon, but that it emerged with increasing vigor at this time. For a brief history of the jury system, see Friedman, *American Law*, 251.

21. Cardozo, *Judicial Process*, 63. Cardozo discusses the reasonable-man standard, which required juries to consult their lifestyles and beliefs. See also Hayden, "Cultural Norms as Law," 45.

22. Gregory, "Proximate Cause in Negligence," 41.

23. Gerald Graff, *Professing Literature*, 121–44.

24. For a more detailed summary of the social scientists' mania for facts, see Shi, *Facing Facts*, 66–78.

25. Sumner, *Forgotten Man*, 426, 433. Readers of sentimental literature "lose the power to recognize truth" (Sumner, "Scientific Attitude of Mind," 1).

26. Ross, *Social Control*, 301.

27. Calvin Thomas, "Literature and Personality," 305.

28. See Shumway, *Creating American Civilization*, 28, and Vanderbilt, *American Literature and the Academy*.

29. J. M. Robertson, "The Theory and Practice of Criticism," quoted in Dingle, *Science and Literary Criticism*, 9.

30. See also Spingarn, "New Criticism" and *Criticism in America*.

31. Hatfield, "Scholarship and the Commonwealth," 391.

32. Spingarn lamented: "What dull creatures those college professors are whenever they talk about art" ("New Criticism," 2).

33. Perry, "Fiction as College Study."

34. American writers, notes Kermit Vanderbilt in his study of the academy, "had only begun to be studied in the colleges, few histories of our infant literature had been attempted, and scholars' interest in the study of our nation's authors had no sense of community within the academy" (*American Literature and the Academy*, 3).

Epilogue

1. I am thinking here of Goux, *Symbolic Economies*: "The original alienation (pain, loss, trace), the implied eclipse, repression, or oppression is the foundation of the world of values and meaning" (60).

2. "Calumet Shop Injury Reports for 1901–1906." The injuries ranged from mashed hands and lost fingers that kept men from work for several days to severe scalp wounds and blinding injuries that disabled workers for life. See also Lightner, "Construction Labor."

3. *Railway Conductor* 5, no. 2 (Feb.1, 1889): 57–58.

4. Searle, "Cold Charity," 179.

5. Baynton, "Disability and the Justification of Inequality," 22.

6. Thomson, *Extraordinary Bodies*, 49.

7. Kudlick, "Disability History," 766.

8. See Thomson, *Extraordinary Bodies*, 1–51.

9. The complete unblushing male is middle class, white, northern, Protestant, urban, and heterosexual, according to Goffman, *Stigma*.

Bibliography

Aaron, Daniel. *The Unwritten War: American Writers and the Civil War.* New York: Alfred A. Knopf, 1973.

Abel, Richard. "A Critique of American Tort Law." In *Critical Legal Studies*, edited by Allan C. Hutchinson, 273–89. New York: Rowman & Littlefield, 1986.

Agnew, Jean-Christophe. "The Consuming Vision of Henry James." In *The Culture of Consumption: Critical Essays in American History, 1880–1980*, edited by T. J. Jackson Lears and Richard Wightman Fox, 65–100. New York: Pantheon, 1983.

Aichele, Gary J. *Oliver Wendell Holmes Jr.: Soldier, Scholar, Judge*. Boston: Twayne Publishers, 1989.

Alberti, John. "The Economics of Love: The Production of Value in *The Golden Bowl.*" *Henry James Review* 12 (1991): 9–19.

Anderson, Godfrey Tryggve, and Donald Lee Anderson. "Nostalgia and Malingering in the Military during the Civil War." *Perspectives in Biology and Medicine* 28, no. 1 (Fall 1984): 156–66.

Aristotle. *The Poetics. "Longinus" on the Sublime; Demetrius on Style.* Cambridge: Harvard University Press, 1973.

Arms, George. "The Literary Background of Howells's Social Criticism." *American Literature* 14, no. 3 (1942): 260–76.

Atkinson, Edward. *The Industrial Progress of the Nation: Consumption Unlimited, Production Unlimited*. New York: G. P. Putnam and Sons, 1890.

Bandes, Susan A., ed. *The Passions of Law*. New York: New York University Press, 1999.

Barker-Benfield, G. J. *The Culture of Sensibility: Sex and Society in Eighteenth-Century Britain*. Chicago: University of Chicago Press, 1992.

Barnes, Elizabeth. *States of Sympathy: Seduction and Democracy in the American Novel*. New York: Columbia University Press, 1997.

Barnett, James Harwood. *Divorce and the American Divorce Novel, 1850–1937: A Study in the Literary Reflections of Social Influences*. New York: Russell & Russell, 1939.

Bartlett, Katherine T., and Rosanne Kennedy, eds. *Feminist Legal Theory: Readings in Law and Gender.* San Francisco: Westview Press, 1991.
Basch, Norma. "The Emerging Legal History of Women in the United States: Property, Divorce, and the Constitution." *Signs* 12, no. 1 (Autumn 1986): 97–117.
———. *Framing American Divorce: From the Revolutionary Generation to the Victorians.* Berkeley: University of California Press, 1999.
Baym, Max I. *A History of Literary Aesthetics in America.* New York: Frederick Ungar Publishing, 1973.
Baym, Nina. *American Women Writers and the Work of History, 1790–1860.* New Brunswick, N.J.: Rutgers University Press, 1995.
———. "Melodramas of Beset Manhood: How Theories of American Fiction Exclude Women Authors." In *The New Feminist Criticism: Essays on Women, Literature, and Theory*, edited by Elaine Showalter, 62–80. New York: Pantheon, 1985.
———. *Novels, Readers, and Reviewers: Responses to Fiction in Antebellum America.* Ithaca, N.Y.: Cornell University Press, 1984.
Baynton, Douglas G. "Disability and the Justification of Inequality in American History." In *The New Disability History: American Perspectives*, edited by Paul K. Longmore and Lauri Umansky, 32–57. New York: New York University Press, 2001.
Beard, Charles, and Mary Beard. *The Rise of American Civilization, 1874–1948.* 2 vols. New York: Macmillan, 1927.
Bederman, Gail. *Manliness and Civilization: A Cultural History of Gender and Race in the United States: 1880–1917.* Chicago: University of Chicago Press, 1995.
Bell, Michael Davitt. *The Problem of American Realism: Studies in the Cultural History of a Literary Idea.* Chicago: University of Chicago Press, 1993.
Bellard, Alfred. *Gone for Soldier: The Civil War Memoirs of Private Alfred Bellard.* Boston: Little, Brown, 1975.
Bender, Karen. "A Lawyer's Primer on Feminist Theory and Tort." *Journal of Legal Education* 38 (1988): 3–37.
Bending, Lucy. *The Representation of Bodily Pain in Late-Nineteenth-Century English Culture.* New York: Oxford University Press, 2000.
Bendixen, Alfred, and Annette Zilversmit. *Edith Wharton: New Critical Essays.* New York: Garland Publishers, 1992.
Bennett, George N. "Introduction." In *A Modern Instance*, by William Dean Howells. Bloomington: University of Indiana Press, 1977.
Benstock, Shari. *No Gifts from Chance: A Biography of Edith Wharton.* New York: Scribner's, 1994.
Berger, Maurice, Brian Wallace, and Simon Watson, eds. *Constructing Masculinity.* New York: Routledge, 1995.

Berk, Gerald. *Alternative Tracks: The Constitution of American Industrial Order, 1865–1917*. Baltimore: Johns Hopkins University Press, 1994.
Berlant, Lauren. "Poor Eliza." *American Literature* 70, no. 3 (1998): 635–68.
———. *The Queen of America Goes to Washington City*. Durham, N.C.: Duke University Press, 1997.
———. "The Subject of True Feeling: Pain, Privacy, and Politics." In *Cultural Pluralism, Identity, and the Law*, edited by Austin Sarat and Thomas R. Kearns, 49–84. Amherst Series in Law, Jurisprudence, and Social Thought. Ann Arbor: University of Michigan Press, 1999.
Bersani, Leo. *A Future for Astyanax: Character and Desire in Literature*. Boston: Little, Brown, 1976.
Binder, Guyora, and Robert Weisberg, eds. *Literary Criticisms of Law*. Princeton, N.J.: Princeton University Press, 2000.
Birken, Laurence. *Consuming Desire: Sexual Science and the Emergence of a Culture of Abundance, 1871–1914*. Ithaca, N.Y.: Cornell University Press, 1988.
Bishop, Joel Prentiss. *Commentaries on the Law of Marriage and Divorce*. Vol. 2. Boston: Little, Brown, 1881.
Bjorkman, Edwin. *Voices of Tomorrow: Critical Studies of the New Spirit in Literature*. New York: Mitchell Kennerly, 1913.
Blake, Nelson. *The Road to Reno: A History of Divorce in the United States*. New York: Macmillan, 1962.
Blanton, Smiley, and Woodbridge Riley. "Shell Shocks of Family Life." *Forum* (Nov. 1929): 282–87.
Bledstein, Burton J. *The Culture of Professionalism: The Middle Class and the Development of Higher Education in America*. New York: Norton, 1976.
Bohlke, Brent L., ed. *Willa Cather in Person: Interviews, Speeches, and Letters*. Lincoln: University of Nebraska Press, 1986.
Boone, Joseph A. "Modernist Maneuverings in the Marriage Plot." *PMLA* 101 (1986): 374–88.
Bourke, Joanna. *Dismembering the Male: Men's Bodies, Britain, and the Great War*. Chicago: University of Chicago Press, 1996.
Brandeis, Louis, and Samuel Warren. "The Right to Privacy." *Harvard Law Review* 4 (1890): 193–220.
Brickman, Lester. "Contingent Fees without Contingencies: Hamlet without the Prince of Denmark?" *UCLA Law Review* 37 (1989): 49–74.
Brodhead, Richard. *Cultures of Letters: Scenes of Reading and Writing in Nineteenth-Century America*. Chicago: University of Chicago Press, 1993.
Brooks, Peter, and Paul Gewirtz, eds. *Law's Stories: Narrative and Rhetoric in the Law*. New Haven, Conn.: Yale University Press, 1996.
———. *The Melodramatic Imagination: Balzac, Henry James, Melodrama, and the Mode of Excess*. New Haven, Conn.: Yale University Press, 1976.

Brown, Gillian. *Domestic Individualism: Imagining Self in Nineteenth-Century America*. Berkeley: University of California Press, 1990.

Brown, Wendy. *States of Injury: Power and Freedom in Late Modernity*. Princeton, N.J.: Princeton University Press, 1995.

Browne, Irving. "Oral Cruelty as a Grounds for Divorce." *Central Law Journal* 46 (1898): 81–86.

Bruckner, Pascal. *The Tears of the White Man: Compassion as Contempt*. New York: Free Press, 1986.

Brudney, Daniel. "Knowledge and Silence: *The Golden Bowl* and Moral Philosophy." *Critical Inquiry* 16 (Winter 1990): 397–437.

Bruhm, Steven. *Gothic Bodies: The Politics of Pain in Romantic Fiction*. Philadelphia: University of Pennsylvania Press, 1995.

Burbick, Joan. *Healing the Republic: The Language of Health and the Culture of Nationalism in Nineteenth-Century America*. New York: Cambridge University Press, 1992.

Burke, Edmund. *A Philosophical Enquiry into the Origin of Our Ideas of the Sublime and Beautiful*. 1757. Reprint, edited by J. T. Boulton, New York: Columbia University Press, 1958.

Burr, Anna Robeson. *Weir Mitchell: His Life and Letters*. New York: Duffield, 1929.

Butler, Judith. "'Dangerous Crossing': Willa Cather's Masculine Names." In *Bodies That Matter: On the Discursive Limits of "Sex,"* 143–66. New York: Routledge, 1993.

———. *Excitable Speech: A Politics of the Performative*. New York: Routledge, 1997.

Cady, Edwin H. "The Neuroticism of William Dean Howells." *PMLA* 61 (1946): 229–38.

———. *The Road to Realism*. Syracuse, N.Y.: Syracuse University Press, 1956.

Calhoun, Cheshire, and Robert C. Solomon. *What Is an Emotion? Classical Readings in Philosophical Psychology*. Oxford: Oxford University Press, 1984.

Calhoun, J. Theodore. "Nostalgia as a Disease of Field Service." In *Medical and Surgical Reporter* 11 (1864).

———. "Rough Notes of an Army Surgeon's Experience during the Geat Rebellion." *Medical and Surgical Reporter* 10, no. 17 (Aug. 22, 1863): 229–30.

"Calumet Shop Injury Reports for 1901–1906." Pullman Archives, Newberry Library, Chicago, Ill.

Cameron, Sharon. *Thinking in Henry James*. Chicago: University of Chicago Press, 1989.

Cannon, Walter B. *Bodily Changes in Pain, Hunger, Fear, and Rage*. Boston: Charles T. Branford, 1953.

Caplan, Eric. *Mind Games: American Culture and the Birth of Psychotherapy.* Berkeley: University of California Press, 1998.

Cardozo, Benjamin. *Law and Literature and Other Essays and Addresses.* New York: Harcourt Brace, 1931.

———. *The Nature of the Judicial Process.* New Haven, Conn.: Yale University Press, 1991.

Carlin, Deborah. *Cather, Canon, and the Politics of Reading.* Amherst: University of Massachusetts Press, 1992.

Carnes, Mark C., and Clyde Griffen, eds. *Meanings for Manhood: Constructions of Masculinity in Victorian America.* Chicago: University of Chicago Press, 1990.

Cassidy, Jessie J. *The Legal Status of Women.* New York: National American Woman Suffrage Association, 1897.

Cather, Willa. *Kingdom of Art: Willa Cather's First Principles and Critical Statements, 1893–1896.* Edited by Bernice Slote. Lincoln: University of Nebraska Press, 1967.

———. *A Lost Lady.* 1923. Reprint, New York: Vintage, 1990.

———. *Not under Forty.* New York: Knopf, 1936.

Chamallas, Martha. "The Architecture of Bias: Deep Structures in Tort Law." *University of Pennsylvania Law Review* 146 (1998): 463–531.

———. "Women, Mothers, and the Law of Fright: A History." *Michigan Law Review* 88 (1990): 814–64.

———. "Writing about Sexual Harassment: A Guide to the Literature." *UCLA Women's Law Journal* 4 (1993): 37–58.

Chandler, Alfred D. "The Organization of Manufacturing and Transportation." In *Economic Changes in the Civil War Era,* edited by David T. Gilchrist and W. David Lewis, 137–51. Greenville, Del.: Eleutherian Mills-Hagley Foundation, 1965.

———. *Scale and Scope: The Dynamics of Industrial Capitalism.* Cambridge: Belknap Press, 1990.

———. *The Visible Hand: The Managerial Revolution in American Business.* Cambridge: Belknap Press, 1977.

———, ed. *The Railroad, the Nation's First Big Business: Sources and Readings.* New York: Harcourt Brace and World, 1965.

Chapman, Mary, and Glenn Hendler, eds. *Sentimental Men: Masculinity and the Politics of Affect in American Culture.* Berkeley: University of California Press, 1999.

Charvat, William. *The Profession of Authorship in America, 1800–1870: The Papers of William Charvat.* Columbus: Ohio State University Press, 1968.

Chisholm, Daniel. *The Civil War Notebook of Daniel Chisholm: A Chronicle of Daily Life in the Union Army, 1864–1865.* Edited by W. Springer Menge and J. August Shimrak. New York: Ballantine Books, 1989.

Chused, Richard. *Private Acts in Public Places: A Social History of Divorce in*

the Formative Era of American Family Law. Philadelphia: University of Pennsylvania Press, 1994.
Civil War through the Camera. Subscription series, Archives of Huntington Library, Pasadena, Calif.
Clark, Michael, and Catherine Crawford, eds. *Legal Medicine in History*. New York: Cambridge University Press, 1994.
Clinton, Catherine, and Nina Silber, eds. *Divided Houses: Gender and the Civil War*. Oxford: Oxford University Press, 1992.
Cooper, Frederic Taber. "Review." *Bookman* 34, no. 3 (1911): 312.
Cotkin, George. *William James: Public Philosopher*. Baltimore: Johns Hopkins University Press, 1990.
Cott, Nancy. "Divorce and the Changing Status of Women in Eighteenth-Century Massachusetts." *William and Mary Quarterly* 33 (1976): 596–610.
Crain, Caleb. *American Sympathy: Men, Friendship, and Literature in the New Nation*. New Haven, Conn.: Yale University Press, 2001.
Crane, Stephen. "*The Monster*." In *Maggie a Girl of the Streets and Other Stories*. New York: Signet, 1995.
———. *The Red Badge of Courage*. 1895. Reprint, New York: Dover Editions, 1990.
———. *Wounds in the Rain: War Stories*. New York: Frederick A. Stokes, 1900.
Crowley, John W. *The Black Heart's Truth: The Early Career of W. D. Howells*. Chapel Hill: University of North Carolina Press, 1985.
Cvetkovich, Ann. *Mixed Feelings: Feminism, Mass Culture, and Victorian Sensationalism*. New Brunswick, N.J.: Rutgers University Press, 1992.
Da Costa, William. "On Irritable Heart: A Clinical Study of Forms of Functional Cardiac Disorder and Its Consequences." *American Journal of the Medical Sciences* 61 (Jan. 1871): 17–52.
Davidson, Cathy N. *Revolution and the Word: The Rise of the Novel in America*. New York: Oxford University Press, 1986.
Davidson, Marshall. "The Thief Goes Free: Stealing Love in Tennessee." *Tennessee Law Review* 56 (1989): 651–60.
Davis, Cynthia J. *Bodily and Narrative Forms: The Influence of Medicine on American Literature, 1845–1915*. Stanford, Calif.: Stanford University Press, 2000.
Davis, Lennard J., ed. *The Disability Studies Reader*. New York: Routledge, 1997.
Dawes, Rufus R. *Service with the Sixth Wisconsin Volunteers*. Edited by Alan T. Nolan. 1890. Reprint, Madison: State Historical Society of Wisconsin, 1962.
Dean, Eric. *Shook over Hell: Post-Traumatic Stress, Vietnam, and the Civil War*. Cambridge: Harvard University Press, 1997.

Delgado, Richard. "Words That Wound: A Tort Action for Racial Insults, Epithets, and Name Calling." In *Words That Wound: Critical Race Theory, Assaultive Speech, and the First Amendment*, edited by Mari J. Matsuda, Charles R. Lawrence III, Richard Delgado, and Kimberle Williams Crenshaw, 89–110. San Francisco: Westview Press, 1993.

de Moulin, Daniel. "A Historical-Phenomenological Study of Bodily Pain in Western Man." *Bulletin of the History of Medicine* 48, no. 4 (1974): 540–70.

Dent, R. W. *Proverbial Language in English Drama Exclusive of Shakespeare, 1495–1616*. Berkeley: University of California Press, 1984.

Dew, Charles B. "Rally Round the Flag." *New York Times*, Feb. 27, 2000, 29.

Diffley, Kathleen. *Where My Heart Is Turning Ever: Civil War Stories and Constitutional Reform, 1861–1876*. Athens: University of Georgia Press, 1992.

Dimock, Wai Chee. *Residues of Justice: Literature, Law, Philosophy*. Berkeley: University of California Press, 1996.

Dingle, Herbert. *Science and Literary Criticism*. New York: Thomas Nelson and Sons, 1949.

Ditzion, Sydney. *Marriage, Morals, and Sex in America*. New York: Basic Books, 1969.

Donovan, Frank P., Jr. *The Railroad in Literature: A Brief Survey of Railroad Fiction, Poetry, Songs, Biography, Essays, Travel, and Drama in the English Language, Particularly Emphasizing Its Place in American Literature*. Boston: Railway and Locomotive Historical Society, 1940.

Douglas, Ann. *The Feminization of American Culture*. New York: Knopf, 1977.

Drinka, George. *The Birth of Neurosis: Myth, Malady, and the Victorians*. New York: Simon & Schuster, 1984.

Dupré, John, and Regenia Gagnier. "The Ends of Economics." In *The New Criticism: Studies at the Intersection of Literature and Economics*, edited by Martha Woodmansee and Mark Osteen, 175–89. New York: Routledge, 1999.

Edel, Leon. *Henry James, A Life*. New York: Harper & Row, 1985.

Eichelberger, Clayton. *Published Comment on William Dean Howells through 1920: A Research Bibliography*. Boston: G. K. Hall, 1976.

Eiselein, Gregory. *Literature and Humanitarian Reform in the Civil War Era*. Bloomington: Indiana University Press, 1996.

Eliot, Charles W. *Educational Reform: Essays and Addresses*. New York: Century, 1909.

Ellis, Havelock. *Man and Woman: A Study of Human Secondary Sexual Characters (Sex, Marriage, and Society)*. 6th ed. London: A. and C. Black, 1926.

———. *Studies in the Psychology of Sex: The Evolution of Modesty, the Phenomena of Sexual Periodicity, Auto-Eroticism*. New York: Random House, 1936.

Ellison, Julie. *Cato's Tears and the Making of Anglo-American Emotion*. Chicago: University of Chicago Press, 1999.

———. "The Gender of Transparency: Masculinity and the Conduct of Life." *American Literary History* 4, no. 4 (1992): 584–606.

Epperly Letters. Gilder Lehrman Collection, on deposit at the New-York Historical Society, New York City (GLC 2715).

Ernst, Morris L., and Alan U. Schwartz. *Privacy: The Right to Be Let Alone*. New York: Macmillan, 1962.

Fahs, Alice. *The Imagined Civil War: Popular Literature of the North and South, 1861–1865*. Chapel Hill: University of North Carolina Press, 2000.

Faller, John I., and Leo W. Faller. *Dear Folks at Home: The Civil War Letters of Leo and John Faller with an Account of Andersonville*. Edited by Milton E. Flower. Carlisle, Pa.: Cumberland County Historical Society and Hamilton Library Association, 1963.

Farland, Maria Magdalena. "*Ethan Frome* and the 'Springs' of Masculinity." *Modern Fiction Studies* 42, no. 4 (Winter 1996): 707–29.

Farrell, Kirby. *Post-traumatic Culture: Injury and Interpretation in the Nineties*. Baltimore: Johns Hopkins University Press, 1998.

Feinberg, Joel. *Harm to Others*. Oxford: Oxford University Press, 1984.

Felman, Shoshana. *Testimony: Crises of Witnessing in Literature, Psychology, and History*. New York: Routledge, 1992.

———. *Writing and Madness: Literature, Philosophy, Psychoanalysis*. Ithaca, N.Y.: Cornell University Press, 1985.

Ferenczi, Sándor. *Psychoanalysis and the War Neuroses*. London: International Psycho-Analytic Press, Vienna, 1921.

Ferguson, Robert, A. *Law and Letters in American Culture*. Cambridge: Harvard University Press, 1984.

———. "The Limits of Enlightenment." In *The Cambridge History of American Literature, 1590–1820*, edited by Sacvan Bercovitch, 496–537. New York: Cambridge University Press, 1994.

Fertig, L. "Maurice Thompson and *A Modern Instance*." *American Literature* 38 (1966): 103–11.

Finley, Karen. "A Break in the Silence: Including Women's Issues in a Torts Course." *Yale Journal of Law and Feminism* 1 (1989): 41–73.

Fisher, Philip. *Hard Facts: Setting and Form in the American Novel*. Oxford: Oxford University Press, 1985.

Fishlow, Albert. *American Railroads and the Transformation of the Antebellum Economy*. Cambridge: Harvard University Press, 1965.

Fisk, Wilbur. *Hard Marching Every Day: The Civil War Letters of Private Wilbur Fisk, 1861–1865*. Edited by Emil Rosenblatt and Ruth Rosenblatt. Lawrence: University of Kansas Press, 1983.

Fite, Emerson David. *Social and Industrial Conditions in the North during the Civil War.* New York: Macmillan, 1910.
Fogel, Robert. *Railroads and American Economic Growth: Essays in Econometric History.* Baltimore: Johns Hopkins University Press, 1964.
Foucault, Michel. *Discipline and Punish: The Birth of the Prison.* Translated by Alan Sheridan. New York: Vintage, 1979.
———. *Madness and Civilization: A History of Insanity in the Age of Reason.* New York: Random House, 1965.
———. "Nietzsche, Genealogy, History." In *Language, Counter-Memory, Practice: Selected Essays and Interviews,* edited by Donald F. Bouchard, 139–64. New York: Cornell University Press, 1980.
Fox, Richard Wightman. "Intimacy on Trial: Cultural Meanings of the Beecher-Tilton Affair." In *The Power of Culture,* edited by Richard Wightman Fox and T. J. Jackson Lears, 103–43. Chicago: University of Chicago Press, 1993.
———. *Trials of Intimacy: Love and Loss in the Beecher-Tilton Scandal.* Chicago: University of Chicago Press, 1999.
Fredrickson, George M. *The Inner Civil War: Northern Intellectuals and the Crisis of Union.* New York: Harper & Row, 1965.
Freedman, Jonathan. *Professions of Taste: Henry James, British Aestheticism, and Commodity Culture.* Stanford, Calif.: Stanford University Press, 1990.
Freeman, Kimberly. "The 'Enormous Fact' of American Life: Divorce in W. D. Howells's *A Modern Instance.*" *American Literary Realism* 36 (Fall 2003): 65–85.
Freud, Sigmund. "On the Grounds for Detaching a Particular Syndrome from Neurasthenia under the Description of 'Anxiety Neurosis.'" In *Standard Edition of the Complete Psychological Works of Sigmund Freud,* vol. 3, edited by James Strachey. London: Hogarth Press, 1962.
———. "Psychoanalysis and War Neurosis." In *Character and Culture,* edited by Philip Rieff. New York: Macmillan, 1963.
Fried, Michael. *Realism, Writing, Disfiguration: On Thomas Eakins and Stephen Crane.* Chicago: University of Chicago Press, 1987.
Friedman, Lawrence M. *A History of American Law.* New York: Simon & Schuster, 1973.
———. "Rights of Passage: Divorce Law in Historical Perspective." *Oregon Law Review* 63 (1984): 649–69.
———. *Total Justice.* New York: Russell Sage Foundation, 1985.
Friedman, Lawrence M., and Jack Ladinsky. "Social Change and the Law of Industrial Accidents." *Columbia Law Review* 50 (1967): 50–82.
Gilbert, James B. *Work without Salvation: American Intellectuals and Industrial Alienation, 1880–1910.* Baltimore: Johns Hopkins University Press, 1977.

Gilchrist, David, and David W. Lewis. *Economic Change in the Civil War.* Greenville, Del.: Eleutherian Mills-Hagley Foundation, 1965.

Gilman, Sander. *Hysteria beyond Freud.* Berkeley: University of California Press, 1993.

Girgus, Sam B. "Bartley Hubbard, the Rebel in Howells's *A Modern Instance.*" *Research Studies* 39 (1971): 315–21.

———. "The New Age of Narcissism: The Sexual Politics of Howells's *A Modern Instance.*" *Mosaic* 19, no. 1 (1986): 33–44.

Glazener, Nancy. *Reading for Realism.* Durham, N.C.: Duke University Press, 1997.

Goffman, Erving. *Stigma: Notes on the Management of Spoiled Identity.* Englewood Cliffs, N.J.: Prentice Hall, 1963.

Goldberg, Jonathan. *Willa Cather and Others.* Durham, N.C.: Duke University Press, 2001.

Goler, Robert. "Loss and the Persistence of Memory: 'The Case of George Delow' and Disabled Civil War Veterans." *Literature and Medicine* 23, no. 1 (Spring 2004): 160–83.

Goodman, Nan. *Shifting the Blame: Literature, Law, and the Theory of Accidents in Nineteenth-Century America.* Princeton, N.J.: Princeton University Press, 1998.

Goodrich, Herbert. "Emotional Disturbance as Legal Damage." *Michigan Law Review* 20 (1921): 497–513.

Gosling, F. G. *Before Freud: Neurasthenia and the American Medical Community, 1870–1910.* Chicago: University of Illinois Press, 1987.

Goux, Jean-Joseph. *Symbolic Economies: After Marx and Freud.* Translated by Jennifer Curtiss Gage. Ithaca, N.Y.: Cornell University Press, 1990.

Graff, Gerald. *Professing Literature.* Chicago: University of Chicago Press, 1987.

Gregory, Charles O. "Proximate Cause in Negligence—A Retreat from 'Rationalization.'" *University of Chicago Law Review* 6 (1938): 36–61.

Griffin, Susan. *The Historical Eye: The Texture of the Visual in Late James.* Boston: Northeastern University Press, 1991.

———. "Scar Texts: Tracing the Marks of Jamesian Masculinity." *Arizona Quarterly* 53, no. 4 (Winter 1997): 61–89.

Griswold, Robert. "Divorce and the Redefinition of Victorian Manhood." In *Meanings for Manhood*, edited by Mark C. Carnes and Clyde Griffith. Chicago: University of Chicago Press, 1990.

———. "The Evolution of the Doctrine of Mental Cruelty in Victorian American Divorce, 1790–1900." *Journal of Social History* 20 (1986): 127–48.

———. *Family and Divorce in California, 1850–1890.* Albany: State University of New York Press, 1982.

———. "Law, Sex, Cruelty, and Divorce in Victorian America," *American Quarterly* 38 (1986): 721–40.

Grossberg, Michael. *Governing the Hearth: Law and the Family in Nineteenth-Century America*. Chapel Hill: University of North Carolina Press, 1985.

Gutman, Herbert G. *Power and Culture: Essays on the American Working Class*. New York: Pantheon Books, 1987.

———. *Work, Culture, and Society in Industrializing America: Essays in American Working Class History*. New York: Vintage, 1976.

Habegger, Alfred. *Gender, Fantasy, and Realism in American Literature*. New York: Columbia University Press, 1982.

Habermas, Jürgen. *The Structural Transformation of the Public Sphere: An Inquiry into a Category of Bourgeois Society*. Translated by Thomas Burger. Cambridge: MIT Press, 1989.

Hale, Nathan G., Jr. *Freud and the Americans: The Beginnings of Psychoanalysis in the United States, 1876–1917*. Oxford: Oxford University Press, 1971.

———. *The Rise and Crisis of Psychoanalysis in the United States*. Oxford: Oxford University Press, 1995.

Halfmann, Ulrich, ed. *Interviews with William Dean Howells*. Arlington: University of Texas Press, 1973.

Hall, Kermit, ed. *American Legal History*. New York: Oxford University Press, 1991.

Haller, John S., Jr., and Robin M. Haller. *The Physician and Sexuality in Victorian America*. Urbana: University of Illinois Press, 1974.

Halttunen, Karen. "Humanitarianism and the Pornography of Pain in Anglo-American Culture." *American Historical Review* (Apr. 1995): 303–35.

Hammond, W. A. "A Few Words about the Nerves." *Galaxy* (Oct. 1868): 493–99.

Hammond, W. A., and Clara Lanza. *Tales of Eccentric Life*. New York: D. Appleton, 1886.

Hans, Valerie P., and Neil Vidmar. *Judging the Jury*. New York: Plenum Press, 1986.

Haralson, Eric. *Henry James and Queer Modernity*. Cambridge: Cambridge University Press, 2003.

Harper, Fowler V., and Mary Coate McNeely. "A Reexamination of the Basis for Liability for Emotional Disturbance." *Wisconsin Law Review* 13 (1938): 426–64.

Haskell, Thomas L. *The Emergence of Professional Social Science: The American Social Science Association and the Nineteenth-Century Crisis of Authority*. Urbana: University of Illinois Press, 1977.

Hatfield, James Taft. "Scholarship and the Commonwealth." *PMLA* 17, no. 1 (1902): 391–409.

Hawthorne, Nathaniel. *The Scarlet Letter.* New York: Rinehart & Co, 1959.
Hayden, Paul T. "Cultural Norms as Law: Tort Law's 'Reasonable Person' Standard of Care." *American Journal of Culture* 15, no. 1 (Spring 1992): 44–55.
Hazel, Harry, and S. L. Lewis. *The Divorce Mill: Realistic Sketches of the South Dakota Divorce Colony.* New York: Mascot Publishing, 1895.
Hedrick, Joan D. *Harriet Beecher Stowe: A Life.* New York: Oxford University Press, 1994.
Hendler, Glenn. *Public Sentiments: Structures of Feeling in Nineteenth-Century American Literature.* Chapel Hill: University of North Carolina Press, 2001.
———. "The Structure of Sentimental Experience." *Yale Journal of Criticism* 12, no. 1 (1999): 145–53.
Herndl, Diane Price. *Invalid Women: Figuring Feminine Illness in American Fiction and Culture, 1840–1940.* Chapel Hill: University of North Carolina Press, 1993.
Higginson, T. W. "A Bit of War Photography." *The Philistine* 3, no. 2 (July 1896): 33–38.
Hindus, Michael S., and Lynne E. Withey. "The Law of Husband and Wife in Nineteenth-Century America: Changing Views of Divorce." In *Women and the Law: A Social Historical Perspective.* Vol. 2 of *Property, Family, and the Legal Profession*, edited by D. Kelly Weisberg, 133–53. Cambridge, Mass.: Schenkman Publishing, 1982.
Hobbes, Thomas. *Leviathan.* 1651. Reprint, New York: E. P. Dutton, 1950.
Hochschild, Arlie Russell. "Emotion Work, Feeling Rules, and Social Structure." *American Journal of Sociology* 85, no. 3 (1979): 551–73.
Hocks, Richard A. *Henry James and Pragmatistic Thought: A Study in the Relationship between the Philosophy of William James and the Literary Art of Henry James.* Chapel Hill: University of North Carolina Press, 1974.
Hoff, Joan. *Law, Gender, and Injustice: A Legal History of United States Women.* New York: New York University Press, 1991.
Holland, Laurence. *The Expense of Vision.* Princeton, N.J.: Princeton University Press, 1964.
Holly, Carol. *Intensely Family: The Inheritance of Family Shame and the Autobiographies of Henry James.* Madison: University of Wisconsin Press, 1995.
Holmes, Oliver Wendell, Jr. *Touched with Fire: Civil War Letters and Diary of Oliver Wendell Holmes Jr., 1861–1864.* Edited by Mark De Wolfe Howe. Cambridge: Harvard University Press, 1946.
Holmes, Oliver Wendell, Sr. "Doings of the Sunbeam." *Atlantic Monthly*, July 1863, 11–12.
Horwitz, Morton. *American Legal Realism.* Baltimore: Johns Hopkins University Press, 1989.

———. *The Transformation of American Law, 1780–1860*. Cambridge: Harvard University Press, 1992.
Howard, June. "What Is Sentimentality?" *American Literary History* 11, no. 1 (1999): 63–81.
Howe, Adrian. "The Problem of Privatized Injuries: Feminist Strategies for Litigation." In *At the Boundaries of Law: Feminism and Legal Theory*, edited by Martha Albertson Fineman and Nancy Sweet Thomadsen, 148–67. New York: Routledge, 1991.
Howe, Irving, ed. *Edith Wharton: A Collection of Critical Essays*. Englewood Cliffs, N.J.: Prentice Hall, 1962.
Howells, William Dean. *Criticism and Fiction*. New York: Harper & Brothers, 1892.
———. *A Modern Instance*. 1882. Reprint, New York: Penguin, 1988.
———. "Reviews and Literary Notices." *Atlantic Monthly*, July 1867, 121.
———. *The Rise of Silas Lapham*. 1885. Reprint, New York: Penguin Classics, 1986.
Huyler, Jerome. *Locke in America: The Moral Philosophy of the Founding Era*. Lawrence: University Press of Kansas, 1995.
James, Henry. *The Art of the Novel*. New York: Charles Scribner's Sons, 1948.
———. *The Bostonians*. New York: Vintage, 1991.
———. *The Golden Bowl*. 1904. Reprint, Oxford: Oxford University Press, 1991.
———. "A Most Extraordinary Case." *Atlantic Monthly*, Apr. 1868, 461–85.
———. *Notes of a Son and Brother*. New York: Scribner's, 1914.
———. *The Tales of Henry James*. Vol. 1, *1864–1869*. Edited by Maqbool Aziz. Oxford: Clarendon Press, 1973.
James, William. "The Place of Affectional Facts in a World of Pure Experience." In *The Writings of William James*, edited by John J. McDermott, 271–77. New York: Random House, 1967.
Jeffords, Susan. *Remasculinization of America: Gender and the Vietnam War*. Bloomington: University of Indiana Press, 1989.
Jenks, Leland. "Railroads as an Economic Force in American Development." *Journal of Economic History* 4 (May 1944): 1–20.
Jolly, Roslyn. *Henry James: History, Narrative, Fiction*. Oxford: Clarendon Press, 1993.
Journet, Debra. "Phantom Limbs and 'Body-Ego': S. Weir Mitchell's 'George Dedlow.'" *Mosaic* 23, no. 1: 87–99.
Kahane, Claire. *Passions of the Voice: Hysteria, Narrative, and the Figure of the Speaking Woman, 1850–1915*. Baltimore: Johns Hopkins University Press, 1995.
Kairys, David, ed. *The Politics of Law: A Progressive Critique*. New York: Pantheon Books, 1990.

Kaplan, Amy. *The Social Construction of American Realism*. Chicago: University of Chicago Press, 1988.

———. "The Spectacle of War." In *New Essays on "The Red Badge of Courage,"* 77–108. New York: Cambridge University Press, 1986.

Kaser, David. *Books and Libraries in Camp and Battle: The Civil War Experience*. Westport, Conn.: Greenwood Press, 1984.

Kasson, John F. *Rudeness and Civility: Manners in Nineteenth-Century Urban America*. New York: Hill and Wang, 1990.

Kimmel, Michael. *Manhood in America: A Cultural History*. New York: Free Press, 1996.

Kipnis, Laura. "Adultery." *Critical Inquiry* 24 (Winter 1998): 289–327.

Kirby, Lynne. *Parallel Tracks: The Railroad and Silent Cinema*. Durham, N.C.: Duke University Press, 1997.

Korobkin, Laura Hanft. *Criminal Conversations: Sentimentality and Nineteenth-Century Legal Stories of Adultery*. New York: Columbia University Press, 1998.

Kostal, Rande. *Law and English Railway Capitalism, 1825–1875*. London: Oxford University Press, 1995.

Krafft-Ebing, Richard von. *Psychopathia Sexualis*. 12th ed. New York: Physicians & Surgeons Book Co., 1925.

Kramer, Matthew H. *Critical Legal Theory and the Challenge of Feminism: A Philosophical Reconception*. Lanham, Md.: Rowman & Littlefield, 1995.

Kudlick, Catherine J. Review Essay. "Disability History: Why We Need Another 'Other.'" *American Historical Review* (June 2003): 763–93.

Kuklick, Bruce. *The Rise of American Philosophy: Cambridge, MA, 1860–1930*. New Haven: Yale University Press, 1977.

Laclau, Ernesto, and Chantal Mouffe. *Hegemony and Socialist Strategy: Towards a Radical Democratic Politics*. New York: Verso, 1985.

Lamb, Jonathan. *The Rhetoric of Suffering: Reading the Book of Job in the Eighteenth Century*. Oxford: Oxford University Press, 1995.

Lange, Carl George, and William James. *The Emotions*. New York: Hafner Publishing, 1967.

Lears, T. J. Jackson. *No Place of Grace: Anti-modernism and the Transformation of American Culture, 1880–1920*. New York: Pantheon Books, 1981.

Leavitt, Judith Walzer, and Ronald L. Numbers, eds. *Sickness and Health in America: Readings in the History of Medicine and Public Health*. Madison: University of Wisconsin Press, 1978.

Lee, Hermione. *Willa Cather: A Life Saved Up*. London: Virago Press, 1988.

Lens, Sidney. *The Labor Wars: From the Molly Maguires to the Sitdowns*. New York: Doubleday, 1973.

Leonard, Jerry D., ed. *Legal Studies as Cultural Studies: A Reader in (Post)*

Modern Critical Theory. Albany: State University of New York Press, 1995.

Leonard, Thomas. *Above the Battle: War in America from Appomattox to Versailles*. New York: Oxford University Press, 1978.

Leubsdorf, John. "Toward a History of the American Rule on Attorney Fee Recovery." *Law and Contemporary Problems* 4 (1984): 9–35.

Leverenz, David. *Manhood and the American Renaissance*. Ithaca, N.Y.: Cornell University Press, 1989.

Lewis, Jan, and Peter N. Stearns, eds. *An Emotional History of the United States*. New York: New York University Press, 1998.

Lewis, Thomas. *The Soldier's Heart and the Effort Syndrome*. New York: Paul B. Hoeber, 1919.

Leys, Ruth. *Trauma: A Geneaology*. Chicago: University of Chicago Press, 2000.

Licht, William. *Industrializing America: The Nineteenth Century*. Baltimore: Johns Hopkins University Press, 1995.

Lightner, David L. "Construction Labor on the Illinois Central Railroad." *Journal of the Illinois State Historical Society* 66 (Autumn 1973): 285–301.

Linderman, Gerald F. *Embattled Courage: The Experience of Combat in the American Civil War*. New York: Free Press, 1987.

Lindgren, Ralph J., and Nadine Taub. *The Law of Sex Discrimination*. New York: West Publishing, 1993.

Linsom, C. K. *My Stephen Crane*. Syracuse, N.Y.: Syracuse University Press, 1958.

Lively, Robert A. *Fiction Fights the Civil War: An Unfinished Chapter in the Literary History of the American People*. Chapel Hill: University of North Carolina Press, 1957.

Livingston, James. *Pragmatism and the Political Economy of Cultural Revolution, 1850–1940*. Chapel Hill: University of North Carolina Press, 1997.

Locke, John. *A Letter Concerning Toleration*. Edited by John Horton and Susan Mendus. New York: Routledge, 1991.

———. *Of Civil Government, Two Treatise*. 1690. Reprint, London: J. M. Dent & Sons, 1924.

Longmore, Paul K., and Lauri Umansky, eds. *The New Disability History: American Perspectives*. New York: New York University Press, 2001.

Lundberg, David. "The American Literature of War." *American Quarterly* 36, no. 3 (1984): 375–88.

Lutz, Catherine A. "Engendered Emotion: Gender, Power, and the Rhetoric of Emotional Control in American Discourse." In *Language and the Politics of Emotion*, edited by Lila Abu-Lughod and Catherine Lutz, 69–91. New York: Cambridge University Press, 1990.

Lutz, Tom. *American Nervousness: 1903, An Anecdotal History*. Ithaca, N.Y.: Cornell University Press, 1991.

Machor, James L., ed. *Readers in History: Nineteenth-Century American Literature and the Contexts of Response*. Baltimore: Johns Hopkins University Press, 1993.

Magruder, Calvert. "Mental and Emotional Disturbance in the Law of Torts." *Harvard Law Review* 49 (1936): 1034–67.

Mailloux, Steven. "The Rhetorical Use and Abuse of Fiction: Eating Books in Late-Nineteenth-Century America." *Boundary* 2, no. 17 (Spring 1990): 156–57.

Mann, Ronald. *The History of the Management of Pain from Early Principles to Present Practice*. New York: Pantheon Books, 1988.

Marshall, David. *The Surprising Effects of Sympathy: Marivaux, Diderot, Rousseau, and Mary Shelley*. Chicago: University of Chicago, 1988.

Marx, Karl. *Communist Manifesto*. Edited by Frederic L. Bender. New York: Norton, 1988.

Marx, Leo. *The Machine in the Garden: Technology and the Pastoral Ideal in America*. New York: Oxford University Press, 1964.

Masur, Louis P., ed. *"The Real War Will Never Get in the Books": Selections from Writers during the Civil War*. Oxford: Oxford University Press, 1993.

Matthiessen, F. O. *Henry James: The Major Phase*. New York: Oxford University Press, 1944.

Mattocks, Charles. *"Unspoiled Heart": The Journal of Charles Mattocks of the 17th Maine*. Edited by Philip N. Racine. Knoxville: University of Tennessee Press, 1994.

May, Elaine Tyler. *Great Expectations: Marriage and Divorce in Post-Victorian America*. Chicago: University of Chicago Press, 1980.

McCormack, Peggy. *The Rule of Money: Gender, Class, and Exchange Economics in the Fiction of Henry James*. Ann Arbor: UMI Research Press, 1990.

McMahon, Carol E. "Nervous Disease and Malingering: The Status of Psychosomatic Concepts in Nineteenth-Century Medicine." *International Journal of Psychosomatics* 31, no. 3 (1983): 15–19.

McPherson, C. B. *Political Theory of Possessive Individualism: Hobbes to Locke*. Oxford: Clarendon Press, 1962.

Medical and Surgical History of the War of the Rebellion, 1861–1865. 6 vols. Washington: Government Printing Office, 1870–88. Archives of the Huntington Library, Pasadena, Calif.

Mendelson, Danuta. *The Interfaces of Medicine and Law: The History of the Liability for Negligently Caused Psychiatric Injury (Nervous Shock)*. Hampshire, Eng.: Ashgate, 1998.

Merish, Lori. *Sentimental Materialism: Gender, Commodity Culture, and Nineteenth-Century American Literature*. Durham, N.C.: Duke University Press, 2000.

Micale, Michael. *Approaching Hysteria: Disease and Its Interpretations*. Princeton, N.J.: Princeton University Press, 1995.

———. "Charcot and the Idea of Hysteria in the Male: Gender, Mental Science, and Diagnosis in Late-Nineteenth-Century France and Britain." In *Medical History* 34 (1990): 363–411.

Michaels, Walter Benn. "The Contracted Heart." *New Literary History* 21:495–531.

———. *The Gold Standard and the Logic of Naturalism*. Berkeley: University of California Press, 1987.

Mill, John Stuart. *On Liberty*. 1859. Reprint, edited by David Spitz, New York: Norton, 1975.

Mitchell, Lee Clark, ed. *New Essays on "The Red Badge of Courage."* New York: Cambridge University Press, 1986.

Mitchell, S. Weir. "The Case of George Dedlow." In *"Autobiography of a Quack" and Other Stories*. New York: Century, 1915.

———. *Clinical Lessons on Nervous Diseases*. Philadelphia: Lea Brothers, 1897.

———. *In War Time*. New York: Century, 1905.

———. *Nurse and Patient, and Camp Cure*. Philadelphia: J. B. Lippincott, 1877.

———. "Phantom Limbs." *Lippincott's Magazine* 8 (Dec. 1871): 563–69.

Morris, David. *The Culture of Pain*. Berkeley: University of California Press, 1991.

"Mr. Howells on Divorce." *Century* 24, no. 2 (1882): 940–41.

Mullan, John. *Sentiment and Sociability: The Language of Feeling in the Eighteenth Century*. Oxford: Clarendon Press, 1988.

Myerson, Abraham. "The Nervous Husband." *Ladies Home Journal* (Sept. 1921): 11–12.

Nelson, Dana D. *National Manhood: Capitalist Citizenship and the Imagined Fraternity of White Men*. Durham, N.C.: Duke University Press, 1998.

Nelson, William T. *A Treatise on the Law of Divorce and Annulment of Marriage*. 2 vols. Chicago: Callaghan, 1895.

Nemiah, John C. "Neurotic Disorders." In *Longman Dictionary of Psychology*, edited by Robert M. Goldenson, 1483–89. New York: Longman, 1984.

"Neurasthenia, the Result of Nervous Shock, as a Ground for Damages." *Central Law Journal* 59 (1904): 83–89.

Nevius, Blake. *Edith Wharton: A Study of Her Fiction*. Berkeley: University of California Press, 1961.

Newfield, Christopher. *Ivy and Industry: Business and the Making of the American University, 1880–1980*. Durham: N.C.: Duke University Press, 2003.

Newman, Kathy. "Wounds and Wounding in the American Civil War: A (Visual) History." *Yale Journal of Criticism* 6, no. 2 (1993): 63–85.

Nietzsche, Friedrich. *On the Genealogy of Morals and Ecce Homo*. Translated by Walter Kaufmann. New York: Vintage, 1969.
Nordau, Max. *Degeneration*. New York: D. Appleton, 1895.
Nussbaum, Martha. "Flawed Crystals: James's *The Golden Bowl* and Literature as Moral Philosophy." *New Literary History: A Journal of Theory and Interpretation* 15, no. 1 (Autumn 1983): 25–50.
———. *Upheavals of Thought: The Intelligence of Emotions*. New York: Cambridge University Press, 2001.
O'Brien, Sharon. *Willa Cather: The Emerging Voice*. New York: Oxford University Press, 1987.
Ogden Papers. Gilder Lehrman Collection, on deposit at the New-York Historical Society, New York City (GLC 6559.01).
O'Neill, William. *Divorce in the Progressive Era*. New Haven, Conn.: Yale University Press, 1967.
Oxenhandler, Neal. "The Changing Concept of Literary Emotion: A Selective History." *New Literary History* 20:103–21.
Pateman, Carol. *The Sexual Contract*. Stanford, Calif.: Stanford University Press, 1988.
Pease, Donald, ed. *New Essays on "The Rise of Silas Lapham."* Cambridge: Cambridge University Press, 1991.
Pernick, Martin S. *A Calculus of Suffering: Pain, Professionalism, and Anesthesia in Nineteenth-Century America*. New York: Columbia University Press, 1985.
Perry, Bliss. "Fiction as College Study." *PMLA* 11, no. 1 (1896): 76–84.
Person, Leland. *Henry James and the Suspense of Masculinity*. Philadelphia: University of Pennsylvania Press, 2003.
Pfister, Joel, and Nancy Schnog, eds. *Inventing the Psychological: Toward a Cultural History of Emotional Life in America*. New Haven, Conn.: Yale University Press, 1997.
Porter, Horace. *Campaigning with Grant*. New York: Century, 1906.
———. "The Philosophy of Courage." *Century Magazine* 36, no. 2 (June 1888): 246–54.
Porter, Roy. "Barely Touching." In *Mind and Body in Enlightenment Thought*, edited by G. S. Rousseau, 45–80. Berkeley: University of California Press, 1990.
Posnock, Ross. *The Trial of Curiosity: Henry James, William James, and the Challenge of Modernity*. Oxford: Oxford University Press, 1991.
Postema, Gerald J. "Public Faces—Private Places: Liberalism and the Enforcement of Morality." In *Morality, Harm, and the Law*, edited by Gerald Dworkin, 77–90. Boulder, Colo.: Westview Press, 1994.
Pound, Roscoe. "Law in Books and Law in Action." *American Law Review* 12, no. 21 (1910): 12–36.

Prioleau, E. S. *The Circle of Eros: Sexuality in the Work of William Dean Howells*. Durham, N.C.: Duke University Press, 1983.
Prosser, William L. *Handbook of the Law of Torts*. 4th ed. St. Paul, Minn.: West Publishing, 1941.
Rathburn, John W. *American Literary Criticism, 1860–1905*. Boston: Twayne Publishers, 1979.
Reed, Edward S. *From Soul to Mind: The Emergence of Psychology from Erasmus Darwin to William James*. New Haven, Conn.: Yale University Press, 1997.
Rein, David M. *S. Weir Mitchell as a Psychiatric Novelist*. New York: International Universities Press, 1952.
Report of Vincent Colyer, on the Reception and Care of the Soldiers Returning from the War. New York: G. A. Whitehorne, Printer, 1865.
Rey, Roselyne. *The History of Pain*. Cambridge: Harvard University Press, 1995.
Rhodes, Elisha Hunt. *All for Union: The Civil War Diary and Letters of Elisha Hunt Rhodes*. Edited by Robert Hunt Rhodes. New York: Orion Books, 1985.
Robinson, Sally. *Marked Men: White Masculinity in Crisis*. New York: Columbia University Press, 2000.
Robinson, Victor. *Victory over Pain: A History of Anesthesia*. New York: Henry Schuman, 1946.
Rogers, Daniel T. *The Work Ethic in Industrial America, 1850–1920*. Chicago: University of Chicago Press, 1978.
Romero, Lora. *Home Fronts: Domesticity and Its Critics in the Antebellum United States*. Durham, N.C.: Duke University Press, 1997.
Rorabaugh, W. J. *The Craft Apprentice: From Franklin to the Machine Age in America*. New York: Oxford University Press, 1986.
Rosen, George. "Nostalgia: A 'Forgotten' Psychological Disorder." *Clio Medica* 10, no. 1 (1975): 28–51.
Ross, Edward. *Social Control: A Survey of the Foundations of Order*. Cleveland, Ohio: Press of Case Western Reserve University, 1969.
Rousseau, G. S., ed. *The Languages of the Psyche: Mind and Body in Enlightenment Thought*. Berkeley: University of California Press, 1990.
Rowe, John C. *At Emerson's Tomb: The Politics of Classic American Literature*. New York: Columbia University Press, 1997.
———. *Henry Adams and Henry James: The Emergence of a Modern Consciousness*. Ithaca, N.Y.: Cornell University Press, 1976.
———. *The Theoretical Dimensions of Henry James*. Madison: University of Wisconsin Press, 1984.
Rowe, John C., and Rick Berg, eds. *The Vietnam War and American Culture*. New York: Columbia University Press, 1991.

Russett, Cynthia. *Sexual Science: The Victorian Construction of Womanhood.* Cambridge: Harvard University Press, 1989.

Ryan, Judith. *The Vanishing Subject: Early Psychology and Literary Modernism.* Chicago: University of Chicago Press, 1991.

Samuels, Shirley, ed. *The Culture of Sentiment: Race, Gender, and Sentimentality in Nineteenth-Century America.* New York: Oxford University Press, 1992.

Sanchez-Eppler, Karen. *Touching Liberty: Abolition, Feminism, and the Politics of the Body.* Berkeley: University of California Press, 1993.

Sandel, Michael. *Liberalism and the Limits of Justice.* Cambridge: Cambridge University Press, 1982.

———, ed. *Liberalism and Its Critics.* New York: New York University Press, 1984.

Scarry, Elaine. *The Body in Pain.* New York: Oxford University Press, 1985.

Schivelbusch, Wolfgang. *The Railway Journey: The Industrialization of Time and Space in the Nineteenth Century.* Berkeley: University of California Press, 1977.

Searle, John Williams. "Cold Charity: Manhood, Brotherhood, and the Transformation of Disability, 1870–1900." In *The New Disability History: American Perspectives*, edited by Paul K. Longmore and Lauri Umansky, 157–86. New York: New York University Press, 2001.

Sedgwick, Eve Kosofsky. "Across Genders, Across Sexualities: Willa Cather and Others." *South Atlantic Quarterly* 88 (Winter 1989): 53–72.

———. *Epistemology of the Closet.* Berkeley: University of California Press, 1990.

———. *Touching Affect: Politics, Emotion, Performativity.* Durham, N.C.: Duke University Press, 2003

Sedgwick, Eve Kosofsky, and Adam Frank, eds. *Shame and Its Sisters: A Silvan Tomkins Reader.* Durham, N.C.: Duke University Press, 1995.

Seltzer, Mark. *Bodies and Machines.* New York: Routledge, 1992.

———. *Henry James and the Art of Power.* Ithaca, N.Y.: Cornell University Press, 1984.

———. *Serial Killers: Death and Life in America's Wound Culture.* New York: Routledge, 1998.

Sennet, Richard. *The Fall of Public Man.* New York: Norton, 1977.

Shamir, Milette. "Hawthorne's Romance and the Right to Privacy." *American Quarterly* 49, no. 4 (Dec. 1997): 746–79.

Shamir, Milette, and Jennifer Travis, eds. *Boys Don't Cry? Rethinking Narratives of Masculinity and Emotion in the U.S.* New York: Columbia University Press, 2002.

Shaw, Robert. *Blue-Eyed Child of Fortune: The Civil War Letters of Colonel Robert Gould Shaw.* Edited by Russell Duncan. Athens: University of Georgia Press, 1992.

Shi, David E. *Facing Facts: Realism in American Thought and Culture, 1850–1920*. New York: Oxford University Press, 1995.
Showalter, Elaine. *The Female Malady: Women, Madness, and English Culture*. New York: Penguin Books, 1985.
———. *Hystories*. New York: Columbia University Press, 1997.
Shrage, Laurie. *Moral Dilemmas of Feminism: Prostitution, Adultery, and Abortion*. New York: Routledge, 1994.
Shumway, David R. *Creating American Civilization*. Minneapolis: University of Minnesota Press, 1994.
Sicherman, Barbara. "The Uses of Diagnosis: Doctors, Patients, and Neurasthenia." In *Sickness and Health in America*, edited by Judith Walzer Leavitt and Ronald L. Numbers, 25–38. Madison: University of Wisconsin Press, 1978.
Silverman, Kaja. *Male Subjectivies at the Margins*. New York: Routledge, 1992.
Singer, William Joseph. "The Legal Rights Debate in Analytic Jurisprudence from Bentham to Hohfeld." *Wisconsin Law Review* (Dec. 1982): 975–1059.
Sklar, Martin. *The Corporate Reconstruction of American Capitalism, 1890–1916: The Market, the Law, and Politics*. Cambridge: Cambridge University Press, 1988.
Smith, Henry Nash. "William Dean Howells: The Theology of Realism." In *Democracy and the Novel: Popular Resistance to Classic American Writers*, 75–103. New York: Oxford University Press, 1978.
Smith, Joseph H. *Telling Facts: History and Narration in Psychoanalysis*. Baltimore: Johns Hopkins University Press, 1992.
Smith-Rosenberg, Carroll. *Disorderly Conduct: Visions of Gender in Victorian America*. New York: A. A. Knopf, 1985.
Southward, E. E., ed. *Shell-Shock and Other Neuropsychiatric Problems*. Boston: W. M. Leonard, 1919.
Spingarn, Joel Elias. *Criticism in America: Its Function and Status*. New York: Harcourt Brace, 1924.
———. "The New Criticism." In *Creative Criticism: Essays on the Unity of Genius and Taste*, 2–44. New York: Henry Holt and Company, 1917.
Springer, Marlene. *"Ethan Frome": A Nightmare of Need*. New York: Twayne Publishers, 1993.
Stanton, Elizabeth Cady. "The Need of Liberal Divorce Laws." *North American Review* 139 (Sept. 1884): 234–46.
Staves, Susan. "Money for Honor: Damages for Criminal Conversation." *Studies in Eighteenth Century Culture* 11 (1982): 279–97.
Stein, Allen F. *After the Vows Were Spoken: Marriage in American Literary Realism*. Columbus: Ohio State University Press, 1984.
Stern, Julia. *The Plight of Feeling: Sympathy and Dissent in the Early American Novel*. Chicago: University of Chicago Press, 1997.

Stone, Lawrence. *The Road to Divorce*. Oxford: Oxford University Press, 1990.

Sumner, William Graham. *The Forgotten Man and Other Essays*. New Haven, Conn.: Yale University Press, 1919.

———. "The Scientific Attitude of Mind." In *Essays of William Graham Sumner*, 2 vols., edited by Albert Galloway Keller and Maurice Davie, 1:43–54. Hamden, Conn.: Archon Books, 1969.

Sundquist, Eric J. *Home as Found: Authority and Genealogy in Nineteenth-Century American Literature*. Baltimore: Johns Hopkins University Press, 1979.

Sussman, Herbert. *Victorian Masculinities: Manhood and Masculine Poetics in Early Victorian Literature and Art*. Cambridge: Cambridge University Press, 1995.

Sussman, Warren. *Culture as History: The Tranformation of American Society in the Twentieth Century*. New York: Pantheon Books, 1984.

Sutliffe, Robert Steward. *Impressions of an Average Juryman*. New York: Banks Law Publishing, 1931.

Sweet, Timothy. "Photography and the Scene of History." In *Traces of War: Poetry, Photography, and the Crisis of the Union*, 78–106. Baltimore: Johns Hopkins University Press, 1990.

Tanner, Tony. *Adultery in the Novel: Contract and Transgression*. Baltimore: Johns Hopkins University Press, 1979.

Thomas, Brook. *American Literary Realism and the Failed Promise of Contract*. Berkeley: University of California Press, 1997.

Thomas, Calvin. "Literature and Personality." *PMLA* 12, no. 3 (1897): 299–317.

Thompson, Maurice. "A Modern Instance of Criticism." *Indianapolis Saturday Herald*, Aug. 18, 1883, 4.

Thompson Letters. Houghton Library, Harvard University, Cambridge, Mass.

Thomson, Rosemarie Garland. *Extraordinary Bodies: Figuring Disability in American Literature and Culture*. New York: Columbia University Press, 1997.

Tompkins, Jane. *Sensational Designs: The Cultural Work of American Fiction, 1790–1860*. New York: Oxford University Press, 1985.

Trachtenberg, Alan. "Albums of War: On Reading Civil War Photographs." *Representations* 9 (1986): 1–32.

Traister, Bryce. "Academic Viagra: The Rise of American Masculinity Studies." *American Quarterly* 52, no. 2 (2000): 247–304.

Trilling, Lionel. *The Liberal Imagination: Essays on Literature and Society*. New York: Viking, 1950.

———. "The Morality of Inertia." In *Edith Wharton: A Collection of Critical*

Essays, edited by Irving Howe. Englewood Cliffs, N.J.: Prentice Hall, 1962.
Turner, James. *Reckoning with the Beast: Animals, Pain, and Humanity in the Victorian Mind.* Baltimore: Johns Hopkins University Press, 1980.
Tuttle, Jennifer. "Empire of Sickness: Literary Professionals and Medical Discourse in the Age of American Nervousness, 1869–1911." Ph.D. diss., University of California, San Diego, 1996.
United States Bureau of the Census. *Special Reports: Marriage and Divorce, 1867–1906.* Washington: Government Printing Office, 1908–1909.
Vance, James. E. *The North American Railroad: Its Origin, Evolution, and Geography.* Baltimore: Johns Hopkins University Press, 1995.
Vanderbilt, Kermit. *American Literature and the Academy: The Roots, Growth, and Maturity of a Profession.* Philadelphia: University of Pennsylvania Press, 1986.
———. "Marcia Gaylord's Electra Complex: A Footnote to Sex in Howells." *American Literature* 34, no. 3 (1962): 365–74.
Veith, Ilza. *Hysteria: The History of a Disease.* Chicago: University of Chicago Press, 1965.
Walton, Priscilla. *The Disruption of the Feminine in Henry James.* Toronto: University of Toronto Press, 1992.
Weinstein, Jeremy. "Adultery, Law, and the State." *Hastings Law Journal* 19 (1986): 215–29.
Weisberg, Richard. *Poethics and Other Strategies of Law and Literature.* New York: Columbia University Press, 1992.
Weisenberg, Theodore H. "The Military History of the American Neurological Association." *Archives of Neurology and Psychology* (1918): 1.
Welsh, Alexander. *Strong Representations: Narrative and Circumstantial Evidence in England.* Baltimore: Johns Hopkins University Press, 1992.
West, Robin. *Narrative, Authority, and the Law.* Ann Arbor: University of Michigan Press, 1993.
Wexler, Laura. *Tender Violence: Domestic Visions in an Age of U.S. Imperialism.* Chapel Hill: University of North Carolina Press, 2000.
Wharton, Edith. "A Cycle of Reading and Reviewing." In *Edith Wharton: The Uncollected Critical Writings*, edited by Frederick Wegener. Princeton, N.J.: Princeton University Press, 1996.
———. *Ethan Frome.* 1911. Reprint, New York: Dover, 1991.
White, G. Edward. *Tort Law in America: An Intellectual History.* Oxford: Oxford University Press, 1980.
White, James Boyd. *Justice as Translation: An Essay in Cultural and Legal Criticism.* Chicago: University of Chicago Press, 1990.
Whitman, Walt. *Specimen Days in America.* London: Routledge & Sons, 1906.

Wilkinson, Warren. *Mother May You Never See the Sights I Have Seen: The Fifty-Seventh Massachusetts Veteran Volunteers in the Army of the Potomac, 1864–1865*. New York: Harper & Row, 1990.

Williams, Raymond. *Marxism and Literature*. Oxford: Oxford University Press, 1982.

Wilson, Christopher. *Labor of Words: Literary Professionalism in the Progressive Era*. Athens: University of Georgia Press, 1985.

Wilson, Edmund. *Patriotic Gore: Studies in the Literature of the American Civil War*. Boston: Northeastern University Press, 1984.

Wolff, Cynthia Griffin. *A Feast of Words: The Triumph of Edith Wharton*. New York: Oxford University Press, 1995

———. "Hot Ethan, Cold Ethan." In *Edith Wharton: New Critical Essays*, edited by Alfred Bendixen and Annette Zilversmit. New York: Garland, 1992.

Woodmansee, Martha, and Mark Osteen, eds. *The New Economic Criticism: Studies at the Intersection of Literature and Economics*. New York: Routledge, 1999.

Woodring, Carl. *Literature: An Embattled Profession*. New York: Columbia University Press, 1999.

Wright, Ellen. "Given Bartley, Given Marcia: A Reconsideration of Howells's *A Modern Instance*." *Texas Studies in Literature and Language* 23, no. 2 (1981): 214–31.

Yeazell, Ruth Bernard. "The Difficulty of Ending: Maggie Verver in *The Golden Bowl*." In *Language and Knowledge in the Late Novels of Henry James*, 100–130. Chicago: University of Chicago Press, 1976.

Young, Elizabeth. *Disarming the Nation: Women's Writing and the American Civil War*. Chicago: University of Chicago Press, 1999.

Index

Aaron, Daniel, 37, 38, 175 (n. 52)
Abandonment: as grounds for divorce, 68–70, 178 (n. 29)
Abel, Richard, 186 (n. 19)
Adultery: in Cather's *Lost Lady*, 6, 19–20, 79–103; as grounds for divorce, 68–70, 94–95, 178 (n. 36); law on, 80–81; and criminal conversation cases, 80–81, 83, 84, 92–98, 180–81 (nn. 13–17), 181–82 (nn. 21–22); voyeuristic framing of, in Cather's *Lost Lady*, 93, 98, 100–102; court case on, 96; proof of, 97–99; as cause of physical disease in betrayed spouse, 133
Affect, 5, 81, 159–61
Agnew, Jean-Christophe, 117, 122
Alcott, Louisa May, 40
American Neurological Association, 173 (n. 22)
Aristotle, 140, 142
Autobiographical writings. *See* Personal/autobiographical writings

Barnes, Elizabeth, 7, 169 (n. 11)
Basch, Norma, 64
Baym, Nina, 7
Baynton, Douglas C., 165
Beard, George M., 29–30, 35
Bederman, Gail, 6
Beecher, Henry Ward, 96
Beers, Henry, 37, 38
Belknap, E. H., 164
Bell, Daniel, 14
Bell, Michael D., 57, 58
Bellard, Alfred, 28, 42
Bellows, Harry, 24
Berlant, Lauren, 6, 16–17
Berlin, Isaiah, 14
Bishop, Joel Prentiss, 75
Bjorkman, Edwin, 137, 139, 155, 185 (n. 15)
Blanton, Smiley, 51
Bleckley, Chief Justice, 163
Body: white male body, 6–7; national body, 24–25, 32, 171 (n. 4); physical injuries during Civil War, 27–29, 38–40, 172–73 (n. 14); and Civil War's fetishization of physicality, 39–40; in James's *Golden Bowl*, 115–16; and emotions, 133–34; in Wharton's *Ethan Frome*, 139, 143, 145–46, 149, 166
The Bostonians (James), 110, 116–17, 127, 129
Brady, Mathew B., 27–28
Bragg, Colonel, 40
Brandeis, Louis, 21, 108–10, 125–26, 128–29, 133–34
Brodhead, Richard, 143
Brown, Wendy, 16–17, 55, 171 (n. 30)
Browne, Irving, 74

Brudney, Daniel, 107
Burbick, Joan, 171 (n. 4)
Burke, Edmund, 140
Butler, Judith, 11, 55, 171 (n. 29)

Cady, Edwin, 57
Calhoun, J. Theodore, 32, 174 (n. 34), 175 (n. 44)
Camp cure for male nervousness, 29, 30, 173 (n. 18)
"A Candidate for Bedlam" (Hammond), 33
Cannon, Walter B., 133–34
Cardozo, Benjamin, 186 (n. 21)
Carpenter, A., 74–75
"The Case of George Dedlo" (Mitchell), 30–31
Cather, Willa: and adultery plot, 6, 19–20, 79–103; on laws, 79; and "the thing not named," 81, 82–83, 180 (nn. 3, 5); on realist novel, 81–82; same-sex sexual desire in works by, 82; and injury law, 179–80 (n. 1); on Wilde, 182–83 (n. 30). See also *A Lost Lady* (Cather)
Chamallas, Martha, 11
Chisholm, Daniel, 39
Chronicle of Daily Life in the Union Army (Rhodes), 41
Civil War: medical views of psychic wounds from, 4–5, 23–25, 29–36; fiction on, 4–5, 25, 34–35, 43–50; weapons of, 6, 172 (n. 13); and soldier's heart, 18, 23–50; and rhetoric of injured national body, 24–25, 32; and heroic masculinity, 25, 26, 28, 29, 57, 165; aesthetic value of literature from, 25, 36–38, 40; historiography of, 26, 172 (n. 8); personal/autobiographical writings on, 26–27, 36–44, 139; physical injuries during, 27–29, 38–40, 172–73 (n. 14); photographs of injured soldiers in, 27–29, 172 (n. 12); medical care during, 30; and nostalgia, 31–33; silence on terrors of battle in, 38–40; women writers on, 40–41; pension records from, 174–75 (n. 43); and malingering, 175 (n. 44)
Commercial law, 90
Compensation hysteria, 36–44
Cooper, Frederic Taber, 19
Copyright, 125
Courage, 29
Crane, Stephen, 18, 43, 46–50, 52, 85, 166, 180 (n. 6)
Criminal conversation cases, 80–81, 83, 84, 92–98, 180–81 (nn. 13–17), 181–82 (nn. 21–22). *See also* Adultery
Criticism and Fiction (Howells), 59, 77
Cruelty: as ground for divorce, 68–71, 74–77, 178 (n. 29), 179 (n. 41)

Da Costa, Jacob Mendes, 23–24, 28, 29–30, 31
Darwin, Charles, 157
Davidson, Cathy N., 56
Dawes, Rufus, 39
Dean, Eric T., Jr., 26
Delgado, Richard, 55
Demos, John, 14
Depression, 34
Diffley, Kathleen, 37, 40, 176 (n. 67)
Dimock, Wai Chee, 53–54, 154
Disability, 164–67
Divorce: in Howells's *Modern Instance*, 2–3, 5–6, 18–19, 53–55, 60–77, 177 (n. 14); and patriar-

chal family, 51–52; as marital shell shock, 51–55; increase in, 64; legal grounds for, 64, 67–71, 94–95, 178 (nn. 29, 36), 179 (n. 41); and verbal cruelty, 64–65, 74–77; Indiana laws on, 67–68; court cases on, 69, 74–76; masculine need to protect women from, 179 (n. 46)
Dix, Morgan, 138
Doctors. *See* Medicine
Douglas, Ann, 142–43, 185 (n. 11)
Douglass, Frederick, 4
Dreiser, Theodore, 85

Edmonds, S. Emma E., 40
Eiselein, Gregory, 175 (n. 45)
Eliot, Charles W., 159
Ellison, Julie, 7, 8–9, 170 (nn. 11–12)
Emotional aura, 81–83
Emotional injury. *See* Male emotional injury
Empathy, 16, 17, 142–44
England, 95–96
Epperly, Christian, 40
Ethan Frome (Wharton): literary critics on, 21–22, 137–43, 154–55, 160–61; Mattie in, 22, 138–39, 143, 145–47, 149–53, 161; narrator in, 22, 138–39, 144, 147–48, 151–54; Zeena in, 22, 138–39, 145–48, 151–54, 161; love between Ethan and Mattie in, 22, 138–39, 149–51; plot summary of, 138–39; bodies in, 139, 143, 145–47, 149, 166; Ethan's disabled body in, 139, 143, 145–47, 166; suicide attempt in, 139, 147, 149, 152–53; preface of, 142, 148, 155; Ethan's silence in, 144–45, 146, 148–49, 161; health of Zeena in, 145, 146, 154; Harmon Gow in, 145, 147; Mrs. Ned Hale in, 147, 148; labor strike in, 151–53; Ethan's labor on farm in, 152; agrarian versus industrial America in, 152–54; Mrs. Frome in, 154

Faller, John, 42
Farwell v. Boston and Worcester Railroad Corporation, 88–89, 180 (n. 9)
Ferenczi, Sándor, 35–36
Fiction: sentimental novels, 4, 18–19, 57, 59–60, 142–44, 186 (n. 25); on soldier's heart, 4–5, 25, 26, 30–31, 34–35, 44–50; by doctors, 30–31, 33–35; on Civil War, 34–35, 43–50; dangers of "feminine" fiction, 56–57, 59–60; women's reading of, 56–57, 59–60; Cather on realist novel, 81–82; psychological novels by Henry James, 110–11, 128, 135. *See also specific authors and titles*
Fiedler, Leslie, 7
Fields, James T., 41
First Amendment, 55–56
First World War. *See* World War I
Fisk, Wilbur, 41–42
Folsom v. Marsh, 184 (n. 16)
Foucault, Michel, 5, 15, 171 (n. 26)
Fox, Richard Wightman, 182 (n. 23)
Frank, Adam, 9
Frederick v. Morse, 180 (n. 14)
Freeman, Kimberly, 177 (n. 14)
Freud, Sigmund, 35, 36, 37, 117, 171 (n. 3), 184 (n. 21)
Friedman, Lawrence, 10, 68, 70, 94

Gilman, Charlotte Perkins, 30
Goffman, Erving, 187 (n. 9)

The Golden Bowl (James): economic discourse in, 20, 105–6, 111, 112, 117, 118, 131; Adam compared to Amerigo in, 20, 118; Amerigo's personal quantity in, 20–21, 48, 108, 110–12, 117–22, 126–31, 133, 164; prevention of pain in, 21, 107, 111, 113–17, 122–23, 127–28, 135; and privacy rights, 21, 108–10, 125–26, 128–29, 133–34, 183 (n. 3); and crack in golden bowl, 21, 113, 116, 121, 122–23, 130; injury and wounds in, 48, 105–13, 126–28, 134; Maggie's marriage to Amerigo in, 105, 108, 113–15, 117, 121–22, 126, 128–33; Charlotte's wounds in, 105, 132; Adam's marriage to Charlotte in, 105–6, 108, 113–14; father-daughter (Adam and Maggie's) relationship in, 105–7, 109–11, 113–15, 122, 126; balance and reciprocity in, 105–7, 118; Maggie's personal nature in, 111, 112, 124; relationship of Adam and Amerigo in, 112; precious objects in, 113–17; Charlotte and Amerigo's sexual relationship in, 114, 115–16, 122, 123, 124, 126–27, 129–30; Fanny Assingham in, 114, 119, 121, 122, 124, 130–31; body in, 115–16; Adam on Amerigo in, 119–20; Maggie on Amerigo in, 119–20; Adam on two houses in, 120–21; ending of, 121–22, 131–33; Maggie's purchase of golden bowl in, 122–23; breaking of golden bowl in, 123–24, 127, 133; legal language in, 132–33; principino in, 183 (n. 11)
Goodman, Nan, 54, 89
Goux, Jean-Joseph, 187 (n. 1)
Graff, Gerald, 157
Graft v. Graft, 69
Greeley, Horace, 69
Gregory, Charles, 156
Griffin, Susan, 28, 185 (n. 22)
Griswold, Robert, 68, 70, 71
Gunshot Wounds and Other Injuries of Nerves (Mitchell), 30

Habegger, Alfred, 57, 58
Habermas, Jürgen, 15
Hammond, William A., 23, 30, 31, 33
Hate speech, 55
Hatfield, James Taft, 160
Hawthorne, Nathaniel, 1–3, 5
Head, M. J., 163, 164, 166
Hedrick, Joan D., 41
Hemingway, Ernest, 40
Hendler, Glenn, 7, 8–9, 170 (n. 11)
Henry, William, 24
Heroic masculinity, 25, 26, 28, 29, 57, 165
Higginson, T. W., 47
Hindus, Michael S., 70–71
Hobbes, Thomas, 11, 12
Hochschild, Arlie Russell, 177 (n. 18)
Hodge v. Wetzler, 181 (n. 14)
Hofer, Johannes, 31–32
Holmes, Oliver Wendell, Jr., 38, 39, 43, 49, 158
Holmes, Oliver Wendell, Sr., 27–28, 29, 42, 172 (n. 12)
Homesickness (nostalgia), 31–33, 174 (n. 34)
Horwitz, Morton, 10, 89, 94
Howard, June, 7, 9, 43, 170 (n. 11)
Howe, Irving, 138, 139, 140
Howells, William Dean: compared to Hawthorne, 2–3; divorce novel by, 2–3, 5–6, 18–19, 53–55, 60–77, 177 (n. 14); on soldier's heart, 18, 49–50, 165; on sentimental novels, 18–19, 57, 59; on Civil War literature, 36–37, 38, 40, 42,

43, 57; realism of, 43, 44–45, 49, 50, 57–59, 81, 138, 139–40; and lack of wartime experience, 46, 49–50, 176 (n. 79); and wounding potential of words, 54–60; on male writers after Civil War, 57; psychological difficulties of, 57, 173 (n. 19); and pain in art, 140. See also *A Modern Instance* (Howells); *and other works*
Hysteria: and women, 31, 146, 173 (n. 21), 185 (n. 14); compensation hysteria, 36–44; and men, 174 (n. 30)
Hystericism, 17

Injury: vocabulary of, 9, 11; work-related injuries, 10, 88–89, 153, 164, 187 (n. 2); etymology of, 11–18, 114–15; civic protection against, 13–14; and disempowerment, 16; prevention of, in James's *Golden Bowl*, 21, 107, 111, 113–17, 122–23, 127–28, 135; physical injuries during Civil War, 27–29, 38–40, 172–73 (n. 14); photographs of, 27–29, 172 (n. 12); ethos of, in nineteenth century, 53; speech-based injury, 54–60, 177 (n. 9); and railroads, 85, 87, 88–89, 164; imagination and pain, 140; as goal of war, 172 (n. 11). *See also* Injury law; Male emotional injury
Injury law: in nineteenth century, 9–10; and industrial workers, 10, 89; and sexual torts, 10–11, 90–100; and gender, 11, 170 (n. 21); and adultery, 80–81; and criminal conversation cases, 80–81, 83, 84, 92–98, 180–81 (nn. 13–17), 181–82 (nn. 21–22); and fellow-servant rule, 88; and railroad injuries, 88–89; history of, 88–91; and assumption of risk, 89; and liability, 89; and jury's ability to read pain properly, 155–56; and negligence, 156, 180 (n. 11); and Cather, 179–80 (n. 1)
In War Time (Mitchell), 34–35

James, Henry: on soldier's heart, 18, 43, 45–46, 49–50, 165; and lack of wartime experience, 28, 46, 49–50, 176 (n. 79); realism of, 44, 49, 58; on dangers of "feminine" fiction, 57; and politics of invalidism, 108, 135; psychological novel by, 110–11, 128, 135; nervousness of, 135, 173 (n. 19); and pain in art, 140; subjectivity of, 184 (n. 17). See also *The Golden Bowl* (James); *and other works*
James, William, 134–35

Kant, Immanuel, 170 (n. 18)
Kaplan, Amy, 59
Kasson, John F., 39
Kipnis, Laura, 88
Korobkin, Laura Hanft, 182 (n. 23)
Kroessin v. Keller, 181 (n. 14)

Labor strike, 151–53
Language: potential of, to wound, 54–60, 177 (n. 9); hate speech, 55; First Amendment speech, 55–56; divorce and verbal cruelty, 64–65, 74–77
Law: on privacy rights, 21, 108–10, 125–26, 128–29, 133–34, 183 (n. 3); on defamatory speech, 56; on divorce, 67–71, 178 (n. 29), 179 (n. 41); Cather on, 79; and criminal conversation cases, 80–81, 83, 84, 92–98, 180–81 (nn. 13–17), 181–82 (nn. 21–22);

Law (continued): on adultery, 80–81, 92–98; in Cather's *Lost Lady*, 83–84, 87; commercial law, 90; and emotional wounds, 133–35; and definition of actual harm, 163; Head's emotional injury claim against railroads, 163, 164, 166; and contingency fees for lawyers, 181 (n. 17); and product liability, 186 (n. 19); and distrust of jury system, 186 (n. 20); reasonable-man standard for juries, 186 (n. 21). *See also* Injury law
Lears, T. J. Jackson, 170–71 (n. 25)
Leonard, Thomas, 37, 38, 175 (n. 52)
Letter Concerning Toleration (Locke), 12, 13
Letters. *See* Personal/autobiographical writings
Leviathan (Hobbes), 12
Lewis, Thomas, 171 (n. 2)
Linderman, Gerald F., 38–39
Lindquist, L., 164
Literary criticism: on Wharton's *Ethan Frome*, 21–22, 137–43, 154–55, 160–61; and universities, 141, 156–57; professionalization of, 156–61; and science of affect, 158–60
Livingston, James, 15
Locke, John, 11–14, 115, 183 (n. 10)
A Lost Lady (Cather): adultery in, 6, 19–20, 79–103; Captain Daniel Forrester in, 19–20, 79–88, 91, 93–94, 100–102, 166; Niel Herbert in, 20, 79–84, 87, 91–94, 96–103, 108; Marian Forrester in, 20, 80, 82, 84–87, 91–94, 96–98, 100–102; physical injuries and accidents in, 80, 84–85, 91, 93, 102, 166; and Captain's silence about wife's adultery, 81, 82–83; "emotional aura" in, 81–82; Frank Ellinger in, 83, 84, 91–93, 97, 98, 100, 102; bank failure and financial problems in, 83, 86–88, 91; Judge Pommeroy in, 83–84, 87, 89–91; lawyers in, 83–84, 87, 92–93, 99–100; Ivy Peters in, 83–84, 87, 101–2; Captain's philosophy of life in, 85–86; home of Forresters in, 85–86, 102; railroad industry in, 85–87, 166; Captain's death in, 91, 93, 94, 102; flood in, 91–92; last conversation between Marian and Frank in, 92–93; Molly Tucker in, 93; Mrs. Beasley in, 93; voyeuristic framing of intimacy in, 93, 98, 100–102; Ned Montgomery in, 96; Adolf Blum in, 97–101; Marian and Frank's secret rendezvous in woods in, 98, 100, 101; jewel imagery of Marian in, 101; Ed Elliot in, 103; last scene of, 103; Marian's death in, 103
Lundberg, David, 37, 38
Lutz, Tom, 30, 108, 184–85 (n. 22)

MacKinnon, Catharine, 11
"A Madness Most Discreet" (Hammond), 33
Magruder, Calvert, 133
Male emotional injury: and guilt, 1–3, 6; and divorce, 2–3, 5–6, 18–19, 50–77; in slave narratives, 4; and Civil War soldier's heart, 4–5, 6, 18, 24–50; in medical literature, 4–5, 23–25, 29–36; compensation for, 6; evidentiary representation of, 6; and adultery, 6, 19–20, 79–103; cultural invisibility of, 7; and vocabulary of injury, 9; in Wharton's *Ethan Frome*, 21–22, 137–55,

160–61; in Civil War's personal/autobiographical writings, 26–27, 36–44, 139; in Civil War fiction, 34–35, 43–50; in James's *Golden Bowl*, 48, 105–13, 126–27; and criminal conversation cases, 80–81, 83, 84, 92–98, 180–81 (nn. 13–17), 181–82 (nn. 21–22); and disability, 164–67
Malingering, 175 (n. 44)
Manhood: heroic masculinity, 25, 26, 28, 29, 57, 165; martial vision of, 29, 44; and suppression of feelings, 39, 78. *See also* Male emotional injury
Marlowe, Christopher, 177 (n. 9)
Marriage: and patriarchal family, 51–52; in Howells's *Modern Instance*, 52–55, 62–65, 67, 72–73; companionate marriage, 63, 64, 66; expectation of happiness in, 63–64; in James's *Golden Bowl*, 105–6, 113–15, 117, 121–22, 126, 128–33; in James's *Bostonians*, 116–17. *See also* Adultery; Divorce
Marx, Karl, 14–15, 153
Masculinity. *See* Male emotional injury; Manhood
Matsuda, Mari, 55
Matthiessen, F. O., 7, 122
May, Elaine Tyler, 63
Medical and Surgical History of the War of the Rebellion, 31, 33
Medicine: and soldier's heart during Civil War, 4–5, 23–25, 29–36, 49; and male nervousness, 29–31; and female nervousness, 30; and neurology, 30, 33, 35, 173 (n. 22); and World War I, 31, 35–36; and nostalgia, 31–33, 174 (n. 34); fictional case study of doctor's psyche, 34–35; and shell shock, 35–36
Melville, Herman, 3
Memoirs. *See* Personal/autobiographical writings
Merish, Lori, 17
Michaels, Walter Benn, 63
Mill, John Stuart, 11, 13, 14, 170 (n. 18)
Miller, Rev. Samuel, 56
Mitchell, S. Weir: and treatment of nervousness, 29, 30, 173 (nn. 18–19); and medical treatment of wounded soldiers, 30, 36, 173 (n. 20); fiction by, 30–31, 34–35; on nostalgia, 33; and American Neurological Association, 173 (n. 22); on hysteria, 174 (n. 30)
A Modern Instance (Howells): divorce case in, 2–3, 5–6, 18–19, 53–55, 60–77; Squire Gaylord in, 2–3, 5–6, 19, 53, 61–62, 67, 71–73, 82, 107–8, 164; compared to other novels, 2–3, 58, 71; Bartley Hubbard in, 3, 5, 19, 52, 53, 61–68, 70, 71–73, 164; Marcia Hubbard in, 3, 6, 19, 52, 61–67, 71–73; Ben Halleck in, 19, 53, 60–68, 71, 73, 166; Olive Halleck in, 19, 66, 67; Mrs. Gaylord in, 19, 72–73; marital shell shock in, 52–55; marriage in, 52–55, 62–65, 67, 72–73; and wounding potential of words, 54–60; Atherton in, 60–62, 65, 68, 73; trial scene in, 61, 71; philosophy of injury in, 61–62; Ben's physical disability in, 62, 166; Henry Bird in, 62; Mrs. Halleck in, 62, 67; arguments by Hubbards in, 64–65; Clara in, 66; Flavia Hubbard in, 66; Kinney in, 72; possible titles for, 76
Modern Language Association (MLA), 140, 159, 160

Mohn v. Tingley, 181–82 (n. 21)
"The Monster" (Crane), 85
"A Most Extraordinary Case" (James), 45–46
Myer, Charles S., 35
Myerson, Abraham, 52

Nash, Henry, 7
Nelson, Dana D., 7, 169–70 (n. 11)
Nervousness: camp cure for men with, 29, 30, 173 (n. 18); male nervousness, 29–31, 135, 173 (n. 19); rest cure for women with, 30. *See also* Soldier's heart
Neurasthenia, 30, 135, 171 (n. 3), 172 (n. 7), 184–85 (n. 22). *See also* Nervousness
Neurology, 30, 33, 35, 173 (n. 22)
Newfield, Christopher, 141
Newman, Kathy, 172 (n. 11)
Nietzsche, Friedrich, 140
Nolin v. Pearson, 180 (n. 14)
Norris, Frank, 85
Nostalgia, 31–33, 174 (n. 34)
Notes of a Son and Brother (James), 105, 176 (n. 78)
"Novel Démeublé" (Cather), 81–82, 180 (n. 3)
Novels. *See* Fiction
Nussbaum, Martha, 171 (n. 28)

The Octopus (Norris), 85
Of Civil Government, Two Treatise (Locke), 12–13
Ogden, Edward, 32
Ogden, Sallie, 32
Old Homestead stories, 32, 41, 176 (n. 67)
"On Being Ill" (Woolf), 31
On Liberty (Mill), 13
Osgood, James R., 52, 66
Overton v. Overton, 182 (n. 21)

Pain. *See* Injury; Male emotional injury
Pateman, Carol, 12, 90
Perry, Bliss, 5, 140, 156, 160
Person, Leland, 112, 117, 118, 131
Personal/autobiographical writings: on Civil War, 26–27, 36–44, 139
Photography, 27–29, 172 (n. 12)
Physicians. *See* Medicine
"The Place of Affectional Facts in a World of Pure Experience" (W. James), 134
"Poor Richard" (James), 45
Porter, Horace, 26, 29, 36, 47
Porter, Roy, 171 (n. 26)
Portrait of a Lady (James), 110
Pound, Roscoe, 69–70
Privacy rights, 21, 108–10, 125–26, 128–29, 133–34, 183 (n. 3)
Professionalization: of literary studies, 141, 154, 156–60, 165; of academic disciplines, 157–60
Property, 12–13, 14
Psychic injury. *See* Male emotional injury
Psychoanalysis, 14–15, 33, 35–36, 161, 171 (n. 26), 184 (n. 21)
Psychology, 14–15, 33, 35–36, 110–11, 133–35, 171 (n. 26), 184 (n. 21)

Railroads, 85–89, 153, 154, 163, 166, 180 (nn. 7, 9)
Realism: of Howells, 43, 44–45, 49, 50, 57–59, 81, 138, 139–40; of James, 44, 49, 58; Cather on, 81–82
Reconstruction genre of Romance, 176 (n. 67)
The Red Badge of Courage (Crane), 44, 46–50, 52, 166
Rhodes, Elisha Hunt, 41, 42
Riley, Woodbridge, 51

The Rise of Silas Lapham (Howells), 53–54, 59
Robertson, J. M., 159
Romero, Lora, 7, 8, 170 (n. 11)
Roosevelt, Teddy, 29
Ross, Edward, 158
Rott v. Goehring, 180 (n. 14)
Rowe, John Carlos, 39
Ryan, Judith, 110

The Scarlet Letter (Hawthorne), 1–3
Scarry, Elaine, 25, 123, 140, 172 (n. 11), 184 (n. 15), 186 (n. 19)
Sedgwick, Eve K., 9
Seltzer, Mark, 112, 114
Sensibility Studies, 8–9
Sentimental novels, 4, 18–19, 57, 59–60, 142–44, 186 (n. 25)
Sentiment and sentimentalism, 9, 15–17, 43, 95, 142–43, 158, 176 (n. 79)
Sexology, 97, 182 (n. 30), 184 (n. 21)
Sexual torts, 10–11, 90–100
Shakespeare, William, 55, 177 (n. 9), 183 (n. 31)
Shamir, Milette, 56
Shaw, Justice, 88
Shaw, Robert, 39–40
Shell shock, 35–36. *See also* Soldier's heart
Shi, David E., 46, 57, 58, 157, 158, 176 (n. 79), 177 (n. 14)
Showalter, Elaine, 31
Simond, L., 96
The Sixth Wisconsin (Dawes), 39
Slave narratives, 4
Smith, Adam, 112
Smith v. Meyers, 182 (n. 24), 183 (n. 33)
Soldier's heart: fiction on, 4–5, 25, 26, 30–31, 34–35, 43–50; and Civil War, 18, 23–50; medical views of, 23–25, 29–36; symptoms of, 24, 30, 31; personal/autobiographical writings on, 26–27, 36–44, 139; and nervousness, 29–30; and World War I, 31, 35–36; and nostalgia, 31–33, 174 (n. 34); as shell shock, 35–36
Speech. *See* Language
Spencer, Herbert, 157
Spingarn, Joel Elias, 160, 186 (n. 32)
Stanton, Elizabeth Cady, 179 (n. 46)
Stern, Julia, 7
"The Story of a Year" (James), 45
Stowe, Harriet Beecher, 40–43, 58, 71, 143
Suffering. *See* Male emotional injury
Sumner, William Graham, 158
Sympathy, 72, 73, 169 (n. 11)

Theodore Tilton v. Henry Ward Beecher, 96
Thomas, Brook, 14, 129
Thomas, Calvin, 140, 159
Thompson, Maurice, 76
Thomson, Rosemarie Garland, 165, 166, 178 (n. 21)
Tilton, Elizabeth, 96
Tilton, Theodore, 96
The Titan (Dreiser), 85
Tompkins, Jane, 4
Tort law. *See* Injury law
Trachtenberg, Alan, 27
Traister, Bryce, 6
Trilling, Lionel, 5, 137–40, 142, 143, 155, 161
Twain, Mark, 58, 72

Uncle Tom's Cabin (Stowe), 41, 42–43, 58, 71, 143
Universities, 141, 156–57

Vanderbilt, Kermit, 186 (n. 34)

Waler, Francis Amasa, 158
Warfare. *See* Civil War
War neuroses. *See* Nervousness; Soldier's heart
Warren, Samuel, 21, 108–10, 125–26, 128–29, 133–34, 184 (n. 16)
Weisenburg, Theodore H., 173 (n. 22)
Wharton, Edith: literary critics on *Ethan Frome*, 21–22, 137–43, 154–55, 160–61; on dangers of "feminine" fiction, 57; on "contracted heart," 63; and purpose of novel, 138, 139; romantic relationships of, 148; nervousness of, 173 (n. 19); in France, 186 (n. 17). See also *Ethan Frome* (Wharton)
"What Is an Emotion?" (W. James), 134
Wheeler v. Abbott, 99
White, G. Edward, 9, 53
Whitman, Walt, 175 (n. 52)
Whitmore v. Whitmore, 74
Wilde, Oscar, 182–83 (n. 30)
Williams, Raymond, 15, 118, 172 (n. 9)
Wilson, Christopher, 59, 176 (n. 76)
Wilson, Edmund, 37, 175 (n. 52)
Withey, Lynne E., 70–71
Wolff, Cynthia Griffin, 148, 185 (n. 15), 186 (n. 17)
Women: and emotion, 7, 8, 15–16, 95; injury to, 11; and sentiment and sentimentalism, 15–16, 43, 59–60; in Howells's *Modern Instance*, 19; rest cure for, 30; and hysteria, 31, 146, 173 (n. 21), 185 (n. 14); Civil War writings by, 40–41; in patriarchal family, 51; and divorce, 51–52; and fiction reading, 56–57; and injury law, 170 (n. 21); and criminal conversation actions, 180–81 (n. 14). *See also* Adultery; Divorce; Marriage
Woodhouse v. Woodhouse, 182 (n. 21)
Woolf, Virginia, 31
Workmen's compensation, 155
World War I, 31, 35–36
Woundedness. *See* Injury; Male emotional injury

"The Yellow Wallpaper" (Gilman), 30
Young, Elizabeth, 26, 37, 40, 172 (n. 6)

Zaretsky, Eli, 14